Dynamics of Media Writing

Second Edition

To my mom, Lynn, who set me up at the dining room table with her old manual typewriter when I was a kid and let me write until my heart was content. To my dad, Frank, who taught me that the best things in life come to he who hustles while he waits. To my wife, Amy, who has been there for me and with me through everything life has thrown at us. And to my daughter, Zoe, who always asks, "Did you put me in your new book?"

Yes, sweet pea, I did.

Sara Miller McCune founded SAGE Publishing in 1965 to support the dissemination of usable knowledge and educate a global community. SAGE publishes more than 1000 journals and over 800 new books each year, spanning a wide range of subject areas. Our growing selection of library products includes archives, data, case studies and video. SAGE remains majority owned by our founder and after her lifetime will become owned by a charitable trust that secures the company's continued independence.

Los Angeles | London | New Delhi | Singapore | Washington DC | Melbourne

Dynamics of Media Writing

Adapt and Connect

Second Edition

Vincent F. Filak
University of Wisconsin–Oshkosh

 |

FOR INFORMATION:

CQ Press
An imprint of SAGE Publications, Inc.
2455 Teller Road
Thousand Oaks, California 91320
E-mail: order@sagepub.com

SAGE Publications Ltd.
1 Oliver's Yard
55 City Road
London EC1Y 1SP
United Kingdom

SAGE Publications India Pvt. Ltd.
B 1/I 1 Mohan Cooperative Industrial Area
Mathura Road, New Delhi 110 044
India

SAGE Publications Asia-Pacific Pte. Ltd.
3 Church Street
#10-04 Samsung Hub
Singapore 049483

Acquisitions Editor: Terri Accomazzo
Content Development Editor: Anna Villarruel
Editorial Assistant: Sarah Wilson
Production Editor: Bennie Clark Allen
Copy Editor: Jim Kelly
Typesetter: C&M Digitals (P) Ltd.
Proofreader: Jennifer Grubba
Indexer: Jean Casalegno
Cover Designer: Scott Van Atta
Marketing Manager: Liz Thornton

Library of Congress Cataloging-in-Publication Data

Names: Filak, Vincent F., author.

Title: Dynamics of media writing : adapt and connect / Vincent F. Filak.

Description: Second edition. | Washington, D.C. : CQ Press, a division of Sage, [2019] | Includes bibliographical references and index.

Identifiers: LCCN 2017051833 | ISBN 9781506381466 (softcover : acid-free paper)

Subjects: LCSH: Mass media—Authorship—Handbooks, manuals, etc. | Journalism.

Classification: LCC P96.A86 F55 2019 | DDC 808.06/63—dc23
LC record available at https://lccn.loc.gov/2017051833

Printed in the United States of America

18 19 20 21 22 10 9 8 7 6 5 4 3 2 1

BRIEF CONTENTS

DETAILED CONTENTS

PREFACE

I always tell people that I learn more from my students than my students learn from me, and this book is the living proof of that truism. Two students helped me understand what this book should be and why it matters to anyone who wants to go into the field of media.

The first was a former editor of mine at the Advance-Titan, the UW Oshkosh student newspaper, who was charged with recruiting a staff of writers. He already had most of the "news" students in our department, and he was still short of bodies. He then went into public relations classes, English composition classes, and any courses that had the word "writing" in the title.

Each time he entered one of those classes, he was met with skepticism, but he presented the newspaper as a great way to get practical job experience in an important field. His pitch consisted of a two-word theme:

"Transferrable skills."

In other words, people who plan to work in a field involving communication will need to know how to ask questions and assess answers. They will need to know how to write effectively and clearly. They will need to understand the legal and ethical rules pertaining to communication.

In the end, he failed more than he succeeded, but he still made an impact on those people who chose to work for him. He also gave me a way to explain what it was I was trying to do in terms of teaching media writing across the various disciplines out there.

The second student was a woman who took my class on writing for the media as a sophomore and hated it. Her complaint was one I had heard too often from students:

"I'm going into PR! Why do I need any of this?"

After passing the class, she ended up on exactly the path she had hoped: She got an internship with a top-flight casino in Las Vegas doing public relations. She parlayed that experience into another internship with an influential public relations firm in New York, where she worked with clients in fashion and video games.

As part of her internship class requirements, she came back and spoke to my class about her experiences. She had the PR students hanging on her every word, but not one of them would ask a question. So I asked one for them:

"If Ashley now could talk to the Ashley who sat in this class back then, what would you tell her?"

The woman's face took on the look of someone who was just forced to eat a piece of rotten fruit. She then sighed and said two things:

"First, listen to this guy. He knows more than you'll give him credit for. Second, learn how to write. Write, write and write some more until you're really good at it, because all I did for my first internship was write like crazy."

The students in the class, especially those in marketing and public relations, suddenly looked as if she had told them that Santa isn't real.

WRITING ACROSS THE MEDIA

This book is rooted in those two stories and should work in a way that I hope will bridge the divides among media students who have, for too long, been taught in silos. Students are often required to declare a major or a sequence and then take classes that insulate them from other disciplines. They also have social identities that relate to those choices. It took me a while, but I finally understood why students had trouble with my course if they weren't "newspaper people." I could talk a good game and lecture about the value of media skills, but at the end of the day, my textbook had the words "news reporting and writing" in bold letters across the cover. The chapters tilted in that direction and either ignored or diminished the importance of things that weren't directly related to "news."

The way this book approaches media writing is about finding common ground among the disciplines. Certain skills matter to you as a media writer, regardless of what part of this field you enter. You need to learn how to research, fact-check and interview. You need to learn proper grammar, style and spelling. You need to work on digital platforms, and you need to do so in an ethical and legal fashion.

Most textbooks on media writing start with writing for a newspaper or a news outlet and then provide a few tidbits about public relations and nothing about advertising. This book looks at the crucial skills that all media writers will need, from understanding an audience to learning the law, before moving into the various niche approaches to media writing. Given the media trend of professionals who work in news before shifting to public relations or work in marketing before shifting to news, these transferable skills are a bedrock for all learners.

The first eight chapters of this book will lay out those skills in a "discipline-neutral" fashion, using examples from news and ads to rock band contract riders and popular movies. The goal is to showcase these skills in a way that makes it clear how each one applies to a particular discipline as well as to the field as a whole.

DIFFERENT NEEDS FOR DIFFERENT PLATFORMS

Although skills matter across the board, a number of things will differ from platform to platform and from area to area. How broadcast journalists write will differ from how newspaper journalists write because of the needs associated with the platform and how the information is consumed. Marketing and advertising will differ in many ways from public relations, especially in terms of audience and approach. You might use the skills in the first half of the book regardless of where you go, but you will likely have to use them in slightly different ways, depending on your job.

The second half of the book will use a chapter-by-chapter approach to outline specific areas of media writing and the key elements associated with each one. Reporting, print writing, broadcast writing, public relations, advertising and marketing will each get a detailed examination, as the first half of the book will function as a lens through which to view these topics.

PROFESSIONAL THOUGHTS

One of the most important portions of the book (at least in my mind) is the "Professional Thoughts" feature in each chapter. The professionals profiled in each chapter have walked the path media-writing students are hoping to walk. In almost every case, these people have transitioned from media discipline to media discipline and found the skills taught in this book to be instrumental in their success.

When I started the book, my goal was to see how many people I could find who started in Media Discipline A and somehow wound up in Media Discipline B, C or Z. Thanks to the downsizing of newspaper staffs, the reworking of PR firms and the general changes to the advertising and marketing game, these people were everywhere, and they all told stories that helped me see how important the basic skills in this book are. The people included in this book took varied paths to reach their current stops in life, although every one of them said that the skills noted in the book as "must-haves" were crucial to their success as they took on new challenges. Their interviews will help readers understand how they adapted to the challenges associated with their career changes and connected with new audiences that sought important information from them.

CENTRAL THEME: ADAPT AND CONNECT

The theme of the book, adapt and connect, is exemplified in the use of **Adapt** and **Connect** breakout boxes in each chapter. The underlying assumption is that the skills you learn in this text can be adapted to fit various disciplines within the field of media in the hope of connecting effectively with your audience.

Each **Adapt** box uses examples and anecdotes to help you see how a skill discussed in one area of the book can be valuable in another way. For example, an **Adapt** box could show you how a topic discussed in a news-writing chapter could benefit you as a public relations practitioner or vice versa. The goal is to show more of the commonalities among the areas of media writing and how truly interlinked the various disciplines are.

The **Connect** boxes reinforce the primary point of the first chapter: You aren't writing for yourself. You are writing for your readers. The ability to understand how audience members function will allow you to better reach them with your words. Each box applies audience-centric approaches to conveying content, thus helping you see ways you can connect to the people you serve.

At the end of each of these boxes (and occasionally scattered elsewhere in the book), you will find **Give It a Try** exercises. The purpose behind these is to let you apply the lesson learned in each breakout box immediately. This will allow you to demonstrate your understanding of the material before you move forward in the text.

EXAMPLES AND BREAKOUT BOXES

Beyond the **Adapt** and **Connect** boxes, several chapters contain examples and breakout boxes to help draw your attention to key ideas and illustrate important concepts. The use of small chunks of text, visual examples and self-contained content elements should help alert you to important topics in easy-to-consume ways. The goal was to use these sparingly and yet effectively, so you didn't become numb to their presence or learn to skip past them. Like everything else in the book, these elements are used only when there is a reason to use them. Keep an eye out for them and give them a look-see before moving on with your reading.

THE BIG THREE

At the end of every chapter, I have highlighted the three most important concepts and skills to remember, rather than trying to provide an overreaching summary of everything discussed. It is my hope that this approach not only gives you a sense of value but also improves your recall of key concepts that will have the most value to you as a reader.

DIGITAL RESOURCES

Access digital resources by logging on to **https://edge.sagepub.com/filakmedia2e.**

SAGE edge offers a robust online environment featuring an impressive array of tools and resources for review, study, and further exploration, keeping both instructors and students on the cutting edge of teaching and learning. SAGE edge content is open access and available on demand. Learning and teaching has never been easier!

SAGE edge for Students provides a personalized approach to help students accomplish their

- **AP Style Quizzes and Exercises** test your students' knowledge of AP style and provide opportunities for them to practice.
- **Media Writing assignments** allow students to broaden their skills and practice writing
- Mobile-friendly **eFlashcards** strengthen understanding of key terms and concepts
- Mobile-friendly practice **quizzes** allow for independent assessment by students of their mastery of course material.
- Carefully selected chapter-by-chapter **Video and Multimedia** content which enhance classroom-based explorations of key topics.

SAGE edge for Instructors supports teaching by making it easy to integrated quality content and create a rich learning environment for students.

- **Test banks** provide a diverse range of pre-written options as well as the opportunity to edit any question and/or insert your own personalized questions to effectively assess students' progress and understanding
- Chapter-specific **PowerPoint®️ slides** offer assistance with lecture and review preparation by highlighting essential content, features, and artwork from the book.
- **Media Writing assignments** allow students to broaden their skills and practice writing
- Chapter **learning objectives** reinforce the most important material.

CONSTANT DIGITAL UPDATES VIA DYNAMICS OF WRITING BLOG

A few of the major complaints about textbooks is that they are out of date before they even hit the shelves and that they lack the interactive elements students enjoy. In an effort to address these concerns, this text has an accompanying digital presence: the Dynamics of Writing blog (**dynamicsofwriting.com**).

The blog covers content outlined in both this text and "Dynamics of News Reporting and Writing," so it covers the field in various ways. It is updated almost daily with additional information, current examples of material discussed in the text and additional interactive elements that will keep students engaged and the material fresh. Professional journalists take part in the blog through interviews and discussions about current events in the media. Guest bloggers frequently post on topics of interest, such as improving local content or covering underrepresented groups. The author has also made the experience more interactive through the inclusion of digital elements, discussion-board opportunities and other web-based options.

This approach to content provision provides students with an opportunity to further their knowledge as they read these thought-provoking posts and seek direct feedback from the author.

ACKNOWLEDGMENTS

This book would not have been half of whatever it is without the generosity of so many professionals in the media world. It is to them that I am truly grateful.

Special thanks to Alex Hummel, Jennifer Morehead, Shay Quillen, Adam Silverman, Suzanne Struglinski, Ken Smith, Pat Finley, Ashley Messenger, Eric Deutsch, Jon Seidel, Lucha Ramey, Erin White, Kate Morgan and Jonathan Foerster for their professional guidance and honest interviews.

Thanks to Daxton "Chip" Stewart for his review of the law and ethics chapter and Robert "Pritch" Pritchard for all his help with the public relations section.

Also, special thanks to Kaylene Armstrong, Angela Bode, Jessica Clary, Kay Colley, Glenn Hubbard, Claudia Ikeizumi, Karilyn Robinson, Fred Vultee, Charlese Watson and Keely Warren, as well as Red Shoes PR, the Lindsey and Asp Advertising and Public Relations Agency at the University of Oklahoma and the Office of Campus Ministry at the University of Notre Dame for their help in procuring valuable examples that help illustrate the key concepts in the book.

It goes without saying that this project would not have been possible without the staff at SAGE, including Matthew Byrnie, who told me "You need to write this book," when I told him what I needed to teach my media-writing course. I also owe special thanks my amazing editors, Terri Accomazzo and Anna Villarruel. I can't thank you enough for all you have done to make this second edition a reality. Also, thanks to Liz Thornton for her marketing prowess and helpful suggestions and Jim Kelly for being the best copy editor I could ever want.

Finally, thanks go out to all the media professionals out there who ply their trade every day in the hopes of informing, engaging and entertaining a wide array of audiences. You are both an inspiration to me and a benchmark for the students I teach.

SAGE wishes to acknowledge the contributions of the following reviewers: Jeff Carter, University of Wisconsin Oshkosh; Brian Sheridan, Mercyhurst University; Lauren Chambliss, Cornell University; and Elizabeth Fish Hatfield, University of Houston–Downtown.

Special thanks are due to Jean Giovanetti of the University of Wisconsin–Oshkosh for developing the student and instructor resources on the "Dynamics of Media Writing" companion website.

ABOUT THE AUTHOR

Vincent F. Filak, PhD, is an award-winning teacher, scholar and college media adviser who serves as a professor of journalism at the University of Wisconsin–Oshkosh, where he primarily teaches courses on media writing and reporting. Prior to his arrival at UWO, he served on the faculty at Ball State University and also taught courses at the University of Missouri and the University of Wisconsin–Madison. He also previously worked for the Wisconsin State Journal and the Columbia Missourian newspapers.

Filak has earned the Distinguished Four-Year Newspaper Adviser award from the College Media Association for his work with the Advance-Titan, UWO's student newspaper. CMA previously honored him as an Honor Roll Recipient for his work as the adviser of the Daily News at Ball State. The National Scholastic Press Association presented him with its highest honor, the Pioneer Award, "in recognition of significant contributions to high school publications and journalism programs."

As a scholar, Filak has received 13 top conference paper awards, including those from the Association for Education in Journalism and Mass Communication, the Broadcast Education Association and the International Public Relations Society of America. He has published more than 30 scholarly, peer-reviewed articles in top-tier journals, including Journalism and Mass Communication Quarterly, Journalism and Mass Communication Educator, Newspaper Research Journal, the Atlantic Journal of Communication, Journalism: Theory, Practice and Criticism, the Howard Journal of Communication, Educational Psychology and the British Journal of Social Psychology. He is also the winner of CMA's Nordin Research Award, which goes to the best research paper completed on a topic pertaining to media advisers within a given year.

He has published several textbooks in the field of journalism, including "Dynamics of News Reporting and Writing" (SAGE), "Convergent Journalism" (Focal) and "The Journalist's Handbook to Online Editing" (with Kenneth Rosenauer; Pearson).

He lives in Omro, Wisconsin, with his wife, Amy, and their daughter, Zoe.

THE BASICS YOU NEED, REGARDLESS OF FIELD

1

KNOW YOUR AUDIENCE

LEARNING OBJECTIVES

After completing this chapter you should be able to:

- Define an audience based on several characteristics, including demographic information, psychographic information and geography.

- Understand what readers want from you as a media professional, how you should deliver it to them and ways in which audiences change over time.

- Discuss the key interest elements that attract most readers, including fame, oddity, conflict, immediacy and impact.

- Identify key needs of audience members and explain how to meet those needs through your writing.

Media outlets today have a singular purpose: Serve the audience. This truism applies to advertising and public relations, where practitioners craft messages to convince clients to create campaigns. In turn, those campaigns release messages that attempt to persuade consumers to purchase a product, trust a candidate for office or change their beliefs about an issue. This statement also relates to the field of news, where print, broadcast and online reporters gather material from sources and craft messages to inform their readers and viewers.

According to research published in the Journal of Communication, media users engage in selective exposure.[1] This means audience members will gravitate to topics they know, writers they like and information providers they trust. This can be good for media professionals who apply strong ethical tenets and good communication skills to reach readers, but it can also be bad, if people insulate themselves too much from outside information and opinion. Analyses conducted in the wake of the 2016 presidential election found that people tend to gravitate toward information that confirms their own ways of thinking, creating what some have termed "media bubbles."[2] This makes it harder, but not impossible, for us to break through to our audience members and inform them about things they need to know.

As audiences continue to fragment and specialize, media professionals can't assume that broad messages or generic bits of information will influence a wide swath of people. Instead, the goal for today's media professionals, regardless of the specialty they practice, is to learn as much as possible about the people they serve and put forth content that targets those people.

The purpose of this chapter is to establish the importance of the audience as it relates to media writing, determine ways to define the audience and explain which information elements attract the most readers.

HOW TO DEFINE AN AUDIENCE

Before you create effective content, you have to define your **audience**. Throughout the various media disciplines, advertising professionals best understand the value of analyzing and segmenting an audience. In order to sell products, advertisers need to know who uses their products, why these people use the products and how best to reach active and potential users. Public-relations practitioners often deal with some of the most difficult audiences to reach, namely, news journalists who can use their media outlets to amplify the practitioners' messages.

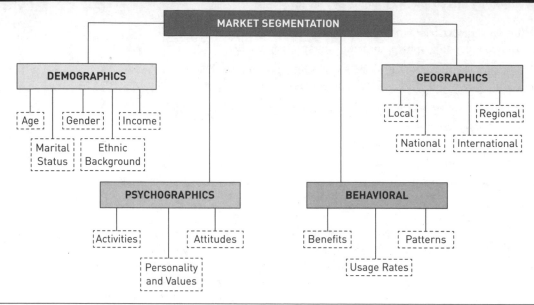

FIGURE 1.1 ■ Market segmentation allows you to figure out who is in your audience and how best to reach them. For media writers, understanding the demographic, psychographic and geographic backgrounds of their readers will help them write better for those people.

PR professionals understand the needs of these fellow media practitioners as well as the needs of the public as they craft a valuable and engaging message. News journalists began to focus on audience centricity a bit later than their colleagues in other areas of the discipline. In years past, reporters viewed **audience segmentation** as unnecessary, because their job was to tell people what mattered based on predetermined news values. In addition, many news outlets held virtual monopolies over geographic areas, thus allowing them to operate with impunity. However, with loss of unilateral control over what people received via news outlets, mainstream news operations now spend ample time catering to their audience.

With the shift of news to digital **platforms**, more people have access to more news than ever. In addition, advertisers are now awash in even greater levels of message competition, and public-relations campaigns are expected to yield greater results with fewer resources than ever. As the internet continues to grow and to create fragmented audiences, all media professionals must be more vigilant in defining and understanding whom they serve. Here are the key ways in which you should look to define your readers:

Demographic Information

The most basic way to define an audience is through **demographics**. These statistics reveal the measurable aspects of a group you hope to reach. Demographics commonly include age, gender, race, education and relationship status.

Marketers traditionally use these population characteristics to divide a larger group into more manageable segments. For example, the purchasing habits of divorced women, ages 54–65, who have no children will differ from the purchasing habits of married men, ages 25–36, who have multiple children living at home. If you targeted both groups with the same types of material and the same products, you probably would fail to reach at least one of those groups.

Websites have also tapped into demographics in terms of audience centricity. For example, the website BuzzFeed has engaged in a series of **microtargeting** posts that Chadwick Matlin calls "demolisticles." These postings target people based on specific interests, such as attending a certain college or growing up in a certain religion.[3] According to an article on Slate, these posts are wildly successful because people have an inherent interest in specific personal attributes and how other people with similar attributes engage in shared experiences.[4] Thus, lists such as "32 Signs You Grew Up in Ealing" and "33 Signs You Went to an All-Girls Public School" tap into that demographic background and highlight the audience members' shared experiences.

Microtargeting has become a huge factor in political campaigns over the past decade. A 2016 Forbes article outlined the ways in which big data analytics are used to find the demographics of voters, as well as other public information about those individuals. Analysts then use this information to target individuals with specific information that is most likely to resonate with them, thus maximizing the impact of the message and minimizing waste.[5]

Geographic Information

People relate well to events that happen near them and care somewhat less about those happening far away. When you consider that a single death can draw more attention than a massive genocide simply based on where the event occurs, you realize that **geographic information** plays a large role in how to target your audience.

Area placement means a great deal to advertisers and event organizers. A person might fit a demographic range for a particular event, such as a 5K run. The person might also have an interest in the charity that the run supports, such as breast cancer awareness or muscular dystrophy. However, if the event takes place 500 miles from where that person lives, it is unlikely the individual will consider participating in it. This is where geography becomes important. Also, advertisers know that the needs of citizens of Madison, Minnesota, are not the same as the needs of those of Madison, Florida, when it comes to snow-removal equipment or alligator deterrents.

People want to know what is happening near them. When a restaurant burns to the ground in a small town, news reporters know that readers likely have eaten at that establishment or know its owners. When a school district requests a tax increase or fires a teacher, the issue of proximity figures prominently into audience members' interest in the issue.

Psychographic Information

Just because someone is your age, your gender and has your level of education, it doesn't necessarily follow that the person has anything in common with you. **Psychographics** allow media professionals to examine an audience based on concepts like personal values, interests and attitudes. This category incorporates topics such as the strength of opinion on certain issues as well as general likes and dislikes associated with certain topics, activities and ideologies.

For example, if you were to examine the demographics of College X, you might find that it has a 55 percent to 45 percent split between men and women, with an age demographic that primarily sits in the 18–24 range. You might find that this school sees about one-third of its students come from within the state and has an 85/15 proportion of white students to those of various other racial groups. College Y might have similar demographics that show a 52–48 split between men and women, a similar age range and about one-half of the students coming from within the state. However, if you were to run a promotion at the first school for a bar's "Drink Like There's No Tomorrow" specials, you would probably do horribly poorly in sales, given that Brigham Young University has a policy and tradition against alcoholic consumption. If you did the same at the second school, you might do pretty well, given West Virginia University's consistent ranking among the top 20 party schools in the country.

CONNECT: THE PERSONIFICATION OF YOUR AUDIENCE

One approach you can take to conceptualize your readers more clearly is to view them in a way that makes them more real for you. Some media specialists refer to this as the **personification** of the audience. This approach to audience understanding has you create a mini-biography about your prototypical reader that lets you to reflect on his or her wants and needs as you approach your writing.

Here are a couple of personification examples:

"Anne is a 50-year-old public school teacher who has lived in the same medium-sized city for her entire life. She always wants to keep up with what is happening all around her, but she places a premium on local information. She still subscribes to the daily newspaper and reads it from cover to cover every day before work. She listens to local news radio during her daily work drives. She will shop where she gets the best deal, and she is an avid coupon clipper. She puts the needs of her two teenage children above her own, in terms of purchase intentions and educational opportunities. She owns a mobile phone, but it is several years old, and she turns it on only for outgoing phone calls."

"Burt is a 19-year-old college sophomore at a small, private college. His school is rooted in a Christian belief system, but Burt puts more emphasis on the quality of his education than the underlying religious aspects of the institution. Burt has limited finances, but he enjoys being at the front of most trends. What his friends think about who he is and how he acts matters a great deal to him. Burt gets all of his information through social media sites and avoids mainstream media. He is never without his phone, and he uses various apps to manage his news, his schedule and everything else around him. He loves cheap eats and other great bargains, but he won't carry around a wad of coupons. He relies on internet codes and digital sharing to find good deals."

Personifying your audience can allow you to better conceptualize who is reading your work. This will also help you figure out if you are meeting the needs of those people you serve.

© iStockphoto.com/wbritten

© iStockphoto.com/PeopleImages

GIVE IT A TRY: Take 10 minutes and look up some basic statistics about the students your school serves. Most universities and colleges have this information on their websites. Then, look into some basic information about media consumption habits associated with people who fall into those statistical categories. Finally, write up a short personification of your audience that mirrors the approach above. Compare and contrast your personification with those your classmates have created. Take particular note of specific similarities and differences you find during your class discussion.

KEY QUESTIONS TO ASK IN SERVING YOUR READERS

As a media professional, you will be expected to ask a lot of questions during your career. Interviewing, which is discussed in Chapter 5, is a key way you will gain knowledge and gather information. However, to fully understand what you must do for your readers, here are three key questions you should ask of yourself:

What Do My Readers Want From Me?

In many cases, media writers write from their own perspectives. In other words, they ask, "What do I want to tell people?" Many writers believe that if a topic matters to them, it should matter to the audience. In some cases, your interests and your audience members' interests will intertwine, especially when you operate in a **niche** area.

If you start a blog that is all about knitting because you really enjoy knitting, you will have a lot in common with knitting aficionados who frequent your site. That said, some of the people will be interested in spinning their own yarn by hand, whereas others might rely solely on processed materials. Some knitters enjoy knitting socks, and some love sweaters. Even more, some sock knitters will only knit "toe up," while others are fervently "top down" knitters. Just because you prefer certain ideas and approaches, you shouldn't become myopic about them.

In writing promotional material for a company, an organization or a department, you can easily fall into a rut of writing lead sentences like "The Boone County Chamber of Commerce will host a comedy event on Saturday to benefit a local charity." It makes sense to you because you are writing what you think is most important: Your organization is doing something.

Don't write for yourself. Write for your readers. Ask yourself, "What is it that will be most compelling to those people who pick up this press release or read this promotional material?" As you answer this question, rely on information elements like fame, oddity and immediacy, which we will discuss below, to amplify the value to your readers.

> *Bill Smith, the only man to ever eat an entire elephant, will perform his comedy routine "One Bite at a Time" on Saturday, with all proceeds going to the Boone County Make-a-Wish Foundation.*

Work for the readers and figure out what those people want from you. If you give it to them, you will likely have a lot of readers who are interested in what you have to say.

How Do My Readers Want the Information?

Think about the last meal you ate. How much did it cost? Did you prepare it or was it prepared for you? Did you eat at a restaurant or did someone deliver the food to you? Did you eat your meal at a leisurely pace, at a table, with other people, or did you grab it on the go?

The point is, you were consuming something based on a variety of factors, and how you needed to eat played a big role in what you ate. If you were in a hurry to get to class this afternoon, a bagel from the school's food cart might have been your best option because you could eat it on the go. A porterhouse steak with mashed potatoes and a side of asparagus might have sounded much better to you at that point, but cost, time and portability made the steak an impossible choice.

© iStockphoto.com/jfmdesign

Companies have been making these kinds of adaptations for years. For example, in 2005, Burger King changed the shape of some of its food containers so that they could more easily fit in a car's cup holder.[6] The new "fry pod" came about after research revealed that more people were eating their food on the go. In selling its Chicken Fries in this carton, the company began to sell more servings per day than its main competitors. Other companies have made similar alterations to their giant drink cups, tailoring the bottom part of the beverage vessels to fit in the spot usually reserved for cans and bottles.

The creation of "frypods" and beverage containers with narrow bottoms allowed Burger King to adapt its packaging to meet the needs of on-the-go consumers who ate in their cars.

Delivering media content to readers is like delivering a pizza to a dorm room in some simple ways. How your readers want to get their information should factor into how you write and how you transmit your content.

Some readers want all of their content in a central location that will allow them to sift through everything at their leisure. Other people want bits of information sent to them as each item becomes available. Still others will want a mix of both forms, depending on the type of content involved.

In many cases, the lives of your readers dictate what they want, and intelligent media professionals will use that to their advantage. A recent Knight Foundation study found that since 2011, smartphone ownership in the United States has increased from 46 percent to 82 percent. As of 2016, 89 percent of smartphone users accessed news on their mobile devices, the study found.[7] Another study, this one by Deloitte, found that mobile devices have become an essential for U.S. citizens, with more than 40 percent of them checking their phones less than five minutes after they wake up. In addition, the study notes that people review text messages, check email and surf the web via the small screen.[8]

To that end, writing in a way that is easy to read on a smartphone and looking for ways to push content out to readers as it becomes available make sense. If you can be a convenient source of information, your readers will hear more of what you have to say.

ADAPT
SHIFTING CONTENT TO SATISFY AN AUDIENCE

When thinking about how to write, you should consider the platform (paper, television, desktop, mobile) and the **outlet** (New York Post, Vogue magazine, ESPN.com).

Some people will want a quick burst of information, and that's it. It could be a notification that a company is having a sale on a particular date or a simple sentence that reveals the results of a football game. Other people will want to sit down and study an extended analysis of why a company's stock is performing well or read a personality profile about a local community leader.

Analyze your audience for outlet and platform preferences. What your readers use and how they use it will help you tailor your approach. Most people won't want to read a 10,000-word profile on their mobile phone screen. However, those same people won't want to wait until a print newspaper arrives on the doorstep to find out who won that night's baseball game.

Take advantage of these preferences. You could use Twitter to alert the readers to that 10,000-word feature, thus piquing their interest and inspiring them to read the full version later on their tablets or laptops. You could pair that sports score alert with a link to other short pieces available on your mobile site, thus sponsoring more audience engagement on the topic while not forcing the readers to shift platforms.

In the end, you want to use the right tool for the right job and meet your readers where they are. Then you can use your writing and promotional skills to guide those readers to additional information that matters to them.

GIVE IT A TRY: Find a story that is of interest to you on a website you frequently visit. Then, boil that story down from the computer version to something you would send out as a tweet or an alert. Make it a single sentence that fits the parameters of what you tend to see on your mobile device.

Does the Audience Change Over Time?

In some cases, audience characteristics remain constant over time, but the members of that audience will change. It is your job to figure out how this will influence your approach to content and what you need to report to your readers.

For example, the magazine Tiger Beat started in September 1965, catering to teenage girls with an interest in music, fashion and the inside scoop on the teen idols. The first magazine featured photos and stories on the Beatles and Herman's Hermits. It offered an "intimate, personal" examination of David McCallum and asked the all-important question: "The Righteous Brothers: Breaking Up?"

A 2016 cover of Tiger Beat offers "Serayah, Olivia Holt, Lilimar and more." It offers a feature on "The best fall trends perfect for you" as well as advice on "Surviving Squads!" The main feature is "We love Peyton List," with a secondary story on "Shawn Mendes: His Next Chapter."

The magazine still meets the audience needs outlined above: teen gossip, music scoops and inside movie information. However, over the 50+ years between the first issue and the most recent one, the audience has changed. The idols of the 1960s don't cause the girls of 2017 to swoon. The people who read the magazine in 1965 have long since moved beyond the makeup tips and teen drama outlined in the pages of Tiger Beat. Although the specific information might change over time, the basic underlying tenets of this magazine have not.

Magazines that cater to teens, brides and fashion will often have audiences that change over time. The editors will keep the content thematically constant, but will alter the stories and photos as the teen idols, wedding standards and fashion trends change.

Magazines often follow this pattern of writing as new members filter in and out of the audience. New parents will want to know if their children are eating properly or if their babies will ever sleep through the night. Engaged men and women will want to know how to plan a wedding, what to do about family drama and how to save enough money to make their dreams come true. In some cases, the underlying questions and answers the audiences have remain the same. In other cases, changes to social norms, trends or technology might lead writers to approach these topics in different ways.

A long-held tradition had the parents of the bride paying for a wedding, so early wedding magazines would list ways to address these issues with parents or how to establish the amount of money available to the couple. Now that tradition isn't as rock solid as it used to be, so while money still must be addressed, writers in this field must look at issues such as how couples can set aside money to pay for their own weddings or how to balance their current financial obligations with their nuptial desires. Even more, second weddings and melding families have become more prominent and thus are likely to be more germane to this generation of brides and grooms.

The core values and interests of a publication can remain the same over time, whether it is a corporate newsletter or a gossip publication. However, writers must continually assess the needs and wants of the audience as the members of that group change and grow over time.

WHAT ATTRACTS AN AUDIENCE?

As media outlets continue to divide audiences along demographic, psychographic and geographic lines, several concepts remain interesting to many audiences. You want your audience to see what you wrote as an important focal point of their lives, and these **interest elements** can help you do that. To remember them, you can use the mnemonic **FOCII**, like the plural of "focus" but with two I's.

Fame

In some cases, it's not what someone does but who is doing the deed that matters. For example, according to drinkinganddriving.org, more than 900,000 people are arrested each year for drinking and driving. However, when retired boxing legend Oscar De La Hoya was arrested on suspicion of committing that offense in January 2017, it became big news. In this case, the status of the person drew the attention of readers and viewers to what is usually a minor criminal offense. The more important the person, the more likely people will pay attention.

Fame falls into two main categories. The first category is for people who are famous over an extended period of time. This can be due to their positions, such as president, prime minister or pope, or to their value to popular culture, such as actors, singers and sports stars. In some cases, fame can rest with the infamous, such as serial killers Jeffrey Dahmer and Ted Bundy. The name Charles Manson still sends shivers up the spines of people, even though he spent the majority of his adult life in prison. The more famous the person, the more the audience members care about what that person is doing.

The second category of fame is based on artist Andy Warhol's well-known statement that "in the future, everyone will be world-famous for 15 minutes." In many cases, circumstance thrusts ordinary people into the spotlight, and they become the center of our attention for a limited amount of time. Once the fervor around them dies down, these people often drift back into anonymity and life moves on. People like Jeff Gillooly, Capt. Chesley "Sully" Sullenberger, Samuel J. "Joe the Plumber" Wurzelbacher and Brian Collins became part of everyday conversations throughout the nation (and in some cases around the world) when they found themselves the subject of media fascination. If most of these names mean nothing to you, it only serves to further the point about this form of fame.

Oddity

"Holy cow! Did you see that?"

When a friend asks that question, he could be pointing out a thunderous dunk at a basketball game, a classic sports car rolling down the highway or someone eating the bark off of a tree in the park. Very rarely will someone be wowed by a free throw, a 5-year-old Toyota Corolla or someone jogging on a trail.

In other words, we like to see rarities.

The reason a video of a cat flushing a toilet gets 4 million views on YouTube is because not all cats flush toilets. The reason sports fanatics celebrate a perfect game in baseball is because of the nearly 190,000 professional games played since 1900, only 21 such games meet the standard of perfection, according to mlb.com. The Hope Diamond mesmerizes people because no other gem of its kind exists.

In the field of media, we focus on these rarities and highlight the elements that make them different from everyday occurrences. Advertising professionals accentuate the aspects of their products that separate them from competing products. These features could include having the lowest price in the field or having the best safety rating among the category's competitors.

Fundraising campaigns often use **oddity** to draw attention to a cause. For example, charities often use gimmicks such as important people who sit on top of a billboard until a certain amount of money is raised.

News is filled with oddities, such as Chuck Shepherd's classic "News of the Weird" features. In these cases, the writers promote weirdness to attract readers. Inept criminals who injured themselves breaking into a bank and had to call 911 for help make for great stories that keep people entertained. Beyond bits of weirdness, the novelty of firsts, lasts and "onlys" also engage audience members, whether the novelty involves the first person to walk on the moon or the only person to vote against the impeachment of a state official.

Conflict

Anytime two or more individuals or groups seek a mutually exclusive goal, **conflict** will arise. The idea of watching people, teams, organizations or nations fight draws on an almost primal desire and tends to attract a lot of attention.

Celebrity feuds and Twitter wars happen frequently and provide a simple way to see one-on-one conflict. In May 2017, late-night talk show host Stephen Colbert attacked President Donald Trump with a series of off-color insults. The president responded a week later, calling Colbert a "no-talent guy" with nothing funny to say.[9] Colbert then used his next show to poke back at Trump, going as far as to ask him to resign.

News publications rely on the FOCII interest elements to determine what stories and photos they want to publish on a daily basis.

Conflict also relates to sporting events, where teams attempt to exert dominance over each other. In some cases, geography can intensify conflict issues in sports. For example, Duke and the University of North Carolina have a strong rivalry in basketball, enhanced to some degree because the schools' campuses are only 8 miles apart. Other rivalries, such as between Ohio State and Michigan or Florida and Florida State, are also geographically enhanced.

Aside from these clear-cut examples, conflict also tends to weave into the day-to-day life of media professionals in every background. Advertising agents want more people to like their products or services as opposed to a competitor's offerings. Drinkers of Powerade are likely to remain loyal to that beverage and thus reject Gatorade's attempts to sway them.

People who raise money for a specific charity or cause know that people tend to set aside a finite amount of money that they will donate in a given period. If the money goes to Cause A, it can't go to Cause B. Conflict can also arise when organizations seek support and funds but are diametrically opposed in terms of philosophy, such as the National Pro-Life Alliance and NARAL Pro-Choice America.

In a news setting, conflict is ever present. When a company wants to build a store, conflict can emerge between that company and other companies that want to put facilities on that land. In addition, members of the boards and councils that approve land use might argue over the value of that type of land use. Citizens could protest the loss of green space associated with the construction.

In looking to serve an audience, you want to understand the multiple facets of an issue. Depending on who wins, the outcome will mean something to the people you serve. It could be good, or it could be bad, but it will matter.

Immediacy

The classic goofball comedy "Talladega Nights: The Ballad of Ricky Bobby" contains the immortal line "If you ain't first, you're last." If you skip past the grammar issues and logical lapses in that sentence, you see that Will Ferrell's statement perfectly captures the importance of **immediacy**.

People want to know what is happening around them at any given point in time, and they want to know before anyone else does. The surveillance need that people possess

© AT&T

AT&T used the idea of immediacy to show that their phones could get information to people more quickly than their competitors.

dominates the digital world, and media professionals need to understand how to meet it. In 2011, AT&T took advantage of the immediacy concept with its series of ads that demonstrated how quickly its phones could get users information on its 4G LTE network. A pair of men were at a football tailgate party while people asked questions such as "Did you guys hear that Chapman rolled his ankle?" or "Did you hear someone stole the other team's mascot?" Each time, one of the men responded with a statement like "That was so 10 seconds ago."

News journalists also value immediacy when they "break" news that is important to readers and viewers. Broadcast journalists cater to this interest element when they interrupt current programming to update people on a developing situation. When the first plane slammed into the World Trade Center on Sept. 11, 2001, television networks cut into their morning shows and went directly to New York City for a visual of the smoldering tower as journalists scrambled for information. Almost 40 years before that event, newspapers rushed out extra edition after extra edition to update citizens on the situation in Dallas, where President John F. Kennedy had been shot and killed.

Today, platforms such as Twitter and Facebook are used to provide users with information on a 24/7 basis. Audience members who choose to follow people, organizations and businesses can get up-to-the-minute updates on everything from product launches to celebrity sightings. As immediacy remains an important interest element, digital platforms and mobile devices will see their value increase exponentially.

Impact

This element of importance helps you explain how the information you put forth will directly affect the readers. In some cases, readers can feel the **impact** on an individual level, such as the amount of money a tax increase will cost each citizen. In other cases, the impact can be felt on a broader level, such as the positive effects that building a theater will have on a community or the negative effects of global pollution.

In most cases, you can measure impact from a **quantitative** or **qualitative** perspective. Quantitative perspectives measure the numerical reach of an impact, and qualitative perspectives examine the severity of the impact.

For example, a newspaper might report the death of a single citizen who was killed in a car crash. Death, something from which you can't recover, is a qualitative impact. In most cases, people have not experienced a fatal car crash, so the story has not only a serious impact but also an oddity factor.

However, that publication might also report ways in which people can deal with an illness, such as a cold. Although you might feel like you are dying when you are sick, you will probably recover from a cold within two weeks. Since the average adult gets two or three colds each year, according to Centers for Disease Control and Prevention, the quantitative reach of the impact is worth noting.

Make sure you examine the ways in which your writing can affect your readers and then focus on that during the writing process.

PROFESSIONAL THOUGHTS
ALEX HUMMEL

Alex Hummel's career has spanned the major areas of media outlined in this text. He started his career as a general assignment and public affairs reporter at the Oshkosh Northwestern, before spending three years running the paper's editorial page.

In 2009, he became the community education and outreach director for the Christine Ann Domestic Abuse Center, where he worked with students, guidance counselors and administrators at K–12 schools, discussing the dynamics of abuse. He also worked with corporations and human resources departments to outline the value of the center and to help cultivate its image in the community.

He shifted his career again in 2011, when he became the director of news services and public relations at the University of Wisconsin Oshkosh. In that role, he created promotional campaigns for the third-largest school in the UW System and worked with print, broadcast and online journalists during times of triumph and tragedy. In January 2015, he took a new job as the associate vice president for communications for UW System administration before returning to UWO as a special assistant to the chancellor in 2016.

At each stop in his career, he said, his underlying set of media production and writing skills allowed him to succeed in his work.

"I think of these skills as elemental skills and, yes, they are transferrable from job to job," he said. "It's just about testing yourself as a storyteller, as a documentarian and as a communicator. The things that translated immediately with immense value were writing and interviewing....Those skills are imbued with you. I love having those skills."

Hummel said it doesn't matter how people define "news" or "information" and which platforms people use to disseminate content. He said his audience's needs and how well he meets those needs matters the most to him.

"What I saw over time was that the news became more personal," he said. "People want to know 'What happened to my kids? What happened to grandma?' That's why Facebook is my favorite channel for reaching people and catering to the audience. We had this opportunity to personalize the day-to-day news."

Although people assume that his main audience is students, Hummel said his job often involves communicating various types of news to niche audiences in ways those readers can access and value.

Alex Hummel

"There are different audiences for everything we do," he said. "There is the general public. There is the legislature. There are members of our alumni community. Then there is our internal community: students, faculty, staff and more. What I'm finding is that we want to make sure we are developing messages and stories that are easy to digest and useful. The journalistic skills I was lucky enough to garner and grow made that work. And that's really what journalism is all about."

Hummel said all good media professionals have the same basic goals, and they go about meeting those goals in similar ways as they reach their audiences.

"I think if you are able to write, produce, edit or anything like that as a journalist, develop a style as a public relations professional in putting out pitches and news releases or sell products and pitch ideas in advertising, you are reaching an audience," he said. "In all of these things, you are effectively demonstrating that you respect your audience members and you want to help them. Each of these things is like an invitation to them to learn something from your storytelling."

One Last Thing

Q: If you could tell students anything about media writing or anything you have seen in your time in the field, what would it be?

A: Condition yourself to dabble in all kinds of media. Learn how to take good photos. Learn how to shoot and edit good video. Write with words and write with pictures. People think "Oh, I should make a video," but don't get fixated on the devices or the technology. Keep it focused on the skills, not the stuff. Content is king, because I'm not just making you a video or sending you a press release. What I'm really doing is telling you a story.

WHAT AUDIENCES NEED TO KNOW AND HOW TO MAKE THEM CARE

The interest items outlined in this chapter can help you draw an audience, but once you have your readers' attention, you need to communicate with them in an effective way. If you focus on what the audience members need, you will improve the likelihood that your writing will do its job well. Outlined below are three key needs and the questions they evoke as well as the best ways to meet those needs and answer those questions:

Key Need: Value

Question: Why Does This Matter to Me as a Reader?

Media professionals often write their copy from the wrong perspective. They construct a story, a pitch or a proposal to emphasize the issues they see as important or ideas they would prefer as consumers. However, the audience and the writer aren't always on the same page regarding **value**, and since the audience matters most, the writer needs to adapt.

When rookie news writers cover stories on topics like tuition increases, they tend to focus on the numbers from a collective perspective. It sounds stunning when they write "School officials said the university would collect an additional $12.4 million from students due to this increase." The number sounds big and it sounds scary, but it lacks value to the individual readers who will see their tuition bills rise.

Self-interest is a human trait that media writers need to embrace. The people who are reading news releases, watching commercials, analyzing marketing pitches or surfing a news site aren't doing so for the greater good of humanity. They are looking at the very basic question of "what's in this for me?" Good writers will look for the opportunity to present the value of material in a way that clearly answers that question.

Meet the Need: Explain

Answer: Show Your Reader a Personal Impact

As a writer, you should use your expertise to help other people understand important concepts. The more difficult each concept is, the slower you need to explain it and the more detailed you should be in your descriptions.

In the tuition-increase example, the writer needs to explain the value on an individual level: What does this mean to me, as a student, in terms of the dollars and cents I need to come up with to stay in school? This is where self-interest drives the value.

A good writer would note, "This tuition increase means the average student will pay $130 more each semester to attend the university." In explaining the tuition increase this way, the journalist would create a more direct line between the story and the reader. Students who read this sentence can figure out whether they need more hours at their jobs or need to take out additional loans.

Regardless of the media platform you use or the purpose of your communication, you want to present your readers with value. Look for ways that you can effectively give your readers a clear sense of why they should buy a product, donate to a cause, take part in an activity or look at a specific side of an issue. People are more likely to pay attention to items and look at issues if they know what is in it for them.

Key Need: Engagement

Question: Can You Tell It to Me in an Interesting Way?

When small children dislike a book or television show, their complaint is usually voiced in a specific and clear way: "This is BORING!" The material the child is consuming might have value or contain interesting information, but the way in which it is being put forth has not engaged the child's interest.

Contrast this with the reaction of children who loved the "Harry Potter" book series. These school-age children would line up with their parents for hours outside of bookstores in anticipation of the midnight release of each new volume. They would voraciously tear into the books and read until they had consumed every page. Clearly, author J. K. Rowling tapped into something when it came to **engagement**.

The most important information in the world doesn't matter if the people who need it aren't paying attention.

Meet the Need: Stimulate

Answer: Tell a Story That Will Pique Reader Interest

How you tell a story is the difference between having an enraptured audience and having people who are bored stiff. The way you emphasize certain elements of your story will determine how well you stimulate your readers.

For example, children enjoy stories that contain characters who are like them. Successful children's novelists like Beverly Cleary and Barbara Park tapped into this with main characters who were dealing with the trials and tribulations of children. Stories about the "Stupid Smelly Bus" and sibling conflicts at age 8 helped engage children because the tales met the readers at their own level.

This basic idea can translate well to help pique the interest of your readers. If you work in a field where you are promoting financial growth products, chances are your readers will want basic numbers and facts. Use a direct approach in your writing that will outline the best numbers first and use them to draw readers into your work. If you work for the National Marrow Donor Program, instead of using numbers to draw in your readers, you might use a more narrative approach, focusing on a single individual. This personal approach, known as using an exemplar, will create an emotional tie between the readers and message, as you put a human face on a larger issue.

Key Need: Action

Question: What Can I Do With What You Just Told Me?

A classic New Yorker cartoon by Robert Weber has two people sitting on a couch at a party. One says to the other, "I used to be in advertising. Remember 'Buy this, you morons'? That was mine." Although most advertisers would avoid this kind of blunt and insulting statement, the underlying concept has merit: You have to tell people what to do if you want to succeed in this field.

Advertising copy often has a clear **action statement** because advertisements should persuade consumers to purchase the product. However, most other forms of writing fall short in this crucial area.

In opinion columns or persuasive pitches, action is about telling people what to do if they agree with you. Most writers assume this element is implied, but you don't want to rely on the readers to take that last step alone. You want to bring the main idea home and help your readers see what they should do next.

For example, when students write opinion pieces in the student newspaper that complain about the parking conditions on campus, they can clearly demonstrate value to the readers. On most campuses, parking is often at a premium, and students usually feel they don't get enough of it.

The column can then engage the readers with anecdotes about students who have to park several miles from the main part of campus. The writer can then support these claims with numbers that show how students get far less good parking than do faculty members.

At the end of reading the column, the readers will likely see the writer's point and feel the writer's outrage. However, if there's no action element present, the writer leaves the readers wondering, "OK, now what?" Should they complain to administrators? Boycott the parking system? Ride bikes to school? Do a sit-in at the parking office?

Meet the Need: Propose Options

Answer: Offer Readers Ways To Act

When you have the opportunity to tell people what you want them to do with the information you provided, you should do so. This concept extends beyond opinion pieces or promotional material and can be useful across all forms of writing.

In advertisements, the action is clearly implied: If you like what we are saying, go buy our products. However, other levels of writing in advertising require a more nuanced explanation of how action should occur.

For example, a creative pitch (see Chapter 13) should include not only the campaign ideas but also how much money should be spent, what types of ads should be purchased and how long the campaign should take. In addition, information such as start and end dates need to be explicit.

In terms of news, if you write stories about tax increases or changes to public policy, do so far enough in advance to give people a chance to attend meetings where officials will debate these issues. You can also include contact information so the members of your audience can reach out to the decision makers.

If you promote events, you must include time, date and place information so people know where to go and when to get there. You also could include other helpful information, such as whether tickets are necessary.

If you write "how-to" pieces, you should address every important issue at each step in a process so that people can make sure they are doing it right. In some cases, images can be extremely helpful, but your writing alone should be able to do the job properly.

THE BIG THREE

Here are the three thoughts you should take away from this chapter:

1. **Focus on the readers:** You are the writer, but you aren't writing for yourself. You are writing for an audience that has specific wants and needs. The better you understand who these audience members are and what they need, the better chance you will have in reaching them.

2. **Content is king:** You need to reach people on a variety of platforms and devices, but what you tell these people will always trump any element of technology. If something is important, well written and communicated effectively, people will read it. Focus on the ways in which you can meet your audience's needs as you create your content.

3. **Rely on core interest elements:** Fame, oddity, conflict, immediacy and impact are the primary interest elements for media writers. When you start writing content and you are unsure what to do, consider each of these elements and look for ways to emphasize them as you try to reach your readers. This will provide you a solid foundation upon which you can build the rest of your work.

KEY TERMS

action statement 15
audience 3
audience segmentation 4
conflict 11
demographics 4
engagement 15
fame 10
FOCII 9

geographic information 5
immediacy 11
impact 12
interest elements 9
microtargeting 4
niche 7
oddity 10
outlet 8

personification 6
platforms 4
psychographics 5
qualitative 12
quantitative 12
value 14

DISCUSSION QUESTIONS

1. What media do you tend to consume to gain information? Discuss this in terms of both the outlets you use and the platform or format. For example, do you read the student "newspaper" in print or only online? Do you watch television on your mobile device? What about the content drives you to consume it, and what makes you prefer the platform you use?

2. Of the three types of audience segmentation listed in the chapter, which one is most important to you as a reader? Why do you think this is? Which one is least important to you? Why do you feel that way?

3. Reread the information associated with the three key needs listed near the end of the chapter (value, engagement, action). When you look at the media you consume, do you think the writers do a good job of working through all three needs? Which ones are traditionally handled the best? Which ones are usually handled poorly? Why do you think this is?

WRITE NOW!

1. Review the five interest elements listed in the chapter and determine which ones are most influential when it comes to things you consume in the media. Then determine which ones are least important. Finally, pick a story that interests you from a local media outlet and see which interest elements are present and absent. Write up your findings.

2. Find a story topic multiple media outlets have covered and select two articles on that topic that serve different audiences. For example, you might look at a specific movie review that ran in a teen publication versus one that ran in a general-interest publication. You could also look at a story on a political topic on sites that tilt toward one side of the political spectrum or the other. Read through each of these and note how the coverage meets the needs of the audience. How much of the content is similar and how much is different between the two? What are your thoughts on how these publications covered these topics.

3. Explore the demographic details of your school in terms of age, gender, race and the in-state/out-of-state gap. Write a paragraph that outlines these details. Then select another institution that has a similar demographic breakdown and take the same approach. Now, compare and contrast your schools in terms of other details, including geography and psychographics. How similar are your schools and why do you think that is? Use examples to illustrate your point.

NOTES

1. J. G. Webster and T. B. Ksiazek (2012). "The Dynamics of Audience Fragmentation: Public Attention in an Age of Digital Media." Journal of Communication, 62(1), 39–56.

2. J. Schafer and T. Doherty (2017, May/June). "The Media Bubble Is Worse Than You Think." Politico. Accessed at: http://www.politico.com/magazine/story/2017/04/25/media-bubble-real-journalism-jobs-east-coast-215048.

3. J. Lazauskas (2013, Aug. 14). "The Revolution Will Be Listicled." Accessed at: https://contently.com/strategist/2013/08/14/the-revolution-will-be-listicled-why-this-supposed-content-fad-may-have-actually-taken-over/.

4. W. Oremus (2013, July 18). "The Rise of the Demolisticle." Slate. Accessed at: http://www.slate.com/articles/technology/future_tense/2013/07/demolisticles_buzzfeed_lists_crafted_for_specific_demographics_are_social.html.

5. M. S. Brown (2016, May 29). "Big Data Analytics and the Next President: How Microtargeting Drives Today's Campaigns." Forbes. Accessed at: https://www.forbes.com/sites/metabrown/2016/05/29/big-data-analytics-and-the-next-president-how-microtargeting-drives-todays-campaigns/#26406bd36c42.

6. Technology Trends. "Burger King Products—Products—Packaging." Accessed at: https://www.primidi.com/burger_king_products/products/packaging/.

7. Knight Foundation (2016, May 11). "Mobile-First News: How People Use Smartphones to Access Information." Accessed at: https://knightfoundation.org/reports/mobile-first-news-how-people-use-smartphones-acces.

8. Deloitte (2016). "2016 Global Mobile Consumer Survey: US Edition." Accessed at: https://www2.deloitte.com/us/en/pages/technology-media-and-telecommunications/articles/global-mobile-consumer-survey-us-edition.html#.

9. TMZ (2017). "Donald Trump on Stephen Colbert: 'No-Talent' Hack With 'Filthy Mouth.'" Accessed at: http://www.tmz.com/2017/05/11/donald-trump-stephen-colbert-no-talent-filthy-mouth-feud/.

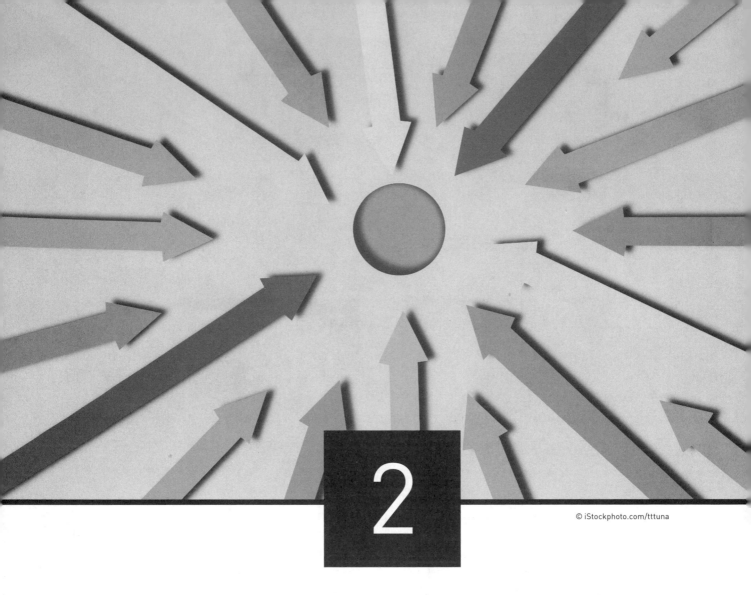

2

BEING ACCURATE, RELYING ON THE FACTS

"By defeating the Soviet Union in the 'Miracle on Ice' game, the 1980 United States Olympic hockey team won the gold medal."

"Mount Everest is the tallest mountain in the world."

"Dr. Jonas Salk, born of Russian-Jewish immigrant parents, invented polio in the 1950s."

If taken at face value and with a quick glance, each of these items would likely be viewed as fact. The movie "Miracle" details the Olympic hockey team's triumph at the Lake Placid games, where they defeated the Soviets and prompted Al Michaels' famous broadcast call: "Do you believe in miracles?" The name "Mount Everest" has become synonymous with giant obstacles to be overcome, and a quick peek at the Wikipedia page for it notes that it is "the Earth's highest mountain." If you Google the words "Salk" and "polio," thousands of entries show up.

However, these three statements are wrong.

The United States did defeat the Soviet Union in the Miracle on Ice game and did win the gold medal in those Olympics. However, winning the game didn't earn the team the medal. After beating the Soviets, the U.S. team had to defeat Finland in the finals to win gold.

Mount Everest is the highest mountain in the world, as mountain height is measured from sea level to the top of the peak. However, the "tallness" of a mountain is traditionally measured from the base of the mountain to its peak. This means that Mauna Kea in Hawaii, which has an appreciable amount of its base underwater, is 33,476 feet tall and thus is taller than Mount Everest (29,029 feet).

Dr. Jonas Salk was born of Russian-Jewish immigrant parents and was involved in polio research in the 1950s. That said, he invented the polio vaccine, not polio itself.

It would be easy to dismiss these errors as insignificant or a bit of nerd-level trickery. "Aw, you know what I meant," is often the complaint people make when confronted with errors like these.

However, you can't be almost right most of the time if you work in a media organization. You have to be entirely right all of the time or at least push yourself toward that goal. Accuracy is the most important aspect of your job, regardless of whether you are publishing a newspaper, broadcasting a news report, issuing a press release or sending out an advertisement. A factual inaccuracy can crush the best writing, the most creative ad and the most innovative campaign.

As you collect information as a media writer, make sure your content is as accurate as possible.

In this chapter, we will outline why accuracy should be at the forefront of your mind. We will also examine where most people get tripped up in the world of facts. Finally, we will discuss how best to check the accuracy of your work and how to avoid major pitfalls along the way.

WHY IS JOURNALISM SUCH A PICKY FIELD?

In the movie version of the Neil Simon play "Biloxi Blues," the main character maintains a journal in which he writes his thoughts about people and life in general during his time at a boot camp in 1945. When one of his musings leads to a confrontation among several men, he finds himself understanding the power of the written word:

"People believe whatever they read. Something magical happens once it's put down on paper. They figure no one would have gone to the trouble of writing it down if it wasn't the truth. Responsibility was my new watchword."

If you take that concept and pair it with the line famously attributed to Mark Twain about how "a lie can travel halfway around the world while the truth is still putting on its shoes," you can see why journalism requires the utmost attention to accuracy.

The goal of good media writers is to inform the readers of something that will benefit the media organization and the audience members. This shared bond of trust is what keeps people showing up at public events, heading to the stores and reading news stories. The more mistakes we make in journalism, the harder it is to maintain that bond. Even more, not everyone who publishes information, sends out tweets or reaches out to the public in other ways shares our professional duty to the truth. As you will see later in this chapter, many people have no problem starting rumors and spreading lies. For some people, it is a joke, whereas for others it is a chance to take advantage of an unsuspecting public. In any case, this misinformation makes it harder on media practitioners who hold themselves to a higher standard.

WHY MEDIA PROFESSIONALS MATTER MORE THAN EVER

The role of media professionals has changed a great deal over the past several decades. In the pre-internet era, newspapers and TV newscasters selected and presented information, giving certain stories and ideas a sense of importance. This selection process, known as **gatekeeping**, allowed media officials to determine what people would and would not see. Public-relations practitioners were often limited in how they sent their messages to the public, as news reporters could pick and choose which events were covered and which topics were highlighted. Advertisers had fewer venues they could use to publish advertisements, because of the limited number of broadcast channels and the presence of only one or two newspapers per geographic region.

Today, the internet has opened up the floodgates of information, making the job of professional media operatives different but even more crucial. Anyone can start a website and post content of any kind. Facebook, Twitter, Instagram and other social media channels give people the opportunity to spread information quickly. Public-relations practitioners and advertisers no longer need to rely on newspapers or TV stations to reach potential audience members with important content.

However, these endless possibilities can overwhelm readers and viewers, leaving them at the mercy of unscrupulous or uninformed individuals. Therefore, media writers are important not only as content creators but also as tour guides. They help people separate fact from fiction, reality from myth and honesty from dishonesty.

Your goal as a media practitioner, regardless of the area in which you work, is to establish a bond of trust with your readership and do your best to present accurate information. In doing so, you will help guide your readers as they decide what to think, what to believe and what to do. Every time you provide accurate information, you give your readers another reason to believe what you tell them. However, any error, no matter how minor, can destroy all the good work you have done.

ADAPT
THE FIGHT AGAINST FAKE NEWS

© LAWeekly.com

Fake news takes on a variety of meanings, depending on who uses the term. To some people, fake news includes satire sites like The Onion, which seek to mock news or poke fun at public figures. Others argue that any partisan news that fails to reflect their own worldview falls into the category of fake news. Still others see fake news as being hoaxes that internet trolls use to trick journalists and readers into believing and spreading false information. As a media professional, producing or sharing incorrect information is something you need to avoid, regardless of whether it comes from a source who has an axe to grind or a person who just wants to fake you out.

Hoaxes crop up on social media often and gain momentum when people fail to check sources or question the veracity of the information. In July 2017, the most recent version of the "Facebook friend hacker hoax" emerged when warnings ping-ponged all around the site, thanks to friends' warning everyone they knew not to accept a friend request from Jayden K. Smith. The shared message states that Smith was trolling Facebook users and that becoming friends with Smith would give him access to all of your connections and information on Facebook.[1] Snopes.com, a fact-checking

site, has noted the emergence of more than a dozen similar hoaxes[2] throughout the years.

In many cases, the desire to be first on an important development can lead you astray. On July 6, 2013, Asiana Airlines Flight 214 crashed as it approached San Francisco International Airport, setting off a frenzy of media coverage. As part of its coverage on July 12, KTVU-TV in Oakland announced a major scoop: the names of the pilots involved. Unfortunately, a National Transportation Safety Board intern had duped the station, giving the journalists a series of fake and offensive names, including "Capt. Sum Ting Wong" and "Wi Tu Lo." Although the intern was fired, KTVU-TV was forced to apologize, and the news outlet eventually fired three longtime staffers as a result of the gaffe.[3] In this and other cases, bad journalistic attempts at humor can lead to problematic errors and other miserable experiences.

Unlike in previous eras, fake news is everywhere, and it is becoming exceedingly difficult to distinguish it from real news. To help you avoid getting faked out, here are some helpful tips:

- **Consider the source:** Where information comes from is crucial in determining how much credence you should put into a story. Think about when you were in grade school and you heard some unbelievable story from "that one kid" on the playground who always was making stuff up. Chances are, you learned to stop believing him after you discovered that there wasn't a pool on the roof of the gym and that there was no such thing as "No Pants Wednesday." However, when your teacher or the principal told you something, you tended to give it serious consideration. Apply the same basic rule when you consider information you find online. "Who told you

(Continued)

(Continued)

that?" should be one of the first questions you ask when you get information that doesn't seem to pass the smell test. Also, as copy editor Jennifer Morehead notes later in this chapter, it makes sense to rely on official sources like .gov sites instead of places like "IAmTheMasterOfAllCoolThings.blogspot .com."

- **Strength exists in numbers:** If you get information from a single source online, don't pass it along without looking for similar information from other sources. Just because the source you found isn't one you know all that well, it doesn't always follow that the information isn't accurate. Sites outside of the mainstream media break news and share information all the time. However, if the information is incredibly important or shocking, the mainstream media outlets will follow up with their own stories. However, if you find only once source for your story that the president of the United States is actually an alien from Saturn, it's a pretty safe bet you're looking at some level of fake news.

- **The root of the rumor:** Along the same lines as the previous point, just because a quick Google search reveals dozens of stories on a given topic, it doesn't always follow that the information is true. Some sites frequently refer to their own content only and create an echo chamber of information that lacks external support. Good media writing will have multiple and varied sources. Most media outlets will find similar sources, but they don't all tend to rely on the same people. In other words, if 12 media outlets produce a story on the importance of a new drug or the impact of a new virus, all 12 will likely talk to a scientist or a doctor. However, each outlet will likely use different scientists and doctors than the other 11 outlets. If everyone is talking to the same "root source," you have reason for concern.

Dig into stories that cite only a single source or all come back to a single story online before you pass the information along as true.

- **Click the links:** The purpose of links is the same as the purpose of citations in a research paper you would do for a class: Support the claims you are making. However, just because a link exists, it doesn't always follow that the information behind it will support or validate the claims in a story. Click the links and see where they lead you. Does the information at the other end of that click really support the key aspects of what author says it does? Does the link lead you to a credible outside source, or does it link to only other stories by the same author, spouting the same general information? The more you examine the links and the sources to which they lead, the less likely you are to believe something that isn't true.

- **Be suspicious:** One of the best ways to avoid letting fake news trick you is to be a bit paranoid about every piece of information you receive. The Russian proverb "Trust, but verify" should guide you through anything you read. Independently verify the information in a piece before you pass it along to others. Check the quality of the sources before you put your own reputation on the line. A good way to process "facts" in a piece is to assume everything you see is incorrect until you can prove it to be true. Some people may say that's a bit too paranoid, but it's better to be overly suspicious than to be wrong.

GIVE IT A TRY: Think you can tell fake news from the real deal? Check out this online quiz called "Factitious," which was developed by a veteran journalist and a game designer through the game lab at American University. The quiz provides you with clues as to the source as well as hints after the fact to help you sharpen your fake-finding skills: http://factitious.augamestudio.com.

MAKING SURE YOU ARE SURE

Journalists often use the line "if your mother says she loves you, go check it out" as a basic rule for accuracy. In other words, don't assume that something is true, even if you believe it to be. A mild sense of paranoia will keep you on your toes and force you to view every fact you

PolitiFact is one organization that examines the claims of politicians and rates how accurate they are through the use of its "Truth-o-Meter."

use with a sense of suspicion. This can help you make sure that you are sure before you state something with certainty.

Some things may seem unworthy of your attention, but you should realize that someone is always watching. One famous example comes from the contract of the rock band Van Halen in 1982. The "rider," which lists specific demands the band makes beyond the common contract language, was 53 pages long and told promoters that they needed to provide M&M's candy but added this: "Warning: absolutely no brown ones." This requirement forced some employee at the venue to pick through the bowls of candy and remove all the brown and tan M&M's. The band members later explained that this was not a case of being ridiculous with their demands, but rather a way to test the staff at the venue. If brown M&M's were in the bowls, they assumed that bigger issues, such as lighting, staging and security, might also be suspect.[4]

The lesson here is a simple one: If your readers can't trust you with the simple issues, how can you expect them to trust you with the bigger ones?

Basic Fact Checking

A simple **fact check** can take a significant amount of time if you do it right. You need to examine each fact you put into anything you write and then look for any way in which that item might be inaccurate or misleading. Here is a short list of steps to take during a basic fact check:

Check Spelling

Accuracy is about making sure you are right, and to that extent, you need to spell all words correctly. If you have a document full of typos or misspelled words, you will have serious credibility issues. You should always run a computer-based spell check on every piece you do and examine each spelling suggestion carefully. Don't click the "replace all" button or rapidly click the "replace" button as errors pop up. Look at each offering the software provides, and then pick the right replacement.

You also need to do a line-by-line examination of your pieces for words that might be spelled properly but weren't what you meant to write. For example, if you want to study something carefully, you want to "assess" it, not "asses" it. Perhaps the most embarrassing example of a properly spelled improper word choice came in September 2010, when the South Bend, Indiana, school district posted a billboard that alerted people to the "15 best things about our pubic schools."[5]

In each case, the word was spelled properly, but it wasn't an accurate representation of what the writer meant. Spell check doesn't catch your best intentions, so carefully reread your work for any spelling errors or word glitches.

Review Proper Nouns

The spell-check function on most word-processing programs will catch errors in the spelling of common words. However, the names of people, places and things often look like mistakes to the electronic dictionaries.

If you misspell someone's name or the name of someone's group, you will insult that person and make him or her less likely to work with you. That is why you need to do a letter-by-letter examination of every proper noun in anything you write.

When you interview a source, as you will learn how to do in Chapter 5, have the person spell his or her name. It also helps to ask at that point how the source wishes to be cited in your work. Richard Smith could prefer Rich, Rick or Ricky, so it helps to ask. As you take notes on this, write each letter in your notebook carefully so you can go back and check your finished piece against your notes.

If you need to use other material to check a proper noun, use a source you trust, such as a company directory or an official website. Again, go letter by letter to make sure you get it right. Also, take a quick check of any style guides your organization might use. The stationery might list your group as "Smith-Rock Corporation," but your style guide might require that all references in formal documents refer to it as "Smith/Rock Corp." "The Associated Press Stylebook" also is helpful in standardizing official company names and titles.

Finally, check the entire document for consistency. If one part of your news story mentions "Gov. Charles Smith," and five sentences later, he is referred to as "Smyth," one version of the name is obviously wrong. You should also check what you wrote against other pieces you or your organization already published. If one press release lists your boss as Chairman Mike Smith and the second one lists him as Assistant Chairman Mike Smith, you will likely confuse your readers. Even worse, if your audience is a media outlet, that confusion will then be broadcast to a larger population, and the error will continue to propagate.

Look Into The Numbers

Media professionals often joke that they got into journalism because they can't do math. Like it or not, math is a part of this field, and you need to come to grips with it, because numerical errors can create a lot of problems for you and your readers.

Look at math in your writing and make sure it's right. In obituaries, do the math from the person's birth date to his or her death date and make sure the age is right. Just because someone was born in 1940 and died in 2017 doesn't mean the person was 77 years old.

When someone is talking about money or percentages, take the time to walk through the math. Think of it like a story problem from grade school. "OK, if the tax brought in $50,000 and the fees brought in $90,000, how does that add up to $150,000?" You might locate math errors that need to be addressed, or you might be missing part of the equation that makes this odd-looking math make sense.

Understand the difference between percentages and percentage points. If your company institutes a policy stating that it donates 10 percent of its profits to charity, you might need to write a press release about that. If your company says that it plans to increase that amount by 50 percent next year, this means it will be donating 15 percent of its profits to charity (10 percent × 0.5 = 5 percent plus the original 10 percent = 15 percent). If it says that it will increase its donation by 50 percentage points, you have a huge increase (10 percent + 50 percentage points = 60 percent).

Always do the math yourself to double-check any figures you want to use. Also, make sure to check back with the source of those figures to verify your understanding and your approach to the math.

Check Places

When you list places for your events, double-check the addresses against a map and a directory. If you hold an event at 1111 S. Main St. and you list it as 1111 N. Main St., you might be a bit lonely. Also, differences exist among streets, avenues, boulevards and more.

In some large metropolitan areas, like Manhattan, both streets and avenues are numerically based, so you need to know whether you are heading to Fifth Street or Fifth Avenue.

If you decide to include a set of directions, make sure the directions work. Drive or walk the route yourself or have someone who isn't familiar with the area examine the route to see if it makes sense. Physically doing this will help you find out if you missed a turn or if you accidentally have someone going the wrong way down a one-way street.

CONNECT
THE TELEPHONE GAME

If you want to connect with your audience in terms of accuracy, you can think of a game that almost always ends with a disconnect. Children often play "telephone," a game where one person whispers something to another person, that person whispers it to the next person, and so on. Somewhere along the way, the message inevitably will be misinterpreted or mangled, and in the end, you will end up with something that is nothing like the original statement.

As you examine your work for accuracy, keep the telephone game in mind. If you don't have a **primary source** or a solid **secondary source**, you run the risk of passing along information that might have been altered. A primary source allows you to take information from someone or something that was present for whatever it is you are researching. These sources can include a person who witnessed a shooting, the original text of a speech or a video of a news conference. Secondary sources are like the second person in the "telephone"

game: They retell or interpret what the primary sources provided them. Wikipedia, a magazine article and a person who is telling you a story they heard from a friend are all examples of secondary sources.

You want to get as close as you can to the original source so you have fewer chances to make errors.

GIVE IT A TRY: Take a trip back to grade school and play a game of telephone in your class. Have one person start with a basic fact and develop a simple sentence. The person should write it down and give it to your instructor. Then, do the whispering part of the game, with each person in a row sharing the sentence until it gets all the way around to the final person. How close was the final version to the original version? Where did it go off the rails? How much effort did it take for you to keep the information accurate? Keep that in mind the next time you see an internet rumor grow and morph over time.

Where to Find Your Facts

When it comes to fact checking, you want to have confidence in the sources of information you use to verify your writing. Here are some places you can go to complete your fact check and verify your information:

Source Documents

Whenever possible, get copies of original documents so you can compare what people have told you with what someone wrote. People have an uncanny way of being inaccurate or confused, while documents tend to remain exactly the way they were written. Even well-known phrases get jumbled over time and require a source check. In the movie "Apollo 13," Capt. Jim Lovell, played by Tom Hanks, utters the famous line "Houston, we have a problem." This sentence became part of the marketing campaign for the movie and remains a pop-culture referent for situations that go haywire. However, the actual Apollo 13 mission transcript demonstrates that the movie line was incorrectly stated and attributed. Initially, pilot Jack Swigert said, "I believe we've had a problem here." When asked to repeat that statement,

PROFESSIONAL THOUGHTS
JENNIFER MOREHEAD

Regardless of the size of the story or overall impact of the piece, Jennifer Morehead subscribes to a simple philosophy when it comes to checking writers' copy for errors.

"I've tried to approach stories of every kind in the same basic way: They *must* be accurate, they *must* be clear. . . . Someone always notices," she said. "Errors in any story, from local crime briefs to big features, erode credibility."

Morehead has served as a copy editor for some of the country's most recognized and exalted news sources. She currently serves as a copy editor at the Washington Post. She edits the Sunday op-ed section and handles copy editing for print and online stories and blogs for the national, foreign, metro, life/arts and business desks. Prior to her stint at the Post, she was a copy editor for the New York Times, the Houston Chronicle, the Seattle Post-Intelligencer and the San Francisco Chronicle.

Morehead said that no writer ever creates perfect copy, but the more mistakes a media organization makes, the less credibility it will have in the eyes of its readers.

"It's easy to think that 'no one will notice' the little stuff," she said. "A misspelled name? A math error? An incorrect statistic from a baseball game that was played in 1973? When dealing with details, keep three words in mind: Someone always notices. How do we know? Because news organizations get multiple emails, tweets, calls and letters every day from readers pointing out even the smallest factual mistakes, not to mention grammatical ones."

To catch and correct these errors, Morehead said she uses several editing techniques, including reading a story multiple times.

"My first read of a story is the fact-checking read," she said. "I start at the beginning, and anytime I come to a proper name, a date, a number (any kind of number, from a percentage to a death toll to someone's age), statistics, a quote from a previously published source (such as another article, a book or a transcript), a title, a time, historical references or just about anything else presented as fact, I check it, most often using the Internet. I most heavily rely on articles from my own publication, for consistency's sake, as well as primary documents or official

websites. If I'm checking the spelling of an astronaut's name, for instance, I go to NASA.gov, not something like ThisIsMyAwesomeSpaceBlog .com."

Jennifer Morehead

Morehead also said she uses her own internal compass to note statements that don't seem entirely accurate so she can check them against other sources.

"I'm also on the lookout for statements that just seem 'off,'" she said. "Real examples I've encountered: No, Robert E. Lee is not buried at Arlington National Cemetery. The movie 'Xanadu' is about a roller disco, not a roller derby. No, Americans don't have a right to the 'ballet'—that would be the ballot."

The editing process for Morehead is about more than parsing arcane grammar rules or picking at a writer's story. She said the value of editing is about making a piece of copy valuable to the people who are reading it.

"Editing is about clarity and getting to the point—choosing the right words to express your idea in an effective way," Morehead said. "The bits of writing that newspaper copy editors do as part of our jobs—headlines and captions—are intended to connect with an audience; successful display type makes readers pay attention. I can imagine either of these skills being useful in a PR or advertising setting. For instance, my mother sometimes writes fundraising letters for charitable causes she's involved in. These letters have to be compelling from the start, so people will continue reading and be moved to respond, hopefully with a check. My mom will often call me to work out those opening lines, and I draw on years of editing good and bad newspaper leads to help come up with attention-grabbing language."

Regardless of the field, Morehead said learning how to fact-check, clean copy and improve writing will provide anyone in media writing with an important set of skills.

"Editing helps you develop attention to detail, fact-checking skills, a wide range of knowledge about all kinds of subjects, and a certain kind of diplomacy and tact that comes from having to nicely explain to writers why they're wrong," she said.

One Last Thing

Q: If you could tell students anything about media writing or anything you have seen in your time in the field, what would it be?

A: In an information economy, where writing and communicating are more important than ever, learning to edit is such a critical skill. It makes you a better writer. It makes you a better reader. It will make you look smarter. It may help you get a date. (My friend is getting married to a man she met online; his grammatically correct, typo-free Match.com profile caught her eye.) And some people will discover that they love it for its own sake. You know who you are.

Lovell said, "Houston, we've had a problem."[6] If you can get your hands on source material, you can cite it with much more certainty. When you are researching a topic, or interviewing a source, seek email correspondence, meeting minutes, official documents and other similar items. Keeping copies of these items handy can be helpful in checking your work.

Dead-Tree Publications

Newspapers, magazines, books and other publications made from "dead trees" aren't always infallible, but at least you know from where they came. You can also see that some publisher thought enough of the content to put forth money to physically produce them. Editors, copy editors and other experts have likely seen the content at some level before it goes to press, so you can feel slightly more confident in this than in a website that has an unknown origin. In addition, most of the dead-tree publications will archive their content both physically and digitally, which allows you to research as far back as the archives reach.

Official Websites

When you use .gov or .edu websites, you are accessing information from a governmental or an educational outlet. In most cases, these can be more trustworthy than .com, .net, or .us sites, which anyone can start. Beyond those sites, you can look at official sites for specific organizations associated with your writing. If you are building a media kit for a client and you want to provide some history about the client's organization, you can use the organization's website as a solid source. If you are writing a news article about the hiring of a chancellor at a local university, you can find biographical data for that person on that university's website and the sites of the chancellor's previous jobs. You can both cite this information and link to it as you support your statements.

Your Own Work

In some cases, you become the expert on a topic as you research it, cover it, publicize it or market it. After a while, you know more about the issue or product than anyone else. When this happens, you can rely on your previous work to prevent you from having to redo all your research every time you work on that topic. If you digitally archive your work, a search can be easy. If you keep boxes of papers around you, it can be more difficult, depending on your approach to organization. However, when you do quality work at the forefront of your research, you can reap the benefits again and again.

EXAMINING THE BROADER ISSUES

You might have everything spelled right and the math done perfectly, but that doesn't mean you have an accurate piece of writing. Anything you produce can have errors that go beyond corrections you can make with a Google search and a dictionary. Bigger concepts, nuanced word choices and similar issues can put you in hot water just as easily as a misspelled name or an incorrect street address. Below is a list of some key areas you should examine before finalizing any piece of writing:

Stick to What People Said

One of the most famous headlines in New York history came from a complete falsehood. In the mid-1970s, the city of New York teetered on the edge of bankruptcy. Officials had asked President Gerald Ford to provide federal funds to help the city stave off the financial crisis. On Oct. 29, 1975, Ford gave a speech in which he explained that he would not bail out the city. The next day's headline in the New York Daily News proclaimed: "FORD TO CITY: DROP DEAD."

The president never used those words and would later say that the headline wasn't accurate and "was very unfair." Even though the headline wasn't in quotation marks (something we will discuss more in Chapter 10), it still sounded as though the president had said those words. Decades later, he continued to speak out against the way in which the paper portrayed him.[7]

Although an extreme example, this headline reveals what can happen when you use poetic license and alter the words associated with your sources. When you rely on words that are "close enough" to what someone told you or you swap similar-sounding words, you can land in a big heap of trouble.

If you interview the CEO of your company for a profile on the company's website, she might say "We're going to make consumer confidence a top priority this year." However, if you write "CEO Jane Johnson said the company will make consumer confidence its number one task," you have significantly altered what she said. "A" top priority means that this is one item of several at the top of the priority list. That's not the same as "the" top priority, which means that it is the most important task on the company's list of priorities. Even worse, if some other news release or profile quoted her saying that something else was "the" top priority, now she looks foolish, and you are to blame.

When you have to write something and attribute it to a source, you want to stick to what the person said. The more you stray from the actual verbiage the person used, the more problems you can cause for everyone involved.

Avoid Vague Terms

Accuracy is often in the details, and the details aren't always easy to find. Journalists tend to try to "write around" these problems with vague terms and soft language. Unfortunately, that usually leads to the kinds of "telephone game" problems discussed elsewhere in this chapter.

The use of certain words has led to a number of online "reporter dictionaries" that humorously define what certain words actually mean when you see them. A few vague words that made the cut:

Recently: The reporter lost the press release with the actual date on it.

Allegedly: Someone did something bad, but we can't prove it.

Reportedly: We stole this from someone else's report.

Unknown: We can't figure it out.

Likely: We can't figure it out, no one will tell us and yet we need to say something about it.

In most cases, you can find terms like this in your own writing, but the reason for their presence is far less funny: You don't have the facts.

If you find yourself saying something like "arguably," it means you want to make a statement of fact, but you haven't done enough research to do so. If you say, "in recent memory," it means you are afraid you didn't look far enough back into the history of something.

Instead of sticking with these and other vague terms, do more research to solidify your claims or attribute the information to a source. Instead of saying "This is arguably the biggest merger in recent memory," tell people exactly what is going on: "The merger of Smith Corp. and Johnson Inc. will create $15.8 billion in revenue, making it the largest merger of this kind since 2001, according to Smith Corp. CEO Bill Smith." Then do more research to back up your statement and make sure you are sure.

Say Only What You Know for Sure

As Chapter 13 notes, people often rely on **hyperbole** to make their points, which leads to suspicious consumers and empty promises. The desire to state that something is "the biggest" or "the first" or anything along those lines can lead writers to create overblown copy that lacks value and that fails to engage readers.

Logical lapses can happen when you state something with absolute certainty that isn't absolute. "All people drink diet soda." How do we know this? How can we assume that every person on the face of the Earth has participated in this behavior? In most cases, stating an absolute is the first step toward trouble. Watch yourself when you see words like "all," "always," "none" and "never," to name a few. The same is true of words like "worst," "only" and "greatest."

When you are writing, you need to make sure you say only what you know for sure. In news, this can be extremely difficult when a breaking news situation has information pouring out of every media outlet and you are worried you might be lagging behind. In the moments after the first plane struck the World Trade Center on Sept. 11, 2001, early reports inaccurately stated that the aircraft was a small Cessna-like plane instead of an

As we say in newsrooms, "If your mother says she loves you, go check it out."

airliner.[8] In the aftermath of the disaster, it became clear that this statement was false. The rush to get information on the air from any possible source led to these early errors. Although speed matters a great deal in news, accuracy always trumps it.

If you are promoting a cause, an event or a sale, the desire to inflate the importance of your efforts can make it difficult to avoid hyperbole. As we noted in Chapter 1, audience members react well to oddities and one-of-a-kind opportunities, so pushing your language in that direction seems like a good idea. However, you must explain how you came to your conclusions. If you state your organization's charity walk is "the largest in the state," you need to quantify that statement. Are you saying it has the most participants or it raises the most money? Does it draw the most spectators or lead to the highest number of overall donors? What makes it the "largest?" If you can't explain it, don't write it.

Find More Than One Good Source for Key Facts

The ability to support an argument often rests on the quality and quantity of your source material. If you were arguing astrophysics with a friend who cited the research of the holder of a doctorate in that field, you would look foolish if you said, "According to my 10-year-old cousin. . . . " The quality of your source is clearly not as strong as the one your friend has cited.

Oddly enough, it doesn't necessarily follow that your cousin is wrong and that the Ph.D. is right. This is where examining multiple sources can come into play. It is possible that your cousin's statement is the same as 99 percent of the people in the astrophysics community and the expert your friend cited is in the minority.

The key is to examine as many sources as you can, assess the quality of those sources and make an intelligent statement based on what you learn.

For example, in 1995, the Million Man March took place in Washington, D.C. The event was a massive gathering of people who came from across the United States to demonstrate positive views of African-Americans in the wake of numerous negative stereotypes. The organizers of the event stated attendance figures between 1.5 million and 2 million people, but the National Park Service initially issued an estimate of 400,000. Park officials later called the estimate a bit low and moved it up into the 600,000 to 850,000 range. A group at Boston University said the number was likely 870,000, but the group's method had an error of plus or minus 25 percent. This means the number could have been anywhere from 655,000 to 1.1 million.[9] In the end, no one knows how many people attended the event.

Always examine the facts from both a qualitative and quantitative angle, and then write only what you can prove or what you can attribute.

THE BIG THREE

Here are the three key thoughts you should take away from this chapter:

1. **Accuracy matters most:** Of all the skills you will learn as you read this book, accuracy is the most important one. A tiny spelling error can crush even the best writers, most creative minds and strongest advocates. Keep accuracy at the forefront of every

action you take during your writing and editing processes.

2. **Look it up:** If you don't know something for sure, look it up. You will feel a lot better when you know you have the right answer. If you are certain you know something, look it up anyway. It will feel great to confirm how smart you are. You always want to

support your statements with the best information available.

3. **People can be cruel:** Don't assume that everyone operates under the same ethical and accuracy guidelines you are expected to use. People start internet rumors for their own amusement. Some groups and organizations don't care if they are accurate or fair when they make statements. Don't assume that all information you find is of high quality. Verify, reassess and scrutinize anything you find and the sources in which you found it before you put your reputation on the line.

KEY TERMS

fact check 25

fake news 23

gatekeeping 22

hyperbole 31

logical lapses 31

primary source 27

secondary source 27

DISCUSSION QUESTIONS

1. Have you ever been the victim of a media hoax? Maybe you heard that your favorite band was getting back together or that a famous actor was dead. How far did you go in checking it out before telling people about it or sharing that information online? When you found out someone "got you" with the hoax, how did you feel?

2. What do you see as the biggest problems regarding accuracy in the media today? This could be the prevalence of minor errors, such as spelling or grammar gaffes. It could also be issues related to bias, which is a charge often leveled against certain PR firms, CNN, Fox News and other media outlets. Why do you think your choice matters most in how people consume information?

3. In some countries, journalists need a license from the government to publish content. The rationale, in some cases, is that licensing creates a common standard of accuracy and integrity among "official" journalists. Do you think licensing journalists is a good idea? Why or why not? Outside of licensing, what do you think should be done to better assure accuracy and limit hoaxes and rumors?

WRITE NOW!

1. Research one internet hoax that has recently circulated. It can be an erroneous report of someone's death, a major factual inaccuracy in a story of great significance or even an internet meme that has taken on a life of its own. Write a few paragraphs about the hoax, explaining what it is, the origin of the hoax and how eventually it became debunked. Then outline at least three things you learned from this and how you would use those bits of knowledge to help you avoid making a similar mistake.

2. Prepare five statements that could be factually accurate but would require research to disprove. In at least one of those statements, make a factual error. Then exchange your list of statements with a fellow student and set about analyzing the list of statements you received. Determine each statement to be true or false, explain why that is the case and then cite a source for each answer.

3. Select a story that interests you from a newspaper, magazine or website. Examine each fact within the story and verify its accuracy. Explain where you found the information that supports your verification. If you find an inaccuracy, explain how you determined the item to be inaccurate.

NOTES

1. Jennifer Earl (2017, July 11). "Who Is Jayden K. Smith? Stop Sharing This Viral Facebook Message." CBS .com. Accessed at: http://www.cbsnews.com/news/stop-sharing-that-viral-jayden-k-smith-facebook-message-right-now/.

2. "Social Media Hacker Warning." Accessed at: http://www.snopes.com/computer/internet/hackermail.asp.

3. P. Matier and A. Ross (2013, July 24). "KTVU Producers Fired Over Asiana Pilots' Fake Names." San Francisco Chronicle. Accessed at: http://www.sfgate.com/bayarea/matier-ross/article/KTVU-producers-fired-over-Asiana-pilots-fake-4685627.php.

4. "Van Halen's Legendary M&M's Rider." Accessed at: http://www.thesmokinggun.com/documents/crime/van-halens-legendary-mms-rider.

5. T. Nudd (2010). "Billboard Touts South Bend's 'Pubic Schools.'" AdWeek. Accessed at: htttp://www.adweek .com/adfreak/billboard-touts-south-bends-pubic-schools-12200.

6. The whole transcript of the radio interplay between the Apollo 13 crew and NASA can be found here: http://apollo13.spacelog.org/page/02:07:55:19/.

7. S. Roberts (2006, Dec. 28). "Infamous 'Drop Dead' Was Never Said by Ford." New York Times. Accessed at: http://www.nytimes.com/2006/12/28/nyregion/28veto.html.

8. CNN.com/Transcripts (2001, Sept. 11). "Phone Conversation With Joe Tractsonburg." Accessed at: http://transcripts.cnn.com/TRANSCRIPTS/0109/11/bn.01.html.

9. The march organizers later changed their estimate to 837,000, with a margin of 20 percent. See http://www.bu.edu/remotesensing/research/completed/million-man-march/ for a full review of the numbers.

She was born in poor country. Her right leg was seriously ~~ormed~~. This was not a great start in life for her, since in country ~~ny~~ dis abled persons suffer great hard ships, such as being hidden or ~~wanted~~ by their families In fact, the day she was born her father — ~~eling~~ ~~shamed~~ by his daughter's deformity – left the family.

Unfortunately her mother sent her to private school where she ~~was educate~~. She had to ~~live~~ leave school when her mother ~~dead~~. died

Many dis abled persons became ~~athlets~~ athletes to follow their dre~~a~~ ~~reover~~ ~~...~~ helped some disabled person

3

GRAMMAR, STYLE AND LANGUAGE BASICS

LEARNING OBJECTIVES

After completing this chapter you should be able to:

- Understand the value of grammar, style and other language basics as they relate to media writing.

- Use a simple sentence diagram to assess the structure and value of a sentence.

- Write sentences with concrete nouns and vigorous verbs.

- Self-edit work to eliminate unneeded words and phrases that damage copy and waste space.

- Distinguish between cases where grammar rules add value and where writers should bend the rules.

- Identify the value of reading copy aloud to enhance clarity.

When faced with the rules and regulations of writing, people often roll their eyes and groan audibly as they try to remember what their third-grade teachers taught them about "who" and "whom." However, the ability to write well comes down to knowing the rules that govern this form of communication. You can't expect people to take you seriously if you can't master the language or demonstrate proficiency in style. When you make small errors in these areas, your readers will wonder how smart you are. After all, if you can't get the little things right, why should they trust you on the big things?

This chapter won't rehash your entire elementary school English experience. Instead, it will focus on a few core issues that can help you the most in your writing. Think of this as a "most bang for your buck" approach to grammar, style and the other basics of media writing.

WHY DO GRAMMAR AND STYLE MATTER?

The most common complaint teachers get from grammatically challenged students is, "It doesn't matter what I actually wrote. You know what I really *meant*!" In spite of several communication errors, writers often feel they made enough of an effort to get the point across so that the receiver can figure out the sender's intent. That might be true, although it is not the most awe-inspiring defense of grammatical failures.

Regardless of the intention of the sender or the decoding skills of the receiver, failure to put the best-crafted message forward will lead to huge problems for everyone involved. Here are a few of the many reasons why writing the cleanest copy possible should matter to you:

Enhanced Trust Between Writer and Reader

The media writer's stock in trade is credibility. Writers earn it from readers after a long time of demonstrating that they deserve it, to. When writers make errors, they make it harder on themselves too maintain that level of trust.

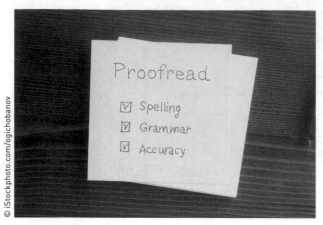

Always check the spelling, grammar and accuracy of your content before you put it out for public consumption.

If you reread that paragraph, you will notice the improper uses of "to" (the **preposition**) and "too" (meaning "also"). Even though you understood what the paragraph was telling you, it's a safe bet you immediately thought, "This book is trying to tell us about grammar, and the writer can't even get "to" and "too" right!" The author's credibility immediately took a hit.

In your media-writing career, you will make many mistakes you cannot avoid. Sources will tell you the wrong thing. Circumstances will change between the time you learn something and the time you publish it. What you meant to write wasn't exactly what you wrote, thus causing a chain reaction of painful errors. Those things are usually outside your control, and yet they still harm your credibility. Given that glum outlook, it would behoove you to make sure you clean up all the simple errors that are within your power to fix.

Improved Understanding

Your audience members have choices where they get their information. Information is no longer solely the realm of a few newspapers and a handful of television stations, but the playground of millions of senders, each with a message to share. The messages that media writers send to the general public are part of a giant informational wave that seems endless and indiscriminate. In short, we are in an age of information overload, and the choices can overwhelm readers.

The more you can do to make your material clear and concise, the better chance you have of drawing readers and retaining them. When people can understand the information, they tend to trust it more. Trust inspires readership habits and thus builds a following among audience members. When you have to fight so hard to be heard among all the voices throughout the media landscape, you should do your best to make sure you are not only heard but also understood.

Consistency Helps Readers

People are creatures of habit, and that means they like consistency. Corporate giants like McDonald's and Starbucks have built their empires on this concept. This is why the restaurants in chains generally have the same menu items, the same ambience and the same decor. The consistency of the overall experience is what keeps people coming back.

Grammar and style provide the same sense of consistency for readers. Even if people can't articulate what bothers them about random capitalization, misspelled words or awkward construction, they still know that it bothers them. If these things bother your readers enough, they will turn to a writer who meets their needs in terms of consistency.

More Tools in the Toolbox

When a novice writer faces an issue such as "Should I use 'who' or 'whom' in this sentence?" the writer usually chooses to work around the problem instead of facing it head on. This also happens for writers who have trouble with complex construction issues, **misplaced modifier** problems and **antecedent-pronoun agreement** trouble.

Master writers understand how to use an indirect object to save a word or two. They know how to move elements around within a sentence to avoid modifier confusion or structural awkwardness. In other words, they have more options to fix the problem because they know how to use the language in ways novices don't.

When you master a grammar rule or learn a writing trick, you put another tool in your writing toolbox. This gives you more ways to fix your writing problems and helps you better communicate with your readers. These writing rules and structural matters may seem complex, but they often start with a few simple elements that you can master through proper sentence construction.

SENTENCE STRUCTURE

You should write clearly and plainly if you want to communicate effectively with your readers. This starts at the sentence level and builds outward. Each sentence should contain a single idea that you think your readers should know, and you should write your sentence to drive that idea home. Think of each sentence like a component in a complex machine. If one component is weak, the whole machine suffers. If a component doesn't fit in properly, the machine will likely fail. To build the best components for your machine, you need to start with the core element of the sentence.

Noun-Verb-Object: The Holy Trinity of Writing

In Chapter 4, you will read about the 5W's and 1H of journalism. The "who, what, when, where, why and how" form the basics of what we tell people in all forms of media writing. Although media writers often claim these basic elements as their own, grammarians know that some of these elements come from the perfect core of every sentence.

A simple sentence builds from a noun-verb structure, which essentially answers a "who did what?" question. In many cases, it incorporates a third element, the object of the sentence, leading to "who did what to whom or what?" construction.

Bill hit Bob.

Jane drank tea.

Carl played the guitar.

As you build each sentence, don't start at the front of the sentence but rather at the core of it, with the noun, verb and object. Then build additional elements onto those pieces, kind of like adding layers to the core of a sphere.

Pick Concrete Nouns and Vigorous Verbs

You need to make the best possible choices for the **noun** and **verb** of each sentence. When writers fail to do this, they feel the need to slather on adjectives and adverbs to prop up their poor choices, just like a lousy cook who pours condiments all over the main course to hide its inherent weaknesses. Don't drown your noun and verb in a sea of modifiers. Instead, go back to these elements and see if you can come up with better choices for each one.

THE SIMPLE SENTENCE DIAGRAM

In years past, teachers forced students to diagram sentences on the blackboard to help them see how each sentence was constructed. The diagram required students to locate the primary elements of the subject and the predicate, as well as order the elements within each of those segments.

Although **sentence diagramming** has gone the way of chalky blackboards, you can fix many writing problems if you know how to use a simple diagram.

Noun	Verb	Direct Object

Look at the diagram, above right.

The first "box" here holds the noun, or the simple subject of the sentence. The second "box" holds the verb, which gives you a sense of the action of the sentence. The third "box" holds the **direct object** of the sentence, if any exists. After you write a sentence, you should look for the elements that fill in these three boxes. If you can't find the words that should fit in the first two boxes, you have a major problem because you can't have a complete sentence without a noun (implied or present) and a verb.

If you fill in these boxes properly, it allows you to assess the degree to which you have a concrete noun or a vigorous verb. You can determine if you used too many adjectives or adverbs because you chose poorly when it came to your noun and your verb.

In other cases, the diagram can help you refocus your approach to information. For example, if you put together a press release for the city regarding a large fire at an area home, this sentence would seem like a good place to start:

Mill Valley firefighters fought a blaze at 121 W. Ash Ave. on Wednesday night, with the electrical fire destroying the home and causing $300,000 in damage.

The sentence has several important elements in it, including the damage amount and the address of the fire. However, if you break down the "who did what to whom/what" elements, this is what you have:

Noun: firefighters

Verb: fought

Object: blaze

The core of your sentence tells your readers that firefighters fought a fire. Isn't that what they normally do, regardless of how big or small a fire is? If you pick different ways to fill in the boxes, you can focus on what makes this situation important:

Noun: fire

Verb: destroyed

Object: home

That approach will get you a sentence like this:
An electrical fire destroyed a home at 121 W. Ash Ave. on Wednesday night, causing more than $300,000 in damage.

In each sentence you write, rely on the simple diagram to focus your purpose, maintain proper order and assess your word choices.

Active Voice: Let Your Verb Do the Work

Active-voice structure is the noun-verb-object approach outlined earlier in the chapter. It has the noun committing an action that affects the direct object of the sentence. **Passive-voice** construction reverses these elements, placing the object first. **Active-voice** writing is beneficial for several reasons:

It Is Shorter

When you need to keep sentences tight and short, which we will discuss later in the chapter, you want to stay active. Consider the following two sentences:

Bill hit the ball.

The ball was hit by Bill.

In each sentence, we learn exactly the same information, but the first sentence has four words while the second one has six. If you wrote the second one, you wasted two words and gave your readers no added value. If each word has to add value to your work, you ended up failing one-third of the time in this short sentence.

It Is Clearer

In a lot of cases, passive voice (the object-verb-noun approach) fails to give you all the information you need. Consider a sentence that a principal issued while explaining the censorship rules the district officials established for the high school newspaper:

There was clear belief that there needed to be or needs to be some level of guidelines developed for the building principal and superintendent to be able to just provide oversight on what items are being published.

In this case, passive voice makes it unclear who had this belief that these guidelines needed to be implemented, primarily because the noun is missing. This might be a case of sloppy writing or a situation in which the writer attempted to hide who was responsible for the changes. A more direct approach might indicate who was concerned with the publication's approach to journalism.

It Strengthens Your Sentence

When you put an active verb into a sentence, it's like dropping a Porsche motor into your car. It's strong, and it will power up your sentence.

When you use passive voice, it's like running your car with a lawnmower engine. You can do it, but you're going to need to augment it substantially, and in the end it still won't be that great.

Vigorous verbs are active verbs. They cut through the jargon and bring strength to your writing. Look at these two sentences used in press releases regarding a "personnel change" and see how much difference active voice and clear purpose can make:

Smith was released from his contract by the company after it was determined that he was responsible for illegally taking department funds.

The company fired Smith after it found he stole department funds.

The words "fired" and "stole" are direct and clear. Most people can easily grasp these ideas. Don't couch your concepts in passive voice. Drive home your point with a strong engine in your sentence.

GIVE IT A TRY: Rework the sentences below to remove passive voice and strengthen the structure. Make sure in your quest to eliminate passive voice that you don't change the meaning of the sentence or eliminate important information from it.

1. Because the car was left unlocked by me, my phone was stolen.

2. The ball was hit to the person playing right field, who was able to make the catch.

3. Although the steamroller was broken, the entire stretch of Highway 41 was paved by the end of the day.

4. "Was the house supposed to be green?" he was asked by his mother when he was done painting.

5. The buffalo chicken sandwiches are eaten in great quantities in the dorm cafeteria.

SENTENCE LENGTH

The length of each sentence will control the pace and flow of your writing. Short sentences can feel powerful, or they can leave your readers feeling like they are in stop-and-go traffic on the freeway. Long sentences can create motion and fluidity, or they can give your readers the feeling of talking to an oversugared 4-year-old who just got off a roller coaster.

Think about the way you punctuate your sentences and the length to which you allow them to grow like moving traffic. Commas work like "yield" signs, while periods bring you to a stop. The number of words in each sentence is like the amount of time you spend between each stop you make. With that in mind, consider the value of short, medium and long sentences.

ADAPT

THE "GROCERY SHOPPING APPROACH"

Many college students have experienced the need to shop for food with a limited budget. The phrase "I have $20 to last me until Tuesday" is an often-lamented part of this process, but it leads to some remarkable comparison-shopping and bargain-hunting efforts.

When funds are short and needs are many, shoppers compare the benefits of a 2-liter bottle of soda against those of a 12-pack of cans. They choose generic cereal that offers twice the volume for half the price instead of the name-brand version. Smart shoppers find items on clearance sale and buy them in bulk.

If you can shop like that, you can write like it, too.

Consider each word you use as a dollar you would spend. Every chance you get, try to save a dollar and use it somewhere better.

Earlier in the chapter, we looked at active and passive voice, the former of which can save you a couple words without any extra work. Beyond active voice, think about using **indirect objects** instead of **prepositional phrases**:

Bill gave the ball to Albert.

Bill gave Albert the ball.

Tucking "Albert" between the verb and the direct object saves you a word. It might not seem like much, but if you can do it frequently, you can pick up a lot of spare change you can use elsewhere.

You can also trim a word or two if you can eliminate unneeded helping verbs.

Pat was trying to fix the car last night.

Pat tried to fix the car last night.

As is the case with any bit of bargain shopping, you need to keep reality in mind when you make your choices. You can't eat toothpaste and potatoes for a whole week just to prove your frugality. The same thing applies to your writing: Don't cut just to cut. Make sure your writing is thrifty, not cheap.

GIVE IT A TRY: Select several sentences from a news story or a press release and rewrite them to tighten them up. Avoid making cuts that would change the meaning of the sentence or limit its descriptive power. Instead, look for opportunities to swap out several words for one or two better words or eliminate extraneous words. You can also rewrite the sentences to eliminate passive voice or improve the verb structure.

Short Sentences Pack a Punch

A short sentence can bring home a point in a hurry, regardless of the writing you do. In 1995, after a 17-month absence from the game of basketball, superstar Michael Jordan made his intention to return to the Chicago Bulls and the National Basketball Association known with a simple two-word press statement, faxed to media outlets throughout the country:

"I'm back."

The power of that simple sentence drove the sports-media world into a commotion for the next several months. Not every one of your sentences of that length will pack a similar punch, but short sentences do create some strong impact within your writing.

As noted at the top of this section, a few words and a period can force your readers to slam on the brakes and take notice of what you wrote. The use of a short sentence can draw notice to a particular aspect of your writing.

At the beginning of his congressional campaign, Sen. Blaine Borthright said he planned to avoid attack ads, keep his focus on the issues and create a discussion with his opponent about their differences.

That pledge ended Monday.

A series of advertisements aired across all three statewide networks several times during the day, calling out challenger Jimmy Jonas as being a spender, a cheater and a liar. In addition, Borthright sent a statement to several media outlets notifying them that he planned to cancel all three scheduled debates he planned with Jonas.

The second sentence gives your readers a reason to stop and see what happened before motoring on to the next several sentences. Attention-getters like this are helpful in small doses but shouldn't be overused, for fear of destroying the overall flow of your writing.

Medium Sentences Set the Pace

When dealing with the written word, sentences of about 17 to 23 words have a solid and inherent pace to them. These medium-sized sentences usually contain one or two key points and help move from the sentence above to the sentence below with intrinsic transitions. If you just want readers to naturally consume your content without slowing down or speeding up, build a noun-verb structure and augment it with crucial additions until you reach the 17- to 23-word zone.

Long Sentences Roll On and On

Media writers usually frown upon long sentences, but just like every other tool, they have their purpose. When you want to create a sense of an ever-expanding area, complete with green grass, rolling hills and endless forest, a lengthy sentence can be helpful to keep things flowing. Long sentences can also create a sense of speed or a feeling of unyielding chaos.

As with short sentences, you should have a reason for using long sentences. When you find a reason to break past the 23-word barrier on standard body-copy sentences, you can rely on longer sentences to create a specific feel in your writing. However, you shouldn't rely too heavily on these, as they will exhaust your readers and limit your effectiveness as a writer.

HELPFUL HINTS
GRAMMAR VERSUS CLARITY

Grammar has a bad reputation because the rules of the English language are riddled with exceptions, oddities and generally painful reasoning. This is why when we teach children the rules that govern the language, we come up with poetic ways to help them keep track of things that don't make sense, such as "I before E, except after C, unless it's in 'EH' as in 'neighbor' or 'weigh.'" Take spelling rules like that and couple them with grammar terms like **split infinitive** and **dangling modifier**, and it's no wonder that people spend more time writing around the rules than they do learning them.

In media writing, the goal is to make sense to the readers and listeners in a way they are used to. With that

(Continued)

(Continued)

in mind, clarity in some cases can trump grammar, because occasionally grammar creates confusion or oddities in structure. For example, the rules pertaining to "who" and "whom" would argue that "whom" should be used as part of an objective-case approach. However, look at this sentence:

Rep. Bill Jones then shouted at Rep. Sue Smith that she didn't know who she was messing with.

The structure is poor, but it sounds about right if you think about someone screaming this across a room as a fight is about to start. Grammar, however, would have this happen:

Rep. Bill Jones then shouted at Rep. Sue Smith that she didn't know with whom she was messing.

Try using that structural approach the next time you get into a bar fight.

Other issues, like split infinitives, lead to bar-fight situations among grammarians but should be viewed in context when considering how much they diminish your ability to connect with your readers:

Mayor Jim Scott said he expected the population of the city to more than double in the next five years.

To fix the split infinitive, you would have to explain the increase but remove the modifiers from between "to" and "double" in the sentence. It is possible but perhaps not advisable:

Mayor Jim Scott said he expected the city's population to increase twofold or more in the next five years.

The point is that you should keep your eye on the primary goal outlined in Chapter 1, which is that the audience should come first. That doesn't mean you should avoid grammar rules or that you don't need to learn them. However, you should focus on getting the message across to your readers in the clearest possible way, even if a grammar rule gets bent along the way.

READ YOUR WORK ALOUD

In Chapter 11, we discuss the way broadcast writing must make sense when spoken out loud, because of the way the journalists send the material and the audience members receive it. However, reading your work aloud has value for all writers, especially when it comes to sentence structure, grammar and clarity.

Writers often miss words, forget to add phrases or repeat ideas when they transfer the information from their brains to their keyboards. When they reread that material, their brains will often fill in those missing pieces or skip the repetition, thus leaving the errors intact.

Reading your copy aloud will help you see whether you wrote "I drove the the car to the park" or "I drove the car to park." It will also help you determine if a sentence is too long or has construction issues.

Take a normal breath and read each sentence aloud. If you find that you run out of air before you get to the end of a sentence, it is likely too long. If you find that you feel "tight" in your chest near the end, you should reread the sentence and look for a few places to trim.

If you have to pause too often, you either used too many commas or you created an awkward structure for your sentence. Edit your work to smooth out the sentence flow and try reading the sentence again.

Problems ranging from too many prepositions to the overuse of personal pronouns will emerge when you read your work aloud. Even if you feel foolish mumbling in front of your computer screen, your readers will eventually appreciate the results.

THE FIVE-MINUTE AP STYLEBOOK

The Associated Press Stylebook serves as the primary source for standardization of content for newspapers, magazines and websites. PR practitioners rely on this guide as well, while advertising (see Chapter 13) and broadcasting professionals (see Chapter 11) use other guiding principles. However, as far as a "bible" for media-writing style, the AP guide is the gold standard.

You can feel overwhelmed if you try to memorize the book, as it is a lot like reading a dictionary, and the rules appear to be contradictory in some cases. In addition, the AP recently changed a number of long-standing rules, including its position on state names and the use of "they" as a gender-neutral singular pronoun. According to the most recent style guide, AP made nearly 200 style changes and updates over the past year. With that in mind, your goal should be to gain familiarity with the kinds of rules the AP has issued. You can then look up specific issues each time you encounter them.

Fred Vultee, an associate professor at Wayne State University who spent more than 25 years as an editor in newspapers, offers his students some quick maxims that account for the majority of the style guide. Here is his "five-minute style guide," reprinted with permission:

The Five-Minute Stylebook

10 Percent of the Rules Cover 90 Percent of Style Questions

People

Capitalize formal titles when they appear before names (The message was sent to **President** Vladimir Putin).

Lowercase titles when they follow a name or stand alone (Bashar Assad, the Syrian **president**, fired his **foreign minister**).

Lowercase occupational or descriptive titles before or after a name (The article was written by **columnist** Joe Bob Briggs).

Refer to adults by given name and family name the first time they appear in a news story (**Michelle Obama**) and by family name only on later references (**Obama**).

Children 17 or younger are usually referred to by both names on first reference and *given name only* on later references. Children in "adult situations"—common examples are international sports and serious crimes in which they are charged as adults—are referred to by *family name only* on later references.

To avoid confusing two people with the same family name, such as husband and wife or mother and son, use both names on later references. A story mentioning Joe Biden and Jill Biden should usually refer to them as **Joe Biden** and **Jill Biden** even after they are introduced if there's any chance of confusion. Sometimes a title can be repeated to make the distinction (Joe Biden could be "Vice President Biden" or "the vice president" on later references; Jill Biden could be "Dr. Biden"). Only rarely, in some feature stories, will you want to refer to adults by given name on later references.

Do not use courtesy titles (Mr., Mrs., Ms.) in news reports except in direct quotes.

Abbreviate military and police titles before names according to a standard reference list such as the one in the AP Stylebook. Don't abbreviate titles when they stand alone or follow a name (**Gen.** Douglas MacArthur, the **general**). Exceptions are allowed for widely used initialisms (The fugitive **CEO** was captured at dawn).

Places

Most stylebooks will have a list of cities that are assumed to be understood without having the name of the state (**Boston**, **New York**, **Los Angeles**) or country (**New York**, **London**, **Cairo**) attached. Follow those guidelines with the usual exceptions for common sense if needed (Books that are popular in **London, Ontario**, might not be popular in **London, England**).

Do not abbreviate the names of U.S. states **except**:

1) In datelines, credit lines, or short forms of party ID: **Debbie Stabenow, D-Mich.**

2) In those cases, abbreviate state names of six or more letters only. (NOTE: the two noncontiguous states, Alaska and Hawaii, are never abbreviated.)

Do not abbreviate such designations as "street" when they stand alone. Only three of these are abbreviated—"street," "avenue" and "boulevard"—and they are only abbreviated when they appear with a numbered address. Do not abbreviate "south" or "north" indicating a part of a road unless it appears with an address (**South Eighth Street**; **221 S. Eighth St.**; **221 Abbey Road**).

(Continued)

(Continued)

Things

Capitalize proper nouns; lowercase common nouns.

Capitalize trademarks (I drank a **Pepsi**) or use a common noun as a substitute (I drank a **soft drink**).

Use abbreviations on first reference only if they are widely known (**CIA** agents helped overthrow the prime minister of Iran). Otherwise spell out the names of agencies on first reference (The U.S. Agency for International Development; **USAID**). If an abbreviation would be confusing, use a common-noun substitute (the State Law and Order Restoration Council; **the council** or **the junta**) on later references. When in doubt, err on the side of clarity. Abbreviations are not as familiar as you think they are.

Generally, don't abbreviate units of measure (pounds, miles, hours, etc.).

Capitalize **shortened versions of proper names**: the Michigan Department of Transportation, the Transportation Department, the Department of Transportation.

Time

Use only the day of the week for events within a week of publication (The summit ended **Saturday**. Negotiators will meet **Thursday**). Use "last" or "next" only if needed for clarity (The summit ended Friday, and the negotiators will meet again **next Friday**).

Never abbreviate days of the week. Use "today" to refer to the day of publication only. Do not use "yesterday" or "tomorrow" except in direct quotes.

Use month and day to refer to events happening a week or more before or after publication. Use cardinal numbers, not ordinal numbers, for dates (The summit began **July 11**. The seminar will be held **March 3**).

Don't use the year unless the event is more than a year before or after publication (He died **March 17, 2007**; the tax will take effect **Jan. 1, 2025**).

Do not abbreviate a month unless it's followed by a date (**January**; **Jan. 1**). Do not abbreviate months of less than six letters (**March**; **March 12, 1998**).

Use lowercase "a.m." and "p.m." to indicate morning, afternoon and night. Use "noon" and "midnight" rather than the unclear "12 a.m." or the redundant "12 noon." Always use figures for time, in this form: **8 a.m.**, **10:30 p.m.**, **1:45 a.m.**

Unless you need to emphasize one element over the others, generally follow time-date-place order: **Trials of collaborators will begin at 2 p.m. April 14 in New York.**

Numbers

The basic rule: Spell out numbers under 10. Use figures for 10 and above.

The main exceptions:

Spell out any number, except a year, that begins a sentence (Twelve students attended. 1999 was an important year).

Use figures for dates, weights, ages, times, addresses and percentages.

For most numbers of a million or more, use this form, rounded off to no more than two decimal places: **1.45 million**, the **$18.1 billion budget**. If the exact number is important, write it out: He received **1,253,667** votes to **988,401** for his opponent.

Spell out numbers used as figures of speech (**Thanks a million**).

Spell out fractions when they stand alone (use **one-half** cup of flour). Otherwise write them as mixed fractions (**1½** cups of flour) or decimals (**1.5** liters of water).

Generally, use a 0 to precede a decimal smaller than zero (**0.75 kilograms**).

Convert metric measurements to English ones.

HOW TO KEEP WRITING TIGHT AND RIGHT

Every writer and every editor has a set of "no-nos" that drive them up a wall and around a bend. (If **clichés** bug you, that sentence probably hurt your brain.) You can't write in a way that pleases everyone, especially if you want to retain your voice in your work. Perfection is an illusion, and demanding it of yourself will set you up for failure in a media world where you must do more work in less time for a wider audience.

Good writers find a middle ground in their writing between grammatical perfection and audience centricity. The list of items below will give you suggestions for fine-tuning your copy.

Write Quickly but Edit Slowly

Many writers make the mistake of thinking they need to be perfect on the first pass. When you work on a piece, the ability to just get the material out of your head should be the first goal. The longer you spend torturing yourself to make sure the writing is perfect, the more you can become tied in knots and the less you will accomplish.

Think of the information in your head as you would consider sand in a sieve. If you need to move a lot of sand from Point A to Point B and you have to carry it in a sifter like that, you know that the longer you spend in one spot, the less sand will make it to your destination. Instead of belaboring anything, just grab everything you can and run with it. Once you get to the destination, you can pick through what's there.

You want to write quickly to make sure you get everything you need poured into that computer file. Then go back through what you wrote once or twice and edit your copy before you let anyone else see it. Once it's on the screen, you can look up words to see if you used them properly, rework awkward sentences and restructure some of your paragraphs. The slow edit will allow you to see what you have done and assess what you have to do next. However, if you don't get the writing done, you will have almost nothing to edit.

CONNECT
INCONCEIVABLE! THE ART OF REVIEWING YOUR COPY CAREFULLY

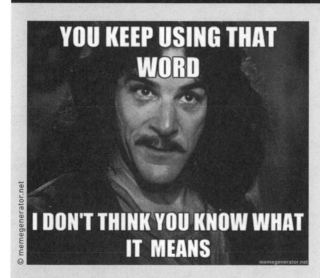

The classic 1980s film "The Princess Bride" features a scene made even more famous through a string of recent memes. The mastermind of a kidnapping, Vizzini, finds that his attempts to evade "The Man in Black" somehow keep failing. He repeatedly notes that it is "inconceivable" that this is happening. Eventually, his conspirator Inigo Montoya tells him, "You keep using that word. I do not think that word means what you think it means."

Journalists often can figure out what a word means by how it sounds or through context clues, but not every word means what we think it means. Getting "close enough" can be embarrassing in many cases and downright humiliating in others. This is why spell check alone isn't the best judge of your copy, and you should take an extra minute to look words up if you aren't sure. If you want people to trust you and consider you a credible source, picking the right words can make all difference to your readers.

In some cases, it's that the word sounds like something that should be what you think it to be. Example:

When it comes to 1990s grunge rock, Nirvana was the penultimate band.

The word "penultimate" sounds like some version of "super-ultimate" or "extra-ultimate." It actually means second to last. So, unless only one band ever came after Nirvana, we have a problem here.

In other cases, the word sounds similar enough to what we were typing to let spell check "fix" it for us. Examples:

Mayor Bill Conroy said he defiantly agreed with the governor, saying he was "100 percent behind our state's leader."

(Continued)

(Continued)

The Nevada Wolves barley beat the Centerville Foxes on Saturday, 42-41, after a late-game touchdown pass to Kyle Moore baled them out.

The word "defiantly" in the first sentence was likely supposed to be "definitely" before the writer got close to the right word and spell check came to the rescue. The second sentence confuses a hardy grain (barley) with a narrow escape (barely). The writer also unintentionally continued the farming theme with the stack-of-hay version of "baled" as opposed to the correct version of it ("bailed").

The advent of the spell check, the digital thesaurus and other quick tools has improved the speed at which people can write but has also diminished the quality of the writing. The spell checker will tell you if a word is spelled properly, with some programs helpfully converting incorrectly spelled words to correctly spelled ones. That doesn't mean that these words are the right words, however, and that can lead to bigger problems.

If you aren't sure on a spelling or a word's definition, it's always best to look it up. If you are using words that "sound" good but you aren't 100 percent sure of their actual meaning, the same thing is true. Readers who know better will start wondering how much faith they should put in your work on the facts and figures in your pieces if you have things like this wrong.

GIVE IT A TRY: Below are several sentences with some word and spelling choices that are suspect. Read through them and identify the words you think are off somehow and then look them up. Define what the suspect word means and then state what you think the proper word should be.

1. Sen. Mark Splan seemed to chaff at the idea that his opponent would distort his military surface record.

2. The district attorney charged the man with three accounts of indecent exposure after police said he was masticating in public in violation of a county ordnance.

3. The rancher led his heard of cattle through afield of winter wheat.

4. In explaining how he knew accounting so well, Jim Jackson refereed to his time working for the IRS, an acronym for the Internal Revenue Service.

5. Jim always takes flack for his political opinions, especially when he complements the president's actions.

6. Sheri liked to flout her wealth, but for all intensive purposes, she was rather levelheaded.

7. He kept his research binder, an agate of all of his work on the topic, in his nap sack.

8. Even though he was inpatient and hated sitting around doing nothing, Officer Donnely volunteered for a steak out Monday, so he could be in observance of criminal activity in the area.

Kill Clichés

A cliché is a worn-out phrase that has lost its meaning and value. With a definition like that, it's no wonder you don't want clichés worming their way into your copy. Every word you use has to add value because you are limited in the number of words you can use. Each word that lacks importance is just one more excuse for your readers to give up on what you wrote and move on.

Return Your Empties

In the days before traditional recycling, bottle manufacturers would implore soda and beer drinkers to "return your empties." For each empty bottle they brought back, users got anywhere from a penny to a dime to use toward future purchases. When it comes to writing, you want to return your empties as well. These "empties" include **empty subjects**, such as "there is" and "there were":

Empty: There were three trees growing on the lot.

Fixed: Three trees grew on the lot.

Empty phrases can pop up in your copy when you overwrite in hopes of sounding stronger or more authoritative.

Empty: Environmental experts have noted the fact that cars need improved gas mileage. (If it weren't a fact, would you put it in a media report of any kind? Probably not.)

Fixed: Environmental experts said cars need improved gas mileage.

Even **empty words** such as "a lot" or "a little" offer no value to your readers. Look to become more specific as you eliminate words that shouldn't be there:

Empty: Frank had a lot of bobbleheads.

Fixed: Frank had 123 bobbleheads.

Empty: I gave her a little more time to finish the test

Fixed: I gave her 10 minutes more to finish the test.

Go through each sentence you write and look for words and phrases that add length, but little else, to your writing and return them with a quick click of your delete key.

Remove Redundancies

As noted earlier in the chapter, you should make the dictionary your best friend when it comes to writing. Redundancies occur when people don't know how a word works or what it means and thus misapply modifiers to it.

The Hope Diamond is a completely unique gem.

"Unique" means one of a kind, so modifying it doesn't work. Something is either unique or it isn't. It's like being dead. You either are or aren't. The word "diamond" refers to a gemstone, thus making "gem" pointless as well.

Ken Rosenauer lists many other redundancies in his editing books,[1] including some of these beauties:

Completely destroy

ATM machine

PIN number

True facts

When you write, question each modifier and see whether it needs to be there. Then eliminate the redundancy before moving on.

GIVE IT A TRY: Locate and remove the redundancies in the following sentences.

1. The armed gunman robbed the bank of money.
2. The athlete told the writer he saw himself as the best ever, having set several all-time records.
3. The free gift came with the magazine subscription.
4. The rally for the GOP party candidate filled up the building to capacity.
5. The captain said he did not receive advance warning of the unexpected attack, thus placing his soldiers in serious danger.

Reduce the Use of Prepositions

One of the favorite winter holiday songs kids learn is based on the poem "The New-England Boy's Song About Thanksgiving Day," by Lydia Marie Child. This classic ditty, which has several versions, creates a sing-song feel from the opening lines:

> *Over the river and through the wood,*
>
> *To grandmother's house we go;*
>
> *The horse knows the way,*
>
> *To carry the sleigh,*
>
> *Through white and drifted snow.*

The reason this stanza has such a clean cadence and smooth pace is the overuse of prepositions. Five of the 26 words are prepositions, and prepositional phrases account for more than half of the lyrics. When you rely heavily on prepositions and prepositional phrases, your writing will not only flow in short spurts, but it will also take on a song-like quality. If you have a sentence with more than two prepositional phrases in it, revise it.

Possessives Versus Plurals (and Other Similar Snafus)

The apostrophe has the ability to add ownership and create contractions. It also can lead to some problematic word constructions when it is misused or misplaced in a sentence. A common mistake people make is in the "its versus it's" area, because this example is the intersection of **possessive** and **contraction**. If an apostrophe is supposed to do both of those things, it is easy enough to see how this can confuse writers. The other aspects of possession, however, should be easy enough to understand:

> *The boy's toy (one boy owning one toy)*
>
> *The boy's toys (one boy owning multiple toys)*
>
> *The boys' toys (multiple boys owning multiple toys)*
>
> *The boys track team (a group of boys that compose a team)*

Other issues are more complicated, such as what happens with last names:

> *It is Joe Smith's toy.*
>
> *It is Bill Jones' toy.*
>
> *I'm keeping up with the Joneses.*
>
> *I like the Joneses' car.*

For special circumstances, such as words that end with "ss" or "x," let the AP Stylebook be your guide. In other words, if you aren't sure, look it up.

Examine Antecedents and Pronouns

We established earlier that each sentence needs a noun and a verb. When a pronoun substitutes for a noun, your writing can become vague or hard to follow. Make sure each sentence has a concrete noun before you work with your pronouns. This antecedent, the word to which the pronoun refers, will help you determine which pronouns to use:

The mayor said he wants to run for Congress. (singular noun, singular pronoun)

The city council members said they don't like the plan. (plural noun, plural pronoun)

When you have a singular noun that isn't **gender neutral**, you can pluralize to avoid awkward construction:

Awkward: A reporter should check his or her copy before he or she submits it.

Better: Reporters should check their copy before they submit it.

Also, watch out for collective nouns or singular nouns that represent multiple people:

Wrong: The city council rejected a bill they said would defund the highway department.

Right: The city council voted to increase its ability to add money to the parks department.

Right: The city council members said they did not like the mayor's attitude.

Right: The Minnesota Timberwolves will play their third game in four nights.

Wrong: Minnesota will use their same starting lineup each game.

Right: Minnesota will use its home court as an advantage.

Each time you use a pronoun, find the antecedent and make sure they match.

GIVE IT A TRY: Consider the following sentences and select the pronoun that best fits the antecedent:

1. The jury rendered (its/their) verdict.

2. Each player on the Milwaukee Bucks will have to give (his/their) maximum effort tonight.

3. The participants said the rally could reach (its/their) goal of world peace.

4. The manager of the Cleveland Cavaliers said (he/they) thought the team had a chance to win a title.

5. (A journalist/Journalists) should check (his or her/their) work before submitting it.

Remove Qualifiers That Couch Your Facts

One of the easiest ways to avoid looking something up is to add a qualifier to your writing. Consider the following:

Andrea Jordan ran one of the fastest 100-meter-dash times in the history of the Smithton Trials.

The attack was the worst shooting on a college campus in recent memory.

Roberto Clemente is arguably the most decorated outfielder in baseball history.

In each case, the writer uses a qualifier to couch his facts, and in each case, all it does is limit the value of the writing.

Instead of using "one of the" to couch "fastest," look up how fast the time was and compare it with the other times. Instead of "in recent memory," determine how you want to quantify the overall damage associated with the shooting, and then make a direct comparison. Instead of relying on "arguably," state your position clearly or attribute the information.

Andrea Jordan ran a 9.84-second 100-meter-dash, which was the third-fastest time in the history of the Smithton Trials.

The attack left 31 people dead, the largest number of shooting fatalities on a campus since the 2007 attack at Virginia Tech.

Right fielder Roberto Clemente earned 12 Gold Glove awards during his career, tying him with centerfielder Willie Mays for the most ever as an outfielder.

When in doubt, look it up. If you still don't know, don't couch it with vague notions and weak qualifiers.

PROFESSIONAL THOUGHTS
SHAY QUILLEN

Shay Quillen began his journalism career working for the Cavalier Daily at the University of Virginia as an undergraduate, where he mixed his love of music and writing. His start as a copy editor at the paper was less of a calling and more of an accident, he said.

"I inadvertently became a copy editor—given a stylebook and virtually no training—and realized I might be anal-retentive enough to eventually get good at the job," he said.

After spending most of the next decade in the music industry, Quillen enrolled in graduate school to study journalism. His affinity for copy editing grew, landing him first as an intern and then as a full-time staff member at the San Jose Mercury News. In 2009, he moved to the San Francisco Chronicle, where he works as copy desk chief for the newsroom's print and online editions.

Although his roles have changed over time, he said the biggest change in his job is in the volume of work that comes his way and how he has to prioritize his efforts.

"You simply have less time to agonize over everything—whether you're working on a blog post that has to get online immediately or a story for print that's moving through an overworked, down-sized desk," he said. "So you have to pick your battles to some degree."

Quillen said accuracy and fairness are at the forefront of everything he does before he moves along to check for spelling and style. Although stylebooks can seem like a maze of arcane rules, Quillen said he sees a lot of value in what they provide for him and his readers.

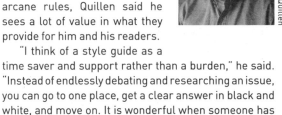

"I think of a style guide as a time saver and support rather than a burden," he said. "Instead of endlessly debating and researching an issue, you can go to one place, get a clear answer in black and white, and move on. It is wonderful when someone has already resolved a matter so you don't have to. That saves you time for worrying about the big stuff."

The purpose of applying grammar and style rules to writing is to improve the connection the paper has with its audience, Quillen said.

"Many readers won't notice inconsistencies in style, but plenty will," he said. "You don't want anything interfering with the communication between the writer and the reader. If the reader is temporarily wondering why something was uppercase in the third paragraph and lowercase in the seventh paragraph, then you're getting in the way.

"Even readers who aren't nitpickers will appreciate the polish and clarity of grammatically correct language, even if it's subconscious," he added. "There is no downside to getting it right."

Getting it right, Quillen said, isn't always about adhering to the letter of the law in grammar. He said the key is to help readers consume your content in the easiest possible way.

"Never, ever, let knee-jerk adherence to a stylebook take precedence over your brain, heart and ear," he said. "If you 'fix' a style problem but end up with a clunky, terrible sentence, you haven't made things better. If you struggle and struggle with a sentence but can't improve it, leave it the way the writer wrote it. Take the Hippocratic oath: First, do no harm. Make sure every change you make to a story actually improves it. If it doesn't, leave it alone."

One Last Thing

Q: If you could tell students anything about media writing or anything you have seen in your time in the field, what would it be?

A: It's easy (and essential) for a copy editor to focus on the little stuff—typos, repeated words, inadvertently italicized commas—but please remember to pull back and get the big picture as well. . . . Think about what would help the reader. What is the package missing? What parts are redundant and would be better cast aside? How can you best draw people in and lead them to the information they're seeking? This line of thinking will help whether you're working on a traditional print publication or a website or a PowerPoint presentation in a business setting. The days when a copy editor could simply worry about getting the written words right are basically over. Think of your role as facilitating communication in every way, whether it's designing a news page or writing web headlines or even shooting and editing video. Take advantage of every opportunity to learn a new skill, and be prepared to keep learning and adapting throughout your career as the industry and technology evolve.

THE BIG THREE

Here are the three key things you should take away from this chapter:

1. **Use active voice:** If you can build an active-voice sentence and it conveys the same meaning and value as a passive-voice sentence, go with the active voice. It will be shorter, stronger and more valuable for your readers. In addition, if you rely on the simple sentence diagram to help you find the noun, verb and object of the sentence, you can see if you're using active voice and if you are using the best noun, verb and object available.

2. **Write quickly, edit slowly:** When you write, get the thoughts out of your head quickly to avoid losing something you want to say. Then go back through what you wrote and analyze it for clarity, precision, focus and value. Edit slowly as you critique each element of each sentence.

3. **Look it up:** Good writers understand that they don't know everything they think they know. Follow their lead as you improve your writing skills, and look up words you don't know and things you don't know for sure. Don't let spell check make you a cautionary tale for critics.

KEY TERMS

active voice 40
antecedent-pronoun agreement 38
cliché 46
contraction 50
dangling modifier 43
direct object 40
empty phrase 49

empty subject 48
empty word 49
gender neutral 51
indirect object 42
misplaced modifier 38
noun 39
passive voice 40

possessive 50
preposition 37
prepositional phrase 42
sentence diagramming 40
split infinitive 43
verb 39

DISCUSSION QUESTIONS

1. How big of a deal is it to you when people use "text speak" ("how r u?") in more formal communication? Do you think it matters in terms of how you think of these people or how others think of you when you do it?

2. How often do you think about your approach to writing in terms of structure, style, grammar and other similar issues? Do you obsess about every comma or figure that the general gist of what you have to say is what matters most?

WRITE NOW!

1. Find a piece of media writing online and highlight the various grammar issues we talked about in the chapter. Look for noun-verb structure, pronoun-antecedent agreement, proper use of possessives and other similar issues. Then rewrite the five worst sentences you found to improve them. Write a three- to five-sentence summary after each rewrite to explain what you did and why you did it.

2. Reread any piece of writing you have crafted over the past semester and find five words you used that you didn't look up, even though you weren't sure what they meant. Look them up and list the

definitions. After that, explain whether you used the words properly. Compare and contrast what you meant against what you wrote. Then find at least two other words that would have been better choices for those sentences.

3. Edit your environment for grammar. Look around the kiosks, bulletin boards and signage near your home and school. See what pieces are well constructed in terms of grammar, style, consistence and more. Explain what worked well on these. Then see which ones have fallen short and explain what went wrong.

NOTE

1. K. L. Rosenauer (2013). "Copycrafting: Editing for Journalism Today." New York: Oxford University Press; K. L. Rosenauer and V. F. Filak (2013).

"The Journalist's Handbook for Online Editing." New York: Pearson.

BASIC MEDIA WRITING

You have spent the majority of your life writing in some format or another. You have written term papers, texted friends, scribbled lecture notes and perhaps even scrawled some graffiti. In each case, you attempted to clearly communicate your thoughts on a valuable topic to a specific audience. Writing in these formats has become second nature because you have a clear understanding as to the rules governing your approach to writing. You know that a tweet needs to be 280 characters or fewer and that your term paper needs to be 10 pages. You know each writing approach has its own style, and each has a specific purpose. In addition, you can easily conceptualize your target audience. You write your term papers for your professor, send texts to communicate with your friends and write class notes for yourself. In each instance, you have a direct connection with the person on the other end of your work.

Media writing can seem more difficult than some of these other forms of writing because it often lacks those parameters. Some pieces are several pages long while others are only a few sentences. In addition, you have to retrain your brain to think about what various audience members need and then meet those needs. It's more about what they want to know and less about what you want to say. Media writing also requires you to focus less on your opinions and more on the facts and opinions you get from sources.

In this chapter, we will look at some of the important elements of good writing that will help you communicate effectively with your readers, regardless of your discipline or your platform. The basic approach to writing discussed here will work just as easily online as it will on paper. The chapter will also explain how to pack a lot of important information into the top of your work so you can draw readers and engage them immediately. Finally, the chapter will explain how to write in a standard media format known as the inverted pyramid and show you why this format has value.

THE "KILLER BE'S" OF GOOD WRITING

Good writing is not an accident or a birthright. Don't believe people who tell you they were "born writers," as if only a select few were granted this gift. Instead, realize that writing is a skill anyone can grow, develop and shape. You can become an incredible writer if you work hard enough at it. These "killer" writing skills are not beyond your grasp.

If you want to be a "killer" writer, you have to "be" a number of other things as well. The list of things below is not exhaustive, but it focuses on things that you can practice until they become part of who you are as a writer.

Be Right

As we saw in Chapter 2, one of the primary things media writing demands of you is **accuracy**. Perfection is unattainable, and yet that is what is expected of you in this field. Obviously, you won't be perfect, but you need to hold yourself to a standard as close to perfection as possible, because accuracy is the essential virtue of media writing.

If you find yourself writing in a news field and you inaccurately report information, your **credibility** will suffer because people will not be able to trust you. In many cases, your readers will attribute this to your being dumb or lazy. Although both of these things are bad, they pale in comparison to what readers will think of you if you work in public relations or advertising and you present inaccurate information. In those cases, the public tends to view you as being purposefully misleading in hopes of profiting from your lies. The idea that you made an honest mistake is unlikely to find accepting ears. This is especially true in an online environment, where people have been burned too often by "fake news" or propaganda-based websites.

Your readers will trust you after you give them a good reason to trust you. After that, trust remains a fragile item, and every time you write, you run the risk of shattering it. Trust is not a boomerang. If you throw it away, it doesn't come back. One of the best ways to retain trust is to be accurate above all else.

Be Tight

Much of the writing students do in school is measured in terms of length, with page counts serving as the demarcation between acceptable and unacceptable submissions. Students have learned a number of tricks to make things longer, including adding adjectives before every noun, increasing the size of the font or even making the periods bigger. (For those of you who are unfamiliar with the "period trick," here it is: http://youtu.be/tt3ac0inzbM.)

In a media setting, you want your writing to be short. Your readers don't want to deal with ever-expanding sentences that ramble on. They also don't have the time to hunt for key information amid paragraph after paragraph of things that don't matter to them. You want to get to the point as quickly as possible and give your readers everything they need to know right away. Twists and turns are for mystery writers, and nine-page descriptions that set the scene are for novelists. If you want to grab a reader on a computer monitor with multiple other distractions available or on a mobile phone screen with limited space, you must tighten your copy until you wring out every unnecessary word.

You can do this during your first draft, although it's usually easier to get the information out of your head and onto your screen without stopping. A good time to start tightening is after you write the whole piece. This allows you to take a good overview of everything you wrote before you start editing.

Be Clear

New writers are afraid of making mistakes, and thus they rely on $5 words and complex **jargon** to hide their insecurities. In most cases, this approach doesn't help their writing, and it tends to confuse their readers. Your job in this field is to say what you mean as simply and clearly as possible.

You need to find the right word to make your point and use it in a straightforward manner. You need to look up concepts that confuse you and describe them in a way that anyone can easily understand. You need to provide your readers with crucial information in a way that they can make sense of it.

Grammar guru Don Ranly lists **clarity** among his seven key "C's" to credibility[1] and for good reason. If people don't understand you, they won't trust you. Make your writing as clear as possible and you will give your readers a good reason to believe what you tell them.

Be Active

In Chapter 3, you got a giant grammar lesson, and here's where it really starts to come into play. Active voice requires you to write in the noun-verb-object format described earlier, but this approach does more than appease the grammar geeks.

Active sentences are tighter sentences. The sentences "Bob hit the ball" and "The ball was hit by Bob" give your reader the same basic information. However, the second sentence contains 50 percent more words than the first one. Sure, it's only two words, but if you convert the sentence to active voice and save those two words, you could use them later when you really need them.

When you write in this format, you want to pick vigorous verbs that are spot on in their descriptions of what is happening. This gives your readers the best chance of easily understanding each sentence. The sentence "Bill hit Bob" lacks the descriptive power of one that states "Bill slapped Bob." Both are active, but the second one improves your clarity as well.

Be Smooth

The **pace** and **flow** of a piece will determine how well it reads. Short sentences disrupt the pace, while longer sentences can make you feel as if the piece is rambling. You want to use medium-paced sentences, which are discussed at length in Chapter 3, of 20 words or so with one or two simple ideas in each one.

Flow is something that comes from putting the sentences together in an order that makes sense. You can think of a good piece like you think of a tree: Each branch smoothly grows from the larger one before it, and it is often difficult to see exactly where one starts and the other stops. When you consider all the branches together, all you see is a complete tree. A bad piece of writing is like a bundle of sticks: Each stick comes from a tree, but the bundle lacks cohesion and organization.

To make your pieces flow better, you want to have a natural order to your writing. Think about how Sentence A can lead into Sentence B in a clear and simple way. Look for things that make the sentences similar, such as talking about the same idea or coming from the same source. Also, look for things that make the sentences different, such as opposing viewpoints on a common topic. Then, use those similarities and differences to connect your sentences as you move through a piece.

Be Quick

Whether your piece is four sentences or 40 sentences, you want to get to the point. Get the most important information to your readers as quickly as possible, and use quickness to keep them interested and engaged. Use tight, medium-paced sentences that help them see what you are saying and why it matters to them. This will keep your readers from becoming bored and will make sure they see the most valuable information in your piece right away.

With all of these things you have to be, it can be daunting to consider writing for the media. However, journalists have developed writing styles to help you meet the needs of your readers. The most tried and true of these formats is the inverted pyramid.

PROFESSIONAL THOUGHTS
ADAM SILVERMAN

Although he has spent his entire professional career at one publication, Adam Silverman has seen a lot of change during his time at the Burlington [Vermont] Free Press. He began at the paper in 2000 as a reporter, covering small towns throughout the state. He went on to cover other areas, such as crime, courts and large towns, before joining the editing team at the paper.

As the associate editor, the No. 2 position in the newsroom, he now coordinates the paper's day-to-day operation. The publication uses a web-first model, in which reporters are expected to break news, use social media, conduct video storytelling and provide frequent updates online. The print edition serves as a tool of depth, offering investigative and narrative journalism as well as vibrant photography and innovative design.

Through all of these changes in his career and to the publication, Silverman said writing remains the most important thing in his newsroom.

"Good writing in all forms connects writers with readers," he said. "Whether you're crafting a piece of long-form journalism or a tweet, your audience will respond to a piece of writing that is accessible, clear and that matters to them."

Silverman said students who want to work in any area of media should work to become well-rounded individuals who possess quality writing and thinking skills.

"There is no doubt these skills are transferrable to other professions—probably any other profession that values clear writing, strong communicating and critical thinking," he said. "These talents are applicable inside and outside of journalism, including fields such as public relations and advertising. Someone who can write well, is adept at social media and can shoot photos and video can thrive in newspapers, television and web-only pursuits, to say nothing of taking those skills with them should they ever want to leave those areas."

Adam Silverman

The most important aspects he seeks in his staff are clarity and brevity, he said, as these attributes allow writers to find the crucial elements of a piece and convey them quickly and effectively.

"A good writer needs to filter the signal from the noise," he said. "That's always been true in journalism, but rarely has it been more important to avoid 'notebook-dumping' than it is today. Although the internet offers infinite space for stories of seemingly endless length, readers lack the patience to spend that much time with a story. And stories rarely need to be extensive tomes. Our job is to boil down, to strip jargon, to make complicated issues accessible and understandable."

One Last Thing

Q: If you could tell students anything about media writing or anything you have seen in your time in the field, what would it be?

A: Write tight. Simplify. Be clear. Avoid pronouns, complicated sentences, passive voice and negative constructions as much as possible. Think about narrative—times when narrative voice works and times when you should seek an alternate approach. Speak with an editor early and often; work collaboratively; file an early draft; and hang around until after your edit. Your editors, and your readers, will be grateful.

THE INVERTED PYRAMID

If you think about the stories you have heard from childhood until today, chances are most of them were told chronologically. Fairytales that start with "Once upon a time" and end with "And they all lived happily ever after" are a perfect example of how we tell stories from beginning to end in the order in which events occurred.

Media writing forces you to break from that mold and make choices about which pieces of information matter most. In writing for the media, you need to write your content in a way that starts with the most important thing and then moves to the second most important thing and then the third most important thing and so forth. This format is called the **inverted pyramid**.

FIGURE 4.1 ■ The inverted pyramid moves through chunks of information in descending order of importance. In this illustration, you can see how the most important elements rise to the top, with elements of lesser value moving down toward the bottom of the piece.

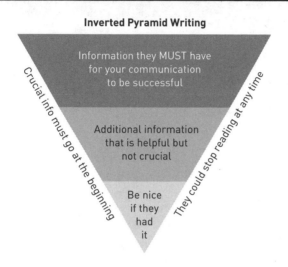

Legend has it that the inverted pyramid became a popular news format during the Civil War, when lines of communication were shaky and editors feared losing touch with their reporters. To make sure the important information about the battles made it from the field to the newsroom, reporters would supposedly transmit their stories backward, starting with the outcome of the battle. They would then outline the number of casualties, the turning point of the battle and so forth. This approach gave the newspaper the key pieces of the story in case the transmission was interrupted.

Whether accurate or merely a part of journalism lore, the idea behind that legend helps outline the importance of telling your story in descending order of importance. If you place the best information near the top of whatever you write, you will improve the chances that a reader will see that information and continue to read your work. In addition, people who read material written in this format can stop at any point and not feel lost or uninformed.

In the digital age, the inverted pyramid has become more popular than ever. People often lack the time to do long and detailed reads of winding narratives and instead want to just know the basics. This approach allows you to tell a reader who won a game, when a big sale will occur or why someone should participate in a charity event, in a simple and efficient manner. A basic inverted-pyramid piece can work well on the front page of a newspaper, the top of a press release or as an alert delivered on a mobile device.

ADAPT
THE INVERTED PYRAMID AS A THINKING TOOL

The inverted pyramid is a helpful tool during both the writing and information-gathering processes. The ability to focus on what matters most will allow you to determine what information you have and what information you need to find. In some ways, you can use the format like a shopping list built from a recipe: You know what should go into the final product, so you need to find those elements.

You can also use this approach after you have finished your writing. When you go through your work, use the inverted pyramid as your guide to determine what information you have and what you need. This will help you find the **holes** associated with your work, and it will also help you keep your eye on your audience as you build your piece.

For example, if you were constructing a press release that celebrates the hiring of your company's president, you would likely interview the president of the company, the outgoing president and a few other key organizational members. As you go through the release, you notice how several sources have attributed the president's work ethic to her favorite high school teacher. That ends up becoming part of your lead and works as a thread throughout the release. That's when you notice the hole: You didn't think to ask the name of the teacher. At that point, you can go back to your source and get the name. Maybe you can take it a step further and interview that teacher.

When you can rely on the inverted pyramid to help you organize your thoughts, you can improve the likelihood that you will remember to cover the most important areas of your piece and plug any holes you find.

GIVE IT A TRY: Here are several statements that have holes in them. Find each hole and then write a sentence that would "fill" the hole.

1. When Seattle Mariners pitcher Felix Hernandez threw a perfect game on Aug. 15, 2012, he became the third pitcher that season to achieve that feat.

2. The Sandy Hook Elementary School shooting, in which 26 people died, was the deadliest school shooting on U.S. soil since 2007.

3. People wishing to donate money to the American Red Cross can do so through the group's website.

4. According to delish.com, you can make sugar cookies with three ingredients.

5. Billionaire and media icon Oprah Winfrey noted that one of her teachers was the person who created a spark for learning in her and inspired her to become a talk show host and entrepreneur.

LEADS: THE PROMINENCE OF IMPORTANCE

The **lead** of an inverted-pyramid piece is meant to capture as much important information as possible. You need to include everything that would matter to people and would entice them to read on. It has to be brief, and yet it has to be laden with information. In many cases, writing a lead can feel as difficult as trying to carry sand in a pasta strainer. Here are some helpful things to think about when you write a lead:

"What Matters Most?" 5W's and 1H and More

Leads traditionally have a focus on the who, what, when, where, why and how of a piece. This is a simple way to hunt through the facts and interview material you gathered for the most valuable information. However, just because something has the **5W's and 1H** in there, it doesn't necessarily follow that you have a good lead. Here's an example:

A 45-year-old woman, whose family needed milk and eggs, paid for her groceries with cash Wednesday morning at Hometown Foods.

In terms of capturing those six elements, this lead is perfect. It has the who (a 45-year-old woman), what (paid for her groceries), when (Wednesday morning), where (Hometown Foods), why (her family needed milk and eggs) and how (with cash). However, it lacks the underlying aspect of what makes a lead worthwhile: valuable information.

When you build your lead, ask yourself, "What would matter most to my readers?" In other words, "Where is the value and how can I condense it into one sentence?" To answer this question, overlay the interest elements outlined in Chapter 1 (fame, oddity, conflict, immediacy and impact) on the story you are trying to tell. Then rely on these elements as you look for ways to show the readers personal value in an interesting way.

Build With the Basics

As mentioned in Chapter 3, the core of a sentence comes down to the noun and the verb (or in some cases, the noun-verb-object trinity). However, most people write sentences the same way they tell stories, which is chronologically. We start at the beginning and work our way through the end of the sentence.

Instead, look for the "who did what to whom" core of your sentence and write that first. If nothing else, it will take care of two of your W's and give you a sense of the focal point of your lead. Then answer the where and the when to emphasize immediacy and geography for your audience. How and why are always tough questions to answer, so if one or both of them drop out of the lead, it isn't the end of the world. That said, you can't get too far into the rest of your piece before you answer those questions.

Here is an example of building a lead outward from the core:

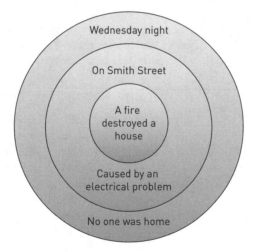

We start at the core with the most important information: Fire destroys home. We then move outward into other interesting elements that touch on the remaining 5W's and 1H: What caused the fire, where it happened, if anyone was around and when it occurred. This allows us to better prioritize what elements must make it into the lead and also gives us a sense of what things can move into a second paragraph if we don't have the room for all of these elements.

Lead Length and Readability

The length of the average lead for an inverted-pyramid piece should be about 25 to 35 words. (Leads for broadcast news stories, professional-to-professional communication and ad copy follow different rules.) A good rule of thumb is to read the lead out loud to see how it sounds and how it feels. If you are running out of air when you get to the end of your lead, the sentence might be too long. If you have to take a second breath, it is definitely too long.

Reading your lead aloud can also help you determine the flow, pace and general feel of your lead. As you read the lead aloud, you can find errors in structure and grammar that might otherwise escape you, such as pairing a plural noun with a singular verb or omitting a key word. If the sentence sounds smooth and you have no problem saying it, you have crafted a well-structured sentence with good flow. If you feel like you have a mouthful of marbles when you try to say the sentence, you have issues that need correction.

You can also determine whether the lead has too many ideas in it. If you think about the word count in terms of a lead's length, you can think about its readability in terms of "weight." If a lead has too much going on in it, the sentence can feel heavy and unwieldy as you read it aloud. Your vocabulary choice can also make your lead feel heavy. If you feel like you are reading a "word a day" calendar instead of a lead sentence, you need to edit your work to improve the readability.

TYPES OF LEADS

Leads are like any other tool you have available to you: If you use the right tool for the right job, you will succeed. If you pick the wrong one, your work can become frustrating to you and your readers. Leads for inverted-pyramid stories that rely on the 5W's and 1H are usually called **summary leads**, in that you are summarizing what happened and explaining why it matters to your readers. Beyond that general term, here are some more nuanced ways of defining lead types and instances in which you can use them effectively:

© iStockphoto.com/hocus-focus

With many people competing for your readers' attention, you need to write strong leads that draw people into your stories.

Name-Recognition Leads

As mentioned in Chapter 1's discussion of FOCII, fame is an important element when it comes to attracting audiences. The more well known someone is, the more likely that person's name will draw readers. **Name-recognition leads** draw on this principle and put the famous person's name at the front of the lead:

President Donald Trump announced Thursday . . .

Pope Francis said Friday . . .

Chancellor David Smith will attend . . .

Use this lead when you think the audience will know the name of someone right away with little or no context. If you are unsure how easily your readers will recognize this person by name, consider taking a different approach.

Interesting-Action Leads

In many cases, the "what" is more intriguing than the "who" when it comes to the lead. For this situation, you want to use an action-based lead in which you delay identifying the person by name and focus more on what the person did or what happened to that person. In many cases, a name will not matter to readers:

BAD: *Chester B. Monroe was arrested Sunday on suspicion of assault at the Springfield County Fair.*

When you use a name in a lead, readers should not think to themselves, "Wait, who is that guy? Should I know him?" By delaying the name of the person and instead giving some descriptors, you can better draw in your readers:

BETTER: *A 43-year-old Springfield man was arrested Sunday on suspicion of assault at the county fair.*

The biggest thing about an interesting-action lead, however, is to explain as clearly as possible what should make that action interesting to your readers:

GOOD: *A 43-year-old Springfield man was arrested Sunday after police say he punched a carnival worker who refused to give him a stuffed bear toy.*

Interesting-action leads are also helpful when you have multiple people involved in something and none of them are well known:

Seven Marconi High School student athletes received full rides to Division I schools, marking the largest number of sports scholarships in school history, Principal Mack Davis said.

In each case, you should name the people shortly after the lead, particularly in the case when one person will be the focal point of the piece. If you think the action will attract more people than the name of any one individual, use this approach.

© iStockphoto.com/Rawpixel Ltd.

A meeting often will contain a lot of information, but you need to find the most important thing that happens and focus on that in your lead.

Event Leads

Whether you are planning them or reporting on them, events are the staple of media writing in many ways. As a PR practitioner who writes about events, you might need to promote the event, gather an audience or gain reporters' attention. As a reporter, you might need to tell people about one thing that is important to them out of the dozen items a group discussed. In any case, an **event lead** can help you locate what matters most and tell your readers about it.

When you write an event lead, focus on what happened at the event, not the event itself. Pieces about meetings or speeches that include the phrase "held a meeting" or "gave a speech" miss the point. Look at the examples below:

> **AWFUL:** *The Smithville College Board of Trustees held a meeting Wednesday where the board members discussed increasing tuition.*

This lead needs help because (a) it starts with a "held a meeting" element, and (b) it doesn't tell the readers what happened with the tuition discussion. Is tuition going up or not? This lead doesn't tell us, and that's probably what most readers would want to know.

> **BAD:** *The Smithville College Board of Trustees held a meeting Wednesday and decided to increase tuition by $500 per student.*

This lead has the same problem as above in terms of relying on the "held a meeting" angle to tell the story. If you see a lead that tells you someone "held a meeting *and…*," whatever comes after "and" is probably where you will find the most important information.

> **BETTER:** *The Smithville College Board of Trustees decided Wednesday to increase tuition by $500 per student.*

This works out fairly well, with a noun-verb structure (trustees decided) and an explanation of what is most newsworthy. However, it keeps the focus on the board of trustees as opposed to the audience. If you can rework this to address the audience members' self-interest, you will have a much stronger lead.

> **GOOD:** *Students at Smithville College will pay $500 more to attend school this year, the board of trustees decided Wednesday.*

This one is the best of the bunch, although it could be better. It shifts the focus to the audience and it sticks with the active voice approach. If you wrote this for the student paper at Smithville College, a lot of people would see value in your story.

Second-Day Leads

Even if you aren't writing for news, the word "new" has value to you. As noted in Chapter 1, immediacy is important to your readers, so the fresher the information, the better your piece will be. You want to give your readers the most recent information at the top of whatever you are writing.

When you are conducting a public-relations campaign, you can notify the public of your goal for the campaign with an event-style lead in your first news release.

> *In memory of a pledge who died of cancer last year, the Alpha Beta fraternity will attempt to collect $10,000 this month for a scholarship in that student's name.*

This lead is simple and tells the story of what the group hopes to accomplish. The next release, however, can't start the same way, because it will confuse readers and rely on old information to tell the story. This is where the **second-day lead** can be helpful as you update information for your audience. Consider these leads:

AWFUL: *In memory of a pledge who died of cancer last year, the Alpha Beta fraternity launched a fundraiser last week to collect $10,000 this month for a scholarship in that student's name.*

BAD: *Five days ago, the Alpha Beta fraternity launched its charity fundraiser for the James Simpson Memorial Scholarship fun, with a goal of $10,000.*

GOOD: *In the first five days of its charity drive for the James Simpson Memorial Scholarship, the Alpha Beta fraternity has raised more than half of its $10,000 goal.*

Notice that the awful lead has done nothing to update the story or even tell readers something beyond what they learned in the initial lead. The bad lead has more news in it than the awful lead, but it still doesn't tell your readers anything of interest or really provide additional information. The good lead focuses on something new and of interest: how the fundraising is progressing.

When the campaign finally comes to a close, you want one more release that again uses a second-day approach to inform your readers of what happened.

BAD: *The Alpha Beta fraternity attempted to raise $10,000 this month to commemorate a student who died of cancer last year.*

BETTER: *The monthlong fundraiser for the James Simpson Memorial Scholarship came to a close tonight, with the group more than reaching its goal of $10,000.*

GOOD: *The Alpha Beta fraternity collected $31,083 in one month for the James Simpson Memorial Scholarship, more than tripling its stated goal.*

The bad lead has the primary problem associated with all of the earlier bad and awful leads: It doesn't tell us anything new. The better lead answers the big question: Did the fraternity meet its goal? (Yes.) However, what makes the good lead the best of the bunch is it provides an exact figure ($31,083) and context (more than triple the initial goal) for the fundraising drive.

You can reshape each of those second-day leads to better emphasize certain aspects of the story or to draw attention to certain interest elements. However, in each case, it is clear that you must put the focus where it belongs: on the newest information.

PROBLEMATIC LEADS AND POTENTIAL FIXES

Throughout this chapter, we have discussed the way in which you have to shift your writing from a chronological format to a value-driven format. Doing this can make you feel uncomfortable and thus drive you to some bad lead-writing choices.

In most cases, you have the right idea in your head for a lead but you don't know exactly how to say it, so you fall back on weak devices and well-worn clichés to do the job for you. This is particularly problematic in public relations, where your audience is filled with other writers who are ready to rip you to shreds, and in advertising, where clarity and innovation are crucial.

Here are a series of problematic leads and a few suggestions on how to improve them. These leads aren't taboo in the sense that you should never use them, but before you choose one of these, you should carefully consider other options.

"You" Leads

Some areas of media writing are more or less forgiving about the use of second person. Broadcast journalism is an interpersonal media, with the anchor or reporter delivering the news in a way that bonds directly to the individual audience members. Thus, the use of "you" isn't as jarring. Newspapers tend to avoid "you," as reporters see second-person writing as sacrificing their objectivity. In advertising, the "you" is often implied in the call to action: You should buy this product.

The big problem with **"you" leads** occurs when they become opinionated and presumptuous. The writer assumes that all readers will react to a situation in the same way or that the writer's value system is the same as the readers'.

> *The Interfraternity Council is hosting a blood drive at the union Friday, and you should donate.*

On its face, the lead seems straightforward and supportive of a good idea. However, this presupposes that everyone can donate blood. Certain restrictions in terms of health, lifestyle, international travel and body size can prohibit some people from donating. Other people might have a serious fear of needles or a propensity to faint, thus making them unwilling to take part. However, the writer essentially is commanding people to skip past all of these issues and get to the blood drive right away.

Instead of approaching the lead this way, you can use a third-person approach and focus more on broader goal-oriented actions.

> *The Interfraternity Council is asking students to attend Friday's blood drive in hopes of breaking last year's collection record of 300 pints.*

In another instance, you could use an anecdote or exemplar to draw in your readers.

> *When he was 8 years old, Beta Theta Pi member Karl Anderson nearly died after severing an artery in his leg while on a camping trip.*
>
> *"The only difference between life and death for me was that someone had donated blood earlier that week in my area," he said. "I lost four pints and if a couple people hadn't taken time to donate, I'd have been a goner."*
>
> *Now the chairman of the Interfraternity Council, Anderson said his goal is to host at least one blood drive on the campus each semester and bring in more donations in each successive event.*
>
> *The group is hosting a blood drive Friday at the union with a goal of exceeding 300 pints.*
>
> *"I know that not everyone can donate," he said. "But people who can, I really hope they do."*

Obviously this is more than a single lead paragraph, but you can see how the example can develop into several sentences on a common theme before getting into the nuts and bolts of the event itself.

Question Leads

Journalism is about questions and answers: You ask questions of your sources, and you report their answers to your audience members. When you use a question lead, you mix up the process.

Question leads often fail because they presuppose that all of your readers would answer in the same way.

Did you ever wonder what it would be like to live in a penthouse in New York City? You're not alone!

This lead presupposes that all readers would see a New York City penthouse as a luxurious and coveted living option. However, if you have readers who hate crowds, love nature and disdain public transportation, you aren't going to hold on to them for very long.

Instead, get to the point of what you are trying to tell people in your lead and then move on.

New York City has seen a rise in penthouse rentals and purchases from small-town, Midwestern buyers who say they want to live the life of big-city celebrities.

A second problem with a question lead comes when you use it in advertising copy, because it heightens the suspicions of your readers.

Wouldn't you like a simple way to feel more energized without having to sleep as much?

Chances are, readers will view this as a come-on akin to the hucksters in the Old West who sold snake oil out of the back of a covered wagon. Instead of asking a question, show your readers you have the ability to support your claim.

People who took XYZ tablets reported feeling more energized while sleeping 1.4 hours less per day, according to a Harvard University study of 1,000 individuals.

If you don't want to sound like a sleazy salesman, don't use a question lead.

Quote Leads

It's not a crime to own a "Quote a Day" calendar, but it shouldn't be your journalistic muse. You can admire the verbal offerings of Albert Einstein, Nelson Mandela or Selena Gomez, but you shouldn't make them the focal point of your lead. This also applies to quoting song lyrics, Bible verses and dictionary definitions.

If you want to capture the essence of a piece, just use a standard lead to tell your readers what happened. If you have a more emotionally driven piece, consider using observation or source anecdotes to make your point.

The problems associated with a **quote lead** also apply to quotes from your sources. (You can learn more about sources in Chapter 5 and more about quotes in Chapter 10.) When you start with a quote, your readers can feel as if they walked into the middle of a conversation.

"I knew I had to kill it by myself. I really didn't want to but nobody else seemed willing, so I grabbed my stick and went to work."

This lead could be the beginning of a horrifying confession of how a serial killer began his bloody career or it could be a story about a gutsy hockey player trying to keep the opposing team from scoring during a penalty situation. In either case, the readers are going to be confused until they get deeper into your piece.

Instead of doing this, start with an anecdote that leads into the quote:

Right winger John Jacoby had played all but three shifts in the state finals on a badly bruised thigh and said the last thing he wanted to do was go out for the final two minutes of a one-goal game.

However, when the team's top penalty killer was whistled for high-sticking, Jacoby said he did what he always does: He gutted it out.

"I knew I had to kill it by myself," he said. "I really didn't want to but nobody else seemed willing, so I grabbed my stick and went to work."

After this, you can add a paragraph that leads your readers into whatever the rest of the story is: a profile of Jacoby, a recap of the state finals or something else that attaches itself to this story.

"Imagine" Leads

Unless you are writing about the John Lennon song, you want to avoid an **"imagine" lead**. First, it is a cliché and a particularly bad one, since you are putting the onus on your readers to do the work for you. Second, it can be problematic if your readers aren't imagining what you are imagining.

Here's a lead for a promotional piece on a new residence hall set up at a university:

Imagine living in a dorm room complete with a refrigerator, stove, washer/dryer combo and private bathroom.

For students who are currently sharing a room and a community bathroom, that might sound great. For nontraditional students who have a house of their own, this would really cramp their style.

Perhaps the most problematic thing about "imagine" leads is that if something is imaginary, why are you writing about it? In most cases, you probably have a real-life example that would serve better as an attention-getter.

Imagine being homeless at the age of 5 with no family and having to fight just to survive.

This is a situation most readers probably haven't faced, so it's tough for them to imagine. It's also likely that they won't stick with the story long enough to find out what is behind that "imaginary" moment.

Instead of telling people to imagine something, show them the reality:

James Carver was born to a drug-addicted mother, abandoned at a church by age 2 and homeless by age 5. During his time on the streets, he slept on a sewer grate to stay warm, fought rats for scraps of food and got his clothing out of thrift-store dumpsters.

Then get to the point of why we are reading about this person by the third or fourth paragraph. He might be speaking at your school, raising money for charity or graduating as a valedictorian of his class.

HOW TO ORDER THE REST OF YOUR PYRAMID

If you have constructed your lead well, you can use it as a road map to help you work your way through the rest of the piece. If you wrote a weak or problematic lead, you will feel as though you are putting a square peg into a round hole for the next several paragraphs. Here are some things that can help you figure out what should come next in your writing:

Determine the Value of Each Fact

The lead will have the majority of the things that matter most in it. Your job at this point is to wade through what remains and make some choices about what will make the cut and what won't. This will help remove a lot of superfluous material and give you a better chance to get a handle on the remaining information. This will also help you figure out if you are missing any crucial pieces that you need to find before you can continue writing.

Consider the following facts from the Department of Transportation regarding an upcoming project:

1. *The Interstate 12 project will begin March 5 and take six months to complete.*

2. *H&J builders have been contracted to complete the job.*

3. *The total job will cost $4.3 million.*

4. *The project will replace the current road surface with more tire-friendly pavement.*

5. *Approximately 42,000 travelers use this road each day.*

6. *Starting April 6, the interstate will be closed for the duration of the project.*

If you could include only three facts from this list in the piece you want to write, you would need to see which facts will matter most to your readers. If you work for a local newspaper, the sixth and fifth facts will likely make the cut, with some discussion of the third and fourth fact for the final spot on your list. If you work for the H&J Construction Newsletter or the company's promotional department, the second fact becomes crucial, while the first, third and fourth facts will also vie for a spot in your work. As you determine value for each fact, you should consider your audience's needs and interests.

Support the Lead

As mentioned earlier, the lead serves as a road map for the rest of your piece, so every sentence that comes after the lead should aid it in telling the story. As you examine each fact, see how it relates to the lead and determine whether it helps drive home the point in that top sentence.

If you find that the story and the lead aren't matching up, you have two options. On one hand, you can see if the piece made a wrong turn at some point and wandered away from the story you originally intended to tell. In a situation like this, you can go back to that point in the piece, correct the problem and get back on track.

On the other hand, you might find that the body of the piece holds more value than the lead does. If this is the case, you can rework the lead so it better fits with the tale you have told. In either case, the lead and the body need to fit together in a way that makes sense.

Descending Order of Importance

The inverted-pyramid structure dictates that you write your story in descending order of importance. This means that the most important bit of information after your lead goes second, the most important information after that goes third and so forth.

You might not be able to discern the overall importance of a particular fact at first glance, which is why doing a self-edit is important in the writing process. Once you have all of the pieces in what you think is the best possible order, go back and look through what you have done to make sure the order is right.

Think back to the list of facts on the Interstate 12 project and consider what order you would place all six of them in if you worked for the DOT or a local newspaper. If you used an inverted-pyramid structure, the fifth and sixth facts would likely be at the top, with the third fact probably staying put and the remaining facts going near the bottom. The two final facts will matter most to your readers, whether you use them as part of a press release or a news story.

In some cases, Fact A will need to precede Fact B for your readers to make sense of each fact. In other cases, you might find facts that take on a greater importance than you first afforded them, which will force you to reorder your facts to get them into the best possible order for your audience members.

© iStockphoto.com/skynesher

Writing in one- or two-sentence paragraphs will help create small chunks of indented text. This approach gives people's eyes little "footholds" like those on a rock-climbing wall and thus makes it easier for your readers to consume content.

Use Small Chunks

The structure of the inverted pyramid forces you to give people chunks of important information in rapid order. To do this without overwhelming your readers, you need to keep those chunks small. The structure relies primarily on one-sentence paragraphs, with a few two-sentence paragraphs thrown in when necessary. In some forms of writing, as you will see in Chapter 10 on print writing, you will have quotes that go longer than that, but these tend to be the exceptions rather than the rules.

Your eyes and your mind can feel overwhelmed when you scan a giant block of text. The small paragraphs, complete with their indents, can give your readers' eyes little "footholds" like those you would see on a rock-climbing wall. The indenting will allow your readers to slowly and steadily move through a piece. When you write in giant paragraphs with almost no indents, the readers can feel as if they are falling down a sheer cliff, with no hope of catching a hold. Take the big chunks and break them up into smaller bites and you will serve your readers well.

Know When to Stop

The inverted pyramid moves from the most important information to the least important information you wish to convey to your readers. However, you don't want to include information that is so low in value it bores your readers. This is where your ability to judge the importance of your facts comes into play. If you don't include enough information, you will leave your readers confused. If you keep adding content for no good reason, you will create bored and disinterested audience members. News reporters often refer to the idea of writing too much as "**notebook emptying**," referring to the notion that since they wrote a fact or a quote in their notes, they should include it in their stories.

CONNECT
WHY ARE YOU DOING WHAT YOU'RE DOING?

In media writing, you don't see a lot of right and wrong answers, but rather better and worse answers. The key to figuring out how to find more "better" answers and have fewer "worse" ones comes down to your thought process as a writer.

As you write your lead and order your paragraphs, consider the question "Why did I do that?" In most cases, when editors or managers question writers in this way, the writers worry that they have done something wrong. A better way of thinking about this question is to consider it a chance to justify your decisions.

In order to connect with the audience, you need to think about what the audience wants to know. This part often gets lost in the daily grind of cranking out copy. To better connect with the readers, you can start answering questions like "Why did you lead with that?" or "Why did you put that near the bottom?"

You need to have a reason behind why you think each piece matters and to what degree you think it does. When you finish writing, go back through you work and justify what you wrote and where you put it in terms of serving your audience. Make sure you can explain to yourself, or your boss, what you did and why you ordered it that way. This will help improve the overall value of your piece and help you reach your audience members on their level.

GIVE IT A TRY: Below are a series of facts on an accident. Place the facts in descending order of importance and then exchange your list with a classmate. See where you agree on the ordering and where you disagree. Justify your organization in hopes of coming to agreement on the best possible order.

Springfield police responded to a report of a two-vehicle accident at Broadway and Sixth Avenue.

Police said the driver of a white minivan drove through a stop sign without stopping.

Traffic was delayed in all directions for 20 minutes because of the crash.

The driver of the minivan was Jane Morris, a 35-year-old mother of three.

The only passenger in the minivan, John Morris, the 38-year-old husband of Jane Morris, was killed in the crash.

The driver of the other vehicle, a red Corvette, was Springfield Mayor Bob Commins.

You need to know when to stop writing. One of the better ways to do this is to examine each fact after you have placed it in your piece and ask if it adds something to the telling of the tale. If the fact is something that would benefit your readers, retain it. If not, cut it. If you have trouble determining this, ask a colleague to read it and give you a second opinion. It takes a lot of practice to figure out exactly where that line sits between too much and not enough information, so that second set of eyes can be helpful during your earliest drafts.

THE BIG THREE

Here are the three big things to take with you as you continue reading the book:

1. **The most important information goes first:** When you work in media writing, you want to take your best shot at getting your audience's attention right up front. This means you need to give them everything that matters as quickly as possible. Don't beat around the bush. Use the inverted-pyramid structure to give them the good stuff immediately.

2. **Rely on the basics:** The best way to have a strong sentence is to stick to the core of what makes a sentence work: noun-verb or noun-verb-object.

Start here when you build each sentence to make sure the core of the sentence is dealing with the issue you think is most important for that sentence. Then augment those pieces with additional information that has value to your readers.

3. **Know when to stop:** You can kill a good piece if you don't know when to stop writing. Make sure that when you write, you know when you have run out of important things to say. If you do this, you will have tightly written pieces and grateful readers.

KEY TERMS

5W's and 1H 62
accuracy 58
clarity 59
credibility 58
event lead 66
flow 59
holes 62

"imagine" lead 70
interesting-action lead 65
inverted pyramid 61
jargon 58
lead 62
name-recognition lead 64
notebook emptying 72

pace 59
question lead 69
quote lead 69
second-day lead 67
summary lead 64
"you" lead 68

DISCUSSION QUESTIONS

1. Of the "killer be's" outlined at the beginning of the chapter, which one do you think is most important, and which one do you think is least important? Why?

2. What are some of the benefits associated with writing in the inverted pyramid? What makes it hard for new journalists to write in this format?

3. Which of the "problem" leads is most bothersome to you as a reader? Why does it bother you and how would you recommend fixing those types of leads?

WRITE NOW!

1. Take the facts in the "Give It a Try" exercise above and create a lead sentence that is between 25 and 35 words long, contains the majority of the 5W's and 1H and has value to the citizens of Springfield.

2. Select a fairytale or other well-known "once upon a time" story and rewrite it in the inverted-pyramid format. Start with a summary lead that focuses on the most important things in the story and then include three to five additional one-sentence paragraphs that provide content in descending order of importance.

3. Write a four-sentence piece based on a news story, press release or other piece of media writing. Remember to use a strong lead sentence and then one sentence per paragraph. Focus on ordering the information from most important to least important. Make sure the piece has solid flow and readability.

4. Select a story with a lead that uses one of the "problematic" devices noted earlier in the story. Rewrite the lead in a summary-lead format.

NOTE

1. Don Ranly. "Seven C's to Credibility." Accessed at: http://www.ranly.com/programs/sevenCs.html.

5

INTERVIEWING

LEARNING OBJECTIVES

After completing this chapter you should be able to:

- Explain how to prepare for an interview by researching your topic and gathering information about your source.

- Understand how to approach a source and conduct an interview in a professional manner.

- Create quality open-ended and closed-ended questions based on the research you conducted on your topic and your source.

- Identify ways to draw additional information from sources through nonverbal cues and concluding questions.

You might not realize this, but you conduct dozens of interviews every day of your life. You ask your roommate how his or her day went. You find out what's going on back home when you talk to Mom or Dad. You figure out how to do an assignment when you ask your professor for guidance. Some of these interviews are simple one-question events, while others stretch across hours. Some are formal and regimented, whereas others are loose and unstructured. The thing that ties them all together is your ability to ask questions in a coherent fashion and gain knowledge from the answers you receive.

In all areas of media, you will interview people as a part of your writing process. You might need to interview a mayor for a news story or your boss for a piece in the company newsletter. If you go into public relations, you could interview your clients as part of a video news release or to learn what they expect of you in an upcoming campaign. If you go into advertising, you will interview company officials to determine how best to craft creative briefs or what to emphasize during the production of advertising copy.

The interview is the most effective tool you have to gather crucial information. When done well, an interview can give you an array of content from which you can choose as you craft your writing. When done poorly, an interview can feel like a bad blind date that will never end.

The purpose of this chapter will be to outline the process of interviewing from preparation through completion. The chapter also will examine the best ways to get the most out of your interviews and how to avoid serious problems as you work with your source.

INTERVIEW PREPARATION

When it comes to a professional interview, preparation is essential. In everyday life, friends and family members will let you beat around the bush and engage in random chitchat. In the professional world, your interview subjects expect you to get to the point immediately.

Preparation will require you to research your source thoroughly before setting up your interview. Beyond simple research, you should approach an interview understanding both the purpose of your interview and why this source matters to your project.

Before you conduct an interview, look through old newspaper files, website profiles and social media accounts to research the person you will interview and to understand the topic of the interview.

PLACES TO DIG

When you are looking for information on an interview subject, here are a few places to look:

Newspaper files: Most papers have their archives digitized, making them easy to access online. However, when you are interviewing someone who has a long history in the field, you will want to check the traditional clipped files as well. Some publications have librarians, who oversee file cabinets full of **clips** on all sorts of topics. Digital and print searches can yield personality profiles written on your subject, articles in which the person was quoted as an expert and information about the person's field on the whole. The information you gather can help you craft your questions and prepare to speak with your source.

Company websites: Many companies provide miniature biographies on their staff members, especially those in the upper echelons of the organizations. Surf a company site to find background on your source, including key biographical, educational and professional information. You can also learn about this person's current interests and professional strengths.

Trade press: In many cases, the importance of a source is germane to people who follow a particular field and not those in the general population. This is where **trade-press** searches come in handy. In some cases, a person is a big deal in a trade or field but hasn't gotten a lot of attention in mainstream newspapers or magazines. What you find here can educate you on both the individual source and the field itself.

Social media: Your source will likely have some presence on social media sites such as Twitter and Facebook. Look here for information about the person's passions, interests and goals. This can help you find an icebreaker question or shape your questions to fit your source's personality. Be careful with this kind of research and approach, because you don't want to look like a stalker. If you start your interview with a statement like "I saw a photo of your grandson last night," you might cause some tension between you and your source.

Other sources: One of the best places to get information about an interview subject is from other people who know your source. People who work with you can offer friendly advice based on their own successes and failures. Friends and colleagues of the source can give you some pointers as well, such as "He won't let you use a recorder" or "Don't call her by her first name." These items can help you start off on the right foot or avoid starting off on the wrong one.

GETTING THE INTERVIEW

How to get an interview varies based on who you are, who your source is and what topic you expect to discuss with that person. Most interviews start with a simple phone call and end just as easily five minutes later. However, interviews also can be spur-of-the-moment things brought about by a lucky happenstance. For example, you might find yourself in an elevator with your school's head basketball coach moments after you find out that the starting point guard broke his leg.

Interviews can also be worked out in advance with painstaking requirements and involve as many as 10 people who need to sign off before you get within 10 feet of your source. Some sources can be tough nuts to crack, and your ability to get your foot in the door, so to speak, is going to be half the battle. Having the best questions in the world will do you little good if you can't get people to talk to you. Here are some things to keep in mind as you work toward getting an interview and gaining the trust of your source:

Understand Your Purpose

Interviews, even within a single media discipline, have various purposes. For example, a news story about a fatal car crash will require several interviews and afford you little time for research and preparation. After you rush to the scene, you would interview any witnesses, anyone who was involved in the crash and the officials working to restore order, such as the police and fire personnel. You could quickly alert your readers to the crash with a tweet or two, based on an interview with a police officer. Then you might write a short story for the web, which would contain most of the 5W's and 1H and other basic information you gathered.

On the other hand, if you are writing a profile on a police commissioner who is retiring after 30 years of service, you need to do a lot of research and prepare many good questions for your interview. The interview you conduct with the commissioner herself is not only crucial to your piece but will need to yield a lot of deep and rich information. If you fail to get a good interview, you will cause irreparable damage to your profile.

The purpose of an interview will dictate what tone you take with your subject, how much time you will need with your source and what types of questions you will prepare. A reporter can try to grill a company's CEO who is suspected of bilking the company out of millions of dollars. However, a spokesperson who interviews the same CEO will need to take a more delicate and probing approach. An interview between a public-relations professional and a client regarding the launch of a charity campaign will have a different tone than that same professional preparing a client for a press conference in the wake of a crisis.

The purpose of an interview will help you determine whether you need five minutes on the phone with a source to confirm some information or several interviews of a few hours each to complete the task at hand. You should convey these needs to your source right away. This will allow the source to prepare for things you will want to know and understand what you think should happen at the interview.

Approaching the Source

In approaching a source, either by phone, in person or through some other means, make sure you display proper manners. When you start things off on the wrong foot, the interview has nowhere to go but downhill. You never know who will answer the phone, what mood that person will be in or if the source will have time for you. When the person on the other end of your conversation greets you, simply starting with "Hello, this is Bill Johnson from the marketing department. Is the head of the finance department there, please?" can get you moving in the right direction. It's an on-point opener, gives the person on the other end a chance to figure out what you want and it shows a modicum of politeness.

Once you get through to the source, introduce yourself and explain your purpose. For a general interview, tell the source who you are and what you want. This will give the source a brief bit of information about your topic, how much time you need and how this interview will be conducted.

In many cases, sources misperceive their value in regard to your work. Some people believe they have no value to you or that you can get the information they have from some other source. Other sources think their time is far too valuable to waste answering your questions. You need to impress upon your sources that they have important information and that your readers need to know it.

If you are planning an in-person interview, which is usually the best way to go, give consideration to where you want to meet the source. Rookie interviewers usually look for "neutral" sites, such as a coffee shop or a restaurant, as a way to reduce their own discomfort with the process. Even worse, some people will ask sources to come to the newsroom or the agency office for interviews. When setting up a meeting with a source, go to the source's turf whenever possible. If you have to interview a client to set up a new campaign, go to the client's office. If you want to get to know the police chief, go to the police department and interview her there. If you want to assemble a press kit for a local homeless shelter, interview the director at his office.

Conducting the interview at your subject's home base does two important things. First, it keeps the source relaxed, which will improve the overall feel and value of your interview. People feel more normal in their personal or work environments, and this will likely lead to longer answers, deeper thoughts and additional pieces of information. Second, it allows you to do some observing, which can help you when you start writing. News features and profile stories benefit from strong visualization opportunities. Your descriptions of the person and the scene allow your readers to see this situation in their own minds.

INTERACTING WITH YOUR SOURCE

When you start your interview, it is best to be conservative in your tone and professional in your approach. Once you get to know the source, either as a part of this interview or through several interviews you conduct over time, you can become more laid back. You can always loosen up later, but if you start too loose, you will feel awkward if your source chafes at your approach.

Regardless of the type of interview you conduct, you need to make sure that you are not hurting your chances of getting important information based on the way you are acting. In an attempt to reduce tension, some people attempt to appear nonchalant. This can give the source a sense that you don't care about the interview or that you aren't serious. One of the best ways to make sure you act appropriately is to mimic your source. If the person is really straitlaced, consider using a lot of courtesy titles, such as "sir," "ma'am" or "professor." If the person is a bit looser, still start conservatively until the person says something like "Hey, just call me Jim."

INTERVIEWING VIA EMAIL OR TEXT

As much as this book pushes you toward interviewing people in person or via telephone, email interviews have value in some cases. When you need quick information from a source who is notoriously hard to reach, a simple exchange of emails, texts, tweets or other digital contacts can make your life a lot easier. That said, email should not be a way to dodge an in-person interview when you feel lazy or scared.

In some cases, sources might be in difficult situations or hard-to-reach areas of the world, and thus the ability to work on an interview digitally can seem appealing. Let's say you need information from a manager at your company about some things that need to make it into an advertising campaign. If that person is stuck in meetings all day, she might not be available for a telephone conversation when you need her most. However, she might pull up your email during one of the more boring parts of a meeting or hit you back quickly with an instant message with the information you need. In another case, you might need some follow-up questions answered from your CEO so you can issue a press release in the morning. If the CEO is halfway around the world, the differences in time zones might make a call difficult, so an email will give this person a chance to time-shift the interview and respond at her discretion.

Email and text interviews have their place in media writing, but they should not be a default option because you are lazy or scared.

One other great aspect of email interviews is that you have a complete digital transcript of what the person wanted to say on the topic. Many sources during telephone or face-to-face interviews will misspeak or say something they don't remember saying. When the interview is published, sources can have "buyer's remorse" and argue that "I never said that!" However, an email has a word-for-word account of what that person had to say.

This is not to say email interviews aren't without their problems. Start with the idea that you really weaken your position as a journalist when you ask only five preset questions and give yourself no real opportunity to follow up. You can always send additional emails with more questions, but that doesn't guarantee you will get answers. Also, it can be difficult to replicate via email the way in which an immediate in-person follow-up question can prod a source to provide a better answers. Even more, when a source has time to create a message, that message might not be as genuine as an initial response given during a live interview.

Some pieces you will write cannot rely mainly on email interviews. Personality profiles, stories steeped in data analysis and news features require one-on-one time with your sources. In the case of the more feature-based writing, you will also need the opportunity to observe your sources, something you can't do via text or email. When it comes to using email to conduct interviews, understand what benefits you receive and what you lose out on as part of the process. As a practical matter, you should also check to see if your organization has any specific rules as to when or how email interviews can be conducted.

INTERVIEWING FOR MULTIPLE MEDIA

When you conduct an interview, you need to think about how you will use the information you gather. In some cases, the material you gather in the interview will serve only as background for other interviews. In other cases, you could use some of the interview material in a print story, a few audio clips to augment a web version of that story and extended video clips of the source as well. Even though this book focuses primarily on writing, consider a few of the issues discussed below:

Several companies manufacture equipment meant to turn your smartphone into a more complete digital recording tool. Tripods like this one can be used to stabilize your phone and avoid shaky video. Other additions include zoom lenses for some smartphone cameras or external microphones to enhance audio recording.

Audio and Video Tools

Technology has made recording audio and video easier and cheaper than ever before. Instead of lugging a giant cassette recorder and microphone to an interview, you can capture audio on a digital recorder that is the size of a candy bar. Video used to require large, shoulder-mounted cameras and multiple VHS or Beta tapes. Now, the average smartphone can capture reasonably decent video if you record in an optimal setting. Smartphone apps are also available to conduct audio recording as well.

Even if you don't plan to work across media platforms, it is a good idea to record your interviews. This will allow you to check facts and quotes or fill in holes in your notes. Since technology isn't perfect, always take good notes just to be safe.

Recording Your Discussion, Repurposing the Material

The rules for recording interviews will vary on your state, your approach and your area of the field. Federal law allows the recording of telephone calls if at least one person involved in the call knows the recording is occurring. This form of recording, often called "**one-party consent**," is also the law of the land in 38 states. The remaining 12 states require "**two-party consent**" for telephone calls, which means both people have to know someone is recording the call. Many states apply their rules for digital communication to in-person conversations as well, although some variations exist from state to state. To make sure you understand the law related to recording, you can check out your state's rules at this website: http://www.rcfp.org/reporters-recording-guide/state-state-guide.

The best way to avoid parsing the law regarding issues of trespassing or wiretapping when it comes to recording interviews is to just ask the source for permission. It is a good idea to start the recording and ask the source, "Can I record this interview?" This will allow you to record your request for permission as well as the source's response. If the source says, "yes," you have that on tape, which allows you to better protect yourself in case the source later raises a concern. If a source says you can't record the interview, explain that you want to record the material to make sure you get things right. This often eliminates a source's fear of **gotcha journalism** and will probably lead to his or her approving your request. However, if a source is adamant that you cannot record the interview, stop the recording and take extremely detailed notes.

You should also make clear to your source what you plan to do with the material you gather. A source who thinks you are doing an interview for a printed company newsletter might be shocked or embarrassed if a video version of the story is published. Let a source know in advance what you plan to do and how you will use the material across media platforms. This will give the person a chance to put on a nicer suit or find a better venue for the interview if video is a concern.

The Right Pieces for the Right Platform

One of the earliest maxims outlined in this book was "the right tool for the right job." This applies here as well when pondering your approach to your interview and your plans for the material you gather. Some pieces of an interview will do better as text copy because the information is tight, short and easy to follow. Other pieces, such as anecdotes, explanations or emotional tales, might be more valuable in an audio or video format.

For example, if you are planning a benefit event to raise money to fight cystic fibrosis, you might conduct an interview with the benefit's chairwoman. You will likely ask the source to confirm and elaborate on the 5W's and 1H of the event. That material can all be covered in a text-based format. However, you might ask the person why she got involved in this event. If she gives you a heart-wrenching tale of how she found out that her son had the genetic disorder, audio or video would better convey the raw emotion of why this event matters and how this illness affects people's lives.

Consider what you plan to do with the material you gather before you start your interview. If you research your topic well enough, you can solicit answers that will take advantage of the strengths of text, audio and video platforms.

ADAPT
OPEN-ENDED AND CLOSED-ENDED QUESTIONS

You have asked questions in many phases of your life, but interviewing seeks to shape your inquiries for a more specific purpose. One of the biggest things you have to understand is when to ask closed-ended questions and when to ask open-ended questions.

Closed-ended questions are meant to gather specific information that can help you nail down facts or clarify specific things within an interview. Examples of these include

Did you approve the plan?

What size hard drive will be in your new laptop?

How old did you say your grandfather was when he died?

In each case, the answer is meant to be short and simple, providing key facts such as "yes," "800 gigabytes" and "85 years old."

Open-ended questions can solicit extended answers from your sources. These questions are helpful when you want to add color, feel or emotion to a story, a proposal or a campaign pitch. Examples of these include

What do you remember about the day you first heard that your son had cancer?

Why did you decide to run for Congress?

How can people who don't understand computers take part in this event?

These questions are meant to offer your subject the opportunity to provide you with a deeper look at an issue. This is also where you can learn information in a more extensive and detailed way.

Adapt your approach to questions to fit the goals you are trying to accomplish in your writing.

GIVE IT A TRY: Interview a classmate about a topic of interest to both of you. Start with four or five closed-ended questions to see what answers you get, and then formulate four or five follow-up questions that are open ended based on your source's answers. This will allow you to see what you can get from each type of question and why in-person opportunities for follow-ups are important.

THE QUESTIONS

Everything that you have done to this point can lead you to a successful interview. However, if you don't spend enough time thinking about your questions, you will crash and burn at the interview itself. The interview is a culmination of preparation and presentation that can lead to crucial information, revealing stories and some truly mind-boggling outcomes. The difference between an outstanding set of interactions with a source and an interview that feels like an awkward dinner party often comes down to the questions.

Preparing Questions

After you do some serious research, you should sketch out your questions. The questions can be used to confirm information (see the breakout box on improving interviewing), troll for quotes or fill in gaps within your research. You need a general sense of what you want to get from the interview and why that information will matter to your readers. You should come up with four or five primary questions that will serve as the skeletal structure of your interview. These will give the source a clear understanding as to what you are going to cover and how you are going to approach the topic. This also will prevent you from missing key points as you go. You can always ask follow-up questions as they arise, but these primary questions can provide you with a good foundation for the interview.

You should write down your questions and keep them handy. If you type your notes during an interview, you can place your questions in your word-processing document and insert the person's answers after each question. Regardless of your approach, you want a tangible copy of the questions so you can review them and make sure you didn't skip a question or let something slip your mind. If you conclude your interview without asking all the key questions, you will need to go back to the source.

Are You Asking What You Think You're Asking?

Doug Williams led the Washington Redskins to a 42–10 win over the Denver Broncos in Super Bowl XXII, earning Williams the MVP honors and making him the first African-American quarterback to start (and win) the NFL's biggest game. However, it was an apocryphal story about a reporter's question that is often most associated with that Super Bowl.

© Keith Allison

Legend has it that during the pregame hype, reporters had asked Williams dozens of questions regarding the significance his race played in this game. During that series of questions, the myth goes, a reporter asked, "So how long have you been a black quarterback?" Williams supposedly replied, "I've been a quarterback since high school. I've been black all my life." According to Murry R. Nelson's book, "American Sports: A History of Icons, Idols, and Ideas," no reporter actually asked the question, and the reporter accused of doing so actually had asked a question meant to squelch the talk of race. However, the legend lives on, and it provides a good lesson for interviewers: Make sure you are asking what you think you are asking.

The legendary question "How long have you been a black quarterback?" a reporter supposedly asked of Doug Williams before the Super Bowl illustrates the importance of making sure you are asking what you think you are asking.

Many times, when you prepare for an interview, you know what you want to ask. However, something gets lost in translation between your brain and your mouth, leading to an awkward or oddly phrased question. Before you ask your questions of a source, ask the questions of yourself or have a colleague look through them. Also, if you read your questions out loud, you can see if the phrasing has varied meanings based on what you emphasize or how you speak. This can help you clean up your questions before you ask them.

As an interviewer, you should think of yourself as a conduit between the source and the audience. To that end, ask yourself what a reader would want to know from the person you are interviewing.

Questions meant to elicit great stories or incredible quotes can be helpful to the readers, but many times, these elements lack value for people who want to know "What does this mean to me?"

Why should a member of the public donate to our charity instead of another charity? How does this proposal help me as a resident of this town? What difference does it make if I take part in your event? If you can get answers to these questions, you can better connect your readers to your work.

When you interview sources, have them put themselves into the shoes of the readers: "What would you say to someone who says 'OK, what's in this for me?'" This can lead the source to think about the topic in a different way and from a specific angle. It can also lead to some good information and some valuable quotes from your subject.

GIVE IT A TRY: In advance of an interview you plan to conduct, write out five or six questions you think will be important to ask the source. Then, examine each question with a classmate to see how each one will help you address the needs of your audience members. If you find that some questions don't achieve that goal, work together to see how best to reconfigure the question to make it work better for your readers.

INTERVIEW FLOW

When you wrote your primary questions, you should have had a general sense as to how you thought the interview would go. This preparation should aid in the natural flow of the interview and make it seem more like a conversation that has a clear and coherent direction. As you move through your questions, you need to make sure you're paying attention to the source and the answers the source is giving you. If you ask Question 1 and in the process of answering Question 1, the source answers Questions 2 and 3, don't stick stubbornly to your list of questions and follow up by asking Question 2. It will make you look dumb, and it will make your source think you aren't paying attention to the answers.

A good interview should have a sense of flow that makes the process feel like a conversation.

© iStockphoto.com/shironosov

You also want to avoid getting into a dialogue with your source, especially if you do more of the talking than your source does. Your goal is to ask questions and make statements that have your subject providing you with important information. Some sources, either through purposeful misdirection or random chance, will reverse the interview and start asking you questions or get you to start talking about yourself. Some back-and-forth banter is fine for establishing trust and camaraderie, but try to get the interview back on track as soon as possible.

PROFESSIONAL THOUGHTS
SUZANNE STRUGLINSKI

Suzanne Struglinski has been on both sides of the interviewing process during her journalism career.

She spent the majority of her career after college as an online and newspaper reporter in Washington, D.C. She spent time at E&E Publishing's Greenwire, an online subscription-based news service focusing on environmental and energy news, before heading to a newspaper job. In 2003, she worked as the Washington correspondent for the Las Vegas Sun, and in 2005, she became the Washington bureau chief for the Deseret News.

During her decade in that realm, she wrote stories on Congress, environmental issues and even political campaigns. When the Deseret News closed its Washington bureau, she worked as a press secretary and in business development.

Today, she serves as the director of membership engagement for the National Press Club, the world's leading professional organization for journalists. Struglinski works with the more than 3,500 current members to ensure they are getting all they need and encouraging other journalists to join.

Struglinski said that in each phase of her career, interviewing was a crucial skill that helped her learn information and tell stories.

"Knowing how to ask the right questions to get the information you need is a critical skill no matter what job you have," she said. "Learning how to have people tell you what they know will help you write a story, a corporate report and many things in between."

As a news reporter, Struglinski said one of the hard parts of the job was extracting information from sources and waiting for information. Now that she has spent time as a source, she said it can be tough to be "on the other side of the notebook."

Struglinski said that when she worked with others to prepare for interviews, her interviewing

skills also came into play, as she made sure her co-workers were ready to handle the assignment.

"When prepping for a press conference or a report release, I would challenge those people who were going to be speaking with tough questions and ask them to explain things to me," she said. "If I did not understand what they were talking about or if they could not answer my questions, we were not ready for prime time."

Now that Struglinski works with reporters, editors and other media professionals who belong to the National Press Club, she still uses her interviewing skills to get to know her members and figure out why they need.

"Really listening to your source is just as important asking the right questions," she said. "You also need to be prepared on how to handle when an interview takes a totally different turn based on an answer to a question or shift in conversation. Your best stories can come from that."

One Last Thing

Q: If you could tell students anything about media writing or anything you have seen in your time in the field, what would it be?

A: Writing is a skill that constantly needs sharpening and improvement but knowing how to string together a sentence properly can really set you apart from the pack. Writing well is not just about memorizing grammar rules or knowing where to put a comma but knowing how to transform a notepad full of facts into a story.

SILENCE AS AN ALLY

Allowing silence to permeate a room can create an odd feeling, especially if you feel nervous or unsure during the interview. Silence is a vacuum, and nature abhors a vacuum, so someone is often forced to fill that void with a statement, question or utterance.

In short, silence is awkward.

Rather than fearing the awkward nature of silence, you can use it to your advantage. After you ask a good, probing question and you receive a solid but unspectacular answer, allow the silence to linger a bit as you look at your source. Instead of being eager to cut off the silence with the next question, put the onus on the source to fill the silence. The silence is just as awkward for the source as it is for you. If you won't say something, the source will.

Silence forces elaboration. Sources who feel guilty about something or feel they have not offered the most complete answer might decide to fill that silence with a little more information. Some sources try to justify an answer or tell you more about why they did something. Silence also allows your sources to go in a direction that has not been predetermined. As you ask questions, you elicit responses based on your queries. This means you are moving a source in a particular direction. However, if you remain quiet for a moment or two, a source might have something important to say that leads you in a different direction. By allowing silence to hang a bit, you open the door to things you had not previously considered.

THE NONVERBAL APPROACH: HOW TO ASK A QUESTION WITHOUT ASKING

If you want to take a course outside of mass communication that can help you interview, consider a class in nonverbal communication. Professional media operatives who learn how to ask questions through facial expressions, body language and other nonverbal interactions can extract a great deal of information from their sources.

It is easy to spot the video stories that rookie broadcasters create, because these journalists lack strong nonverbal skills. In order to demonstrate agreement with their sources, the broadcasters often mutter things like "uh-huh" or "oh, yeah" as the source is speaking. Although this seems normal to most people, when you watch the video of the interview, you can hear these utterances as part of the recording. In learning nonverbal cues, you can quietly nod your head to demonstrate agreement and prompt a source to elaborate on a topic. You can also alter your facial expression, cock an eyebrow or move your head as a way to redirect your source. These things can influence the direction your interview will take.

The key to this kind of thing is that you must be able to maintain eye contact with the source (a pretty good idea even if you aren't using nonverbal tactics). Eye contact shows your interest in what that person has to say. The problem most beginning journalists face with this is that they want to make sure they take good notes. In doing so, they bury their heads in their notebooks and scribble furiously, looking up only to ask the next question on the list. You need to find ways to write notes while not looking at them. Developing a personal version of shorthand can be helpful in this regard so you aren't writing letter-for-letter what the source says. This will take practice, so don't give up if it doesn't work well right away.

Nonverbal cues can prompt an interview subject to elaborate on an answer.

© iStockphoto.com/Siphotography

HELPFUL HINTS
THREE THINGS TO IMPROVE YOUR INTERVIEWS

1. ***Never waste a source's time.*** Don't ask a question you could have answered through background research. In some cases, you can ask for confirmation based on something you read during your research: "President Smith, you were quoted in the Wall Street Journal as saying our company would never agree to binding arbitration with the union. Given the recent court ruling, are you going to maintain that stance when we put out our next media statement?"

   However, if you start asking questions like "So how long has this argument over arbitration been going on?" the company president might lose faith in your abilities as a spokesperson. Make sure you prepare well and ask questions that demonstrate your grasp of the subject.

2. ***Cut through the fog of obfuscation.*** Many people speak in clichés, which limits the value of what they tell you. Other interview subjects use jargon that makes sense to company insiders but to no one else. You need to cut through all of these problematic approaches to the English language and make the interviewee speak to you in a clearer and more direct way. Don't just **parrot** your sources and pass the buck on to your

   readers. Use follow-up questions, offer options for rephrasing ("Could you put that in another way for readers who aren't as well versed on this subject?") and provide opportunities for confirming information ("So, am I right in saying that you believe X?") to cut through the fog and showcase clearer language.

3. ***Avoid loaded questions.*** A **loaded question** is one for which no good answer exists. It can be a leading question, a question based on a faulty assumption or a question that "traps" a person into an answer. The most famous question of this nature is "Senator, have you stopped beating your wife yet?" The reason this is loaded becomes obvious upon attempting an answer: If he says "yes," the senator admits he was beating his wife but has now stopped. If he says "no," it means the beatings continue at the senator's house. The senator can't answer in a way that would explain that he never beat his wife. When you craft your questions, ask each question out loud or imagine it being asked of you. If you can answer the questions fairly, the questions should work well. If you run into a loaded question, rework it to remove the problematic part.

THE END OF THE INTERVIEW (ALMOST)

In many interviews, the last thing a source says is the most important thing you will hear. Here are some techniques to squeeze that last bit of important information out of your interviews:

Just One More Thing

Columbo, the famed detective that actor Peter Falk brought to life in a 1970s TV show of the same name, had a knack for getting exactly what he needed to know by adding "Just one more thing." It always appeared to be an odd thought or a random throw-in question, but at the end of the show, that "one more thing" usually helped him solve the case. Interviewers can use this technique as well. After an interview session, sources will often relax, feeling as though they cleared all the hurdles and dealt with all the topics. They then lower their guard, and it is a perfect time to get in one more question. It need not be a "sucker punch" question or something off-putting, but if it is a serious question delivered in an "oh, by the way" format, you might get a good answer that you did not expect.

Did I Miss Anything Important?

This kind of closing question cedes control of the interview to the subject, so use it only after you feel like you have everything you need. The question is a good one for two reasons. First, you allow a source to discuss something about which you did not think to ask. The source might have something to explain or might offer information on what could be another great story. If you don't ask that question, you could miss a lot. Second, you demonstrate to your source that you care about him

Peter Falk's character in "Columbo" would always get exactly what he needed to know by asking "just one more thing." This approach is an effective interviewing technique that can draw additional information out of your source.

or her as a person. This question serves as a gesture that you want to know what matters to your source. This can be beneficial, especially if you need to come back to that source for more interviews in the future.

Could You Suggest Other People as Sources?

It never hurts to ask for additional sources. The more interviews you conduct, the better you will feel about the information you gather. As people reiterate what you have already learned, you can state the information with more certainty. Conversely, if other people give you conflicting information, you know you need to continue your research and interviewing. You can ask this question in a number of ways depending on what types of sources you need. If you want more people like the source you just interviewed, you might ask, "Is there anyone else you know who agrees with you on this topic?" If you want to get people who oppose your source's view, you can ask "Who doesn't like what you're doing and why?" Either way, if you ask one source for additional sources, you can get more leads for more interviews and drastically improve your work.

FOLLOW-UP INTERVIEWS

In all circumstances, you want to leave an open line for continued communication with your sources. Ask your source for contact information, including office phone, home phone and mobile phone. You can also ask the source for an email address, just in case you need to ask a quick follow-up question or two. You want to make sure that you can get in touch with the source when you need to, whether that's for a follow-up question or an interview on a different topic.

This type of contact is important, especially in situations where something might change at a moment's notice. If you are reporting about an infant who was badly hurt in an accident, you want some kind of contact with hospital officials, police personnel and someone connected with that family. Just because you are factually accurate at 8 p.m., it doesn't mean the situation can't radically change by midnight. If you don't check in with those people before publication, you could end up running a story in the morning paper about a brave toddler, fighting for life while the youngster died just after you filed your story.

THE BIG THREE

Here are the three key things you should take away from this chapter:

1. **Preparation matters most:** If you don't prepare enough for your interview, you will set yourself up for a painful experience. Preparation allows you to ask better questions and feel more confident during the interview. It will also help you get better answers from your sources and thus provide better material to your readers.

2. **Know what you want to get and make sure you get it:** Interviews can go through twists and turn in

some cases, but you should have a good sense of what you need to know before the interview ends. Write down your questions and make sure you get quality answers.

3. **You serve your audience:** Remember that you aren't getting this information for yourself only. You are getting it for people who will be reading what you write. If your interview subject is unclear or reticent, don't be afraid to push for a better answer. You are beholden to your audience members, and you owe them the best answers possible.

KEY TERMS

clips 78
closed-ended question 83
gotcha journalism 82

loaded question 88
one-party consent 82
open-ended question 83

parrot 88
trade press 78
two-party consent 82

DISCUSSION QUESTIONS

1. If you had to interview the head of your school on any topic, what are the key questions you think your audience (other students) would want to have answered? Why do you think these questions would be important?

2. Compare and contrast the three forms of interviewing (in person, telephone, email/chat). What are the benefits of each one and what are

some of the drawbacks? When is it best to use each type?

3. What are some of the things you think are your greatest strengths when it comes to speaking with people, and how do those translate into interviewing skills? What are some of your greatest weaknesses? Why do you think these items are problematic for you?

Chapter 5 ■ Interviewing 91

WRITE NOW!

1. Select an individual you would like to interview on a topic you think would be of importance to students at your school. Research the topic, learn about your source and craft a series of questions. Then conduct the interview. Write a one- to two-page essay about your experience. What went well? What could have been improved, and how could you have done so?

2. Find a transcript or video of a one-on-one interview. Describe the interview, the interviewer and the interview subject. What was the purpose of this interview? In your opinion, was it conducted well? Did anything happen that was particularly revealing or problematic? Write a short paper based on your thoughts and observations.

3. Partner with someone in your class and select a person you agree would be interesting to interview. Each of you should research that person and craft a list of five questions. Then exchange the questions and see where you had similar and different angles on the interview. Discuss why you think you approached the interview the way you did and how the other person's angle might make you reconsider this. Write a short paper that discusses your process, your outcome and your thoughts on the experience.

SUGGESTIONS FOR FURTHER READING

A. Friedman (2013, May 30). "The Art of the Interview." Columbia Journalism Review. Accessed at: http://www.cjr.org/realtalk/the_art_of_the_interview.php?page=all.

S. Israel (2012, April 14). "Nine Tips on Conducting Great Interviews." Forbes. Accessed at: http://www.forbes.com/sites/shelisrael/2012/04/14/8-tips-on-conducting-great-interviews/.

M. Perlich (2007). "The Art of the Interview" (3rd ed.). Los Angeles: Silman-James.

C. Scanlan (2013, March 4). "How Journalists Can Become Better Interviewers." Poynter Institute. Accessed at: https://www.poynter.org/news/how-journalists-can-become-better-interviewers.

G. Sedorkin (2011). "Interviewing: A Guide for Journalists and Writers" (2nd ed.). Crows Nest, Australia: Allen & Unwin.

© iStockphoto.com/badmanproduction

6

WRITING ON THE WEB

Writing for the web can feel freeing, as you are not confined to certain space or time limits often associated with other media formats. You also have access to visual options and interactive elements that you can't use in traditional media. However, you need to keep your focus on what your audience needs instead of how fun it will be to do whatever you want. This means you need to write more tightly than you do in traditional media, keep a sharper focus on your main idea and work to promote your content across multiple media platforms.

(Text is just one of the storytelling options you can use online. Many other books can show you how to build sites or how to use video and audio, but here the focus will remain primarily on writing.)

This chapter will outline how to establish a solid web-based readership. It will also explain what can go wrong when you enter this playing field and how to avoid some of the more damaging mistakes you can make.

WORKING ON THE WEB

One of the challenges associated with web work is that you lack restrictions. This can seem counterintuitive, as restrictions usually make life harder on you. Most traditional media professionals work with size and space limits, thus helping them figure out the word count for a newspaper story or the page length for a press release. Broadcasters work under similar restrictions, with time limits serving as the counterbalance to content. On the web, size, length and time limits have no meaning from a content-provider standpoint. However, just because you write longer, it doesn't follow that your audience members will consume everything you produce. Professionals who work on the web often note that you need to cut your copy in half when you post it online, as readers will spend less time with it than they will with traditional media.

Here are some basic suggestions to help you improve your work and meet the needs of your web-based audience:

Avoid Shovelware

The web is more than an opportunity to give people the same thing they received on another platform. News organizations originally believed that publishing content on the web would undercut their traditional platforms in terms of readership, viewership and advertising. Professionals who work in public relations and marketing saw the web as a way to move past the news media's gatekeepers and establish their own web presences.

However, these professionals often viewed the web the same way they saw their traditional media products. This led to the rise of **shovelware**, in which the sites became giant storage bins of content that was transferred from standard platforms to the web. The people shoveling the content failed to augment the content in any meaningful way, thus leaving audience members seeing nothing more than digital versions of what they already read.

When it comes to your approach to web work, you should avoid shovelware and focus on telling a story in an audience-centric way. Look at what you have available to you in terms of additional content, interactive elements and fresh storytelling opportunities. Treat each piece of writing you put on the web as new content and not last night's leftovers.

Tell the Story With Multiple Elements

The web provides you with many tools that traditional media outlets don't have. Consider how each tool can help you tell a story and use those tools accordingly. A text story might allow you to explain how to fix a dishwasher, but a photo essay with detailed captions might work better. A video option could seem like a good idea, but you might discover that this is too hard to film or that the audience members have trouble doing the steps along with the pace of the video.

Although this book focuses on the writing aspects of storytelling, as you develop your skills in media, you will want to add more tools to your toolbox, including audio, video, graphics and photography. When you tell a story online, you have access to all of these options, so consider each tool in turn and determine how to use it to give your readers what they need.

Write in Easy-to-Use Pieces

As we previously discussed, you want to give your readers the most important information first. Chapter 4 outlines this in detail in its discussion of the inverted pyramid, a writing format where you tell your story in descending order of importance. That said, the traditional inverted pyramid has two drawbacks: web readers have shorter attention spans than traditional-media users, and people can hop anywhere at any time, therefore missing important information. If you write a news story about a bill that would construct a freeway through an area of wetlands, you would likely have comments from environmental experts, highway experts and the government agency that will approve or reject the bill. Regardless of how you build that story, one of those sources will be first, one will be second and one will be third. By the time your readers get to the second source, they could become bored or distracted and not make it to the third source's comments.

To make this work better online and to better fit the "web of information" approach, you want to write in smaller, tighter chunks that tell simple stories. Introduce the topic for your piece in a few short sentences and then offer your readers links to the perspectives of these three sources. People can select which source they will read first, second and third. Each link will move the readers to another page with a mini-inverted-pyramid story that outlines the thoughts of that source. This approach will allow you to keep your writing tight and also provide readers with options for navigating your story.

Other approaches can be equally effective. You can write text-based lists in the form of bulleted items, thus giving your readers short bursts of information on a given topic. If you need to write everything in one large story, use subheadings that help break the material into smaller segments while still drawing their attention to specific aspects of a story.

CONNECT
HOW TO BUILD A NONLINEAR STORY WEB

One of the reasons you need to write in those tight, short pieces is because of how readers have come to use the web as well as how they have come to expect content on it. In most cases, people expect to be able to find everything they desire on a website, but they don't want to sift through content they don't need to see. This means we need to present them with more material, but in more bite-sized chunks. In addition, unlike in the past, you will not control how users arrive on your site, where they go when they get there or in what order they consume the content. This is why nonlinear storytelling is crucial for web-based media writing.

When you visualize storytelling online, think about a visual "web" of information, which will contain multiple points at which people can enter your site and exit it. In between those points, realize that users will take different paths through your site and that those paths will vary in terms of the amount of content, the order in which the content is consumed and overall level of interaction. Here is an example of a simple story web on an issue that might be interesting to students on your campus: the cost of college.

FIGURE 6.1 ■

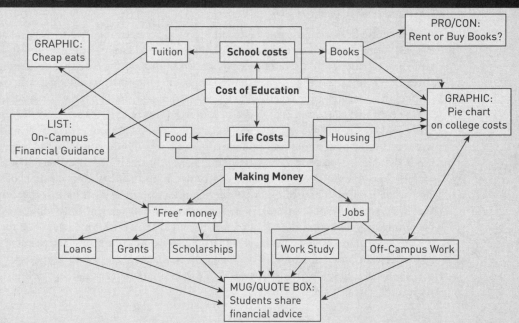

At the center of the web is the idea of the overall cost of college, and you can see several key factors that directly play into that larger topic: tuition, housing, food, books and miscellaneous items. From each of these factors, you can dig into additional angles on these topics. For example, you can do boxes that contain mug shots and quotes from people who are talking about their costs of living or how they pay for certain items, or you could have a bulleted list of how much of the money associated with each charge goes to pay for what aspect of the college experience.

(Continued)

(Continued)

Beyond that, you have other secondary topic areas, such as how to make money to pay for these costs, such as grants, loans, campus jobs and off-campus jobs. In each of these areas, you can see how "chunks" of information can help your readers make sense of the topic quickly. You can include hyperlinks to the job service on campus, the application for grants or services that provide student loans. You can also include contact information for on-campus financial specialists, who can meet with the students to discuss how to finance their education. As you become more adept at other forms of storytelling, such as visuals, audio and video, you can rely on those tools to tell various aspects of this story in different forms.

Certain topics can link you to other sites, such as websites for peer institutions where their costs are listed or university budget documents that outline how much tuition has increased over the past 20 years. The point is to provide your readers a wide array of valuable content and allow them to work through the material as they see fit.

GIVE IT A TRY: Develop a story web based on a topic you think would interest readers on your campus. Place the main idea at the center of the web and then sketch out a few primary elements that are likely to need further examination. From each of these elements, determine what aspects should get a deeper look in a variety of ways. Consider ways to tell the stories, ranging from mini-inverted-pyramid stories to bulleted lists. You should also include options for internal and external linking you would like to explore. Then, write a short paper that explains what you did and why you did it.

Offer Constant Updates

People live in an on-demand world and expect to get what they want whenever and wherever they want it. This is true of everything from books and movies to furniture and food. As a media practitioner, you should meet those needs through your web work, keeping people abreast of things that matter to them and announcing information as soon as you can.

Websites become stale when they fail to provide additional content on a regular basis. You never want your readers arriving at your site thinking, "I already saw all this before." For news sites, you have many options for frequent updates, as your day-in and day-out work will yield new stories and photos. However, you should continue to view the site as more than just a place to dump the daily work you published elsewhere. For corporate and marketing sites, frequent updates can seem daunting at first, but if you plan well, this can become an easy part of everyday life. Consider doing several blogs on various topics that writers update on a given day each week. This will prevent individual writers from becoming overworked while still allowing the site to seem fresh each day. Look for a simple update you can do each day, such as updating people on fundraising activities or the progress of certain projects. Consider what you think the readers need to know most and how often they should know it. Then establish a pattern of updates while remaining flexible for important "breaking news" items.

BLOGGING

When web tools became easier for the public to access and use, many people took advantage of them to create a web presence. In some cases, they wrote about things that interested them, filled niches that mainstream media missed or turned out diary-like content to fulfill their writing desires. Instead of relying heavily on design or interactive elements, the creators focused on writing, logging information in a reverse chronological order. The term "web log" was shortened to **blog** over time as this form of writing grew in popularity and function.

Why Blog?

Many people have accounts on platforms like WordPress or Blogger, where they write for their own needs, but media professionals have adopted the platform and reshaped it to disseminate information and market their products. The reasoning behind hosting a blog will vary based on the area of the field you enter. Let's take a look at the various areas in the field and discuss the importance of blogging in them:

News Blogging

Blogging has benefited traditional news outlets, as it has provided them with the ability to enter a unique area of the digital realm with little investment. Most traditional media outlets maintain a digital presence through standard websites that feature their regular content that already ran in the paper or on TV. The webmaster can easily integrate the blogs into the site and thus extend the brand for this new content. In terms of basic benefits, consider the following:

Blogs can be a valuable way to get a message to interested readers.

- **Provide additional content without cost:** Space and time limit traditional media. A newspaper or magazine has only so much space, and a news broadcast has only so much time to dedicate to content in a given day. Even more, the time in which the content is "due" (the 5 p.m. newscast or the 1 a.m. press deadline) locks journalists into a certain amount of content.

  Blogs free journalists from these strictures while still allowing them to operate under the banner of the traditional media outlet. Bloggers can file multiple posts at various times of day. The content doesn't need to be "stretched" to fill time or "cut" to keep it to a certain amount of space. The author of the blog can decide how long the post should be, based on the value of the content.

- **Take advantage of niche opportunities:** Reporters often rely on a "beat" system to gather news in their coverage area. Traditional beats, such as education, crime, government and sports, make up the staple crop of what audience members tend to see in most newspapers and in most newscasts. In certain areas, publications dedicate reporters to specialty topics germane to that community, such as a nature beat, a farm report or even a casino beat.

  A blog allows journalists to expand their coverage into a small area of interest that might move beyond what most people would come to expect of them. For example, a city government reporter who has an interest in knitting could establish a blog on that topic, or a crime reporter could look into a burgeoning murder-mystery fan-fiction industry through a blog.

  In his book "Engaged Journalism," Jake Batsell notes that niche journalism isn't new, as trade publications and hobby magazines have existed for years. However, he says, the web provides publishers the opportunity to try reaching niche audiences with little risk and without having to guess as to which niche to fill. Niche audiences are often more motivated to seek content than their generalist peers. In addition to their passionate consumption, niche audiences tend to be more loyal to sources that feed their needs.[1]

  If you can reach these consumers through a niche approach, you can draw them to your site and perhaps interest them in additional content you present beyond the blog.

© iStockphoto.com/hocus-focus

Corporations engage in promotional blogging to give readers a better sense of their mission and help humanize the organizations.

- **Sidestep the mainstream:** Blogging provides people interested in creating content the opportunity to do so without having to be attached to a traditional media outlet. News organizations like the Huffington Post and the Drudge Report emerged in the digital era as part of a movement toward freestanding web-based content sites. The blogging approach helped draw readers to these sites that lacked a traditional media outlet and thrive outside of the mainstream.

  The benefit of this approach is that you are able to create content of interest to a small group of people (see the niche argument earlier in the chapter) without the massive overhead costs associated with traditional media.

- **Gather data on your readers:** As mentioned in Chapter 1, understanding your audience is crucial to best serving the people in it. As blogging draws people to your site, you will be able to determine when people most frequently your site, which content they view, where people are when they visit and which posts got the most hits, and that's just the beginning. If your organization uses complex analytics, you can do even more to find out specific details about your readers and thus better target them with future content.

Promotional Blogging

Practitioners who work in advertising and public relations have unique interests when it comes to blogging opportunities. Many of the reasons news journalists blog also apply to marketing professionals. For example, public-relations practitioners can sidestep mainstream media outlets and speak directly to the public through a blog. Marketers or advertisers can use a blog to reach niche communities that have an interest in their organizations or products, providing them with content unavailable in other venues.

However, there are also some additional benefits blogs have for organizations seeking to promote causes or pitch products. Consider these opportunities:

- **Humanize your organization:** Marketing organizations suffer from the misperception that they are monolithic and faceless. Blogging provides these groups with an opportunity to disabuse people of that notion as they present content from the perspective of an individual representative of that group. Blogging can provide people with that "human" touch that isn't often associated with this form of media. For example, a standard website can provide the reader with all the official uses for a specific product, but a blogger can do more on the "day-to-day" uses, providing analogies or personal stories about how he or she has actually used the item. In addition, the blogger can create a personal bond between the company and the audience, much in the same way a celebrity spokesperson or mascot does.

- **Drive traffic to your site:** You need to give people a reason to visit your site frequently, and in many cases, this can be difficult. In the area of news, the constant updates of weather, sports and daily happenings will entice people to check in repeatedly. In the area of public relations or marketing, if nothing on the site has changed from day to day, people won't have a reason to come to your site. It's not like they are going to show up once a day and say, "Yep, that corporate vision is still up there and it hasn't changed since yesterday!" To really drive site traffic, you need to give them something fresh each day (or more), and you need to make it something they want to read.

Blogging allows you to refresh your content and bring people to your site at the same time. For example, if you are blogging about recent changes to an industry, you can include several internal links that will show the readers how your organization has adjusted to those changes. If those changes require certain forms or other material, you can link to that from your post as well, making your blog the central junction point for all the important information on that topic.

It pays to discuss with your coworkers what elements you will include on a blog and why they will matter to your readers.

- **Establish yourself as a thought leader:** Trust and credibility are two elements of media writing that all practitioners desire. If you can constantly demonstrate that you are worthy of these precious commodities, people will turn to you more frequently when they need information on your topic of expertise. A blog gives you the opportunity to demonstrate your knowledge frequently, thus giving you the opportunity to show that you are a thought leader on the topic. Much in the same way that people turn to "Dear Abby" for relationship advice or listen to a sports call-in show to find out what the announcer thinks about a team, people will turn to you for information if you can demonstrate proficiency in covering a topic. In addition, you can be a "go-to" person for news reporters who seek sources in the industry when they want to cover your field. You know a lot about your discipline, and a blog gives you the chance to showcase everything you know.

- **Retain your focus:** Corporate visions and mission statements are meant to direct all members of an organization toward a focal point that demonstrates the group's overall purpose. In many cases, these statements can get lost in the day-to-day noise of running an organization or can be mocked by people inside and outside of the company. Using a blog to present information to the public on a daily basis allows you to retain your focus as an organization as well as a member within it. Think about how old-fashioned teachers would punish students by having them something on the board over and over again. ("The Simpsons" includes this in its weekly opening sequence, with Bart writing something different each time. The best one? "I will not waste chalk.") The idea behind that exercise is to ingrain the idea to the point where it becomes reflexive. If you can publish content on a daily basis that reflects your corporate strategy or your company's vision, you will keep a strong focus on who you are as an institution.

BEST BLOGGING PRACTICES

As you develop your blog, you will find a style and approach that accentuates the value of your content and that helps you bond with your readers. To help you stay focused on providing valuable information, you can draw from the FOCII elements discussed earlier in this book. Beyond relying on those interest elements, here are a few best practices to keep in mind as you establish a blog or take over blogging duties at your organization:

© iStockphoto.com/Rawpixel

Don't Blog Just to Blog

Far too often, people fall prey to **shiny-object syndrome**, leading them to make bad choices. When something new and shiny comes along, some people will say "We need that!" If the person saying it is a 4-year-old child who saw a toy commercial, you can ignore it. If the person saying it is your boss, you will probably have to pay attention.

Blogs are part of a long line of digital tools that have enamored executives, much to the chagrin of people responsible for learning the tools and applying them appropriately. This trend of "We need that!" started with websites and continued with blogs, **podcasts**, **vlogs**, YouTube channels, Twitter accounts and **apps**. Someone higher on the corporate ladder says "We need a blog," and you get stuck building and maintaining one. This leads you to the first and most important rule when it comes to blogging: Don't blog for blogging's sake.

If you build a blog simply to have one, it will lack focus, depth and value. If that happens, you will become bored in updating it, and your readers will be few and far between. Instead, you need to come up with a reason to blog, and you need to maintain a steady stream of content to grow your audience over time.

Focus on Audience Interests

The crucial difference between personal blogs and business blogs is the audience. In a personal blog, you can spend all the time you want complaining about how your Thanksgiving dinner didn't turn out or poking fun at your family members. The personal blog is more of a digital diary, although it is worth mentioning that you can get into trouble for things you post there, even if your blog has no affiliation with your organization.

In their book on blogging for business, Eric Butow and Rebecca Bollwitt explain that blogs can help you inform readers as well as help you get information from the readers. They note that some blogs have used a crowdsourcing approach, in which bloggers reach out to the readers for feedback. This puts the readers in the driver's seat when it comes to outlining specific needs and creating valuable solutions for you and your group.[2] Think about a small yet interesting area of information that would matter to your readers, and you have a ready-made blog topic.

Establish a Tone

Blogging gives you a wider array of options in terms of content and tone. Some blogs will rely heavily on graphics and photos, while others will use text and excerpts from other websites. Beyond that, language, style and tone will vary from blog to blog. A corporate blog that is outlining the company's charitable works will likely have a different tone than a "shock-jock" blog that covers the world of sports.

If you understand your audience members, you can establish a stronger rapport with them and approach them in a tone that matches their expectations. This includes the use of formal or informal language, the presence of more or fewer graphic elements and the level of interactivity allowed on the blog. This can also help you determine the level of decorum on the blog and how involved you will be when it comes to posters who attack one another or use foul language. When you establish a tone, you determine the overall feel of the blog.

ADAPT
KEYS TO GOOD DIGITAL-MEDIA WRITING

Whether you own a blog or post to an organization's website, you will need to adjust your writing and your approach to content. Here are some quick thoughts for how to succeed in the digital realm:

Offer Quick Reads

People head to the web for quick bits of information, not novels. Use short bits of information to give people the most important information first, and then move on. This can be anywhere from a single sentence to a few short paragraphs. If you have something that needs to run longer, you should do a "continue reading" break or a "click here to continue" link so that one post doesn't dominate the whole site and push other information too far down.

Be Timely

The web is about what's happening now, not six weeks ago or six weeks from now. Rely on the immediacy principle outlined in Chapter 1 when you write for a digital platform so you can create strong time pegs for your work. Give your readers information they can use immediately or inform them about something that just happened. Keep it current.

Showcase Additional Content

You can use your connection to your readers to further engage them as active participants on your site. In many cases, people will arrive at your site through a link to a specific post or story. If you incorporate additional links in each post to suggest additional content, you can draw your readers deeper into your site and show them things that matter to them. This can help strengthen the bond between the reader and the organization. This approach can also increase sales or generate better brand identity among your readers.

Don't Just React

Much like their newspaper columnist colleagues, online writers can run the risk of just adding to the noise via reactions to a larger issue. Broader issues can have values on blogs, but if you don't have a stake in the game, your opinion won't add much. The same thing is true regarding tweets that simply say "I agree with X." Think about why you want to react and what you can bring to the discussion on the whole. How is what you have to say adding to the sum of human knowledge? How are you uniquely qualified to add this information? Think about what you want to add beyond a simple reaction.

Update With Changes

When you post information about an ongoing situation, you need to keep abreast of what is happening. You should freshen your digital work with additional content and updates as the situation continues to unfold. These changes can take the form of follow-up posts, much like news writers use second-day stories to follow a trend or as augmentation to the original work.

GIVE IT A TRY: Pick a story that ran in your local paper, student paper or other publication that you enjoy and "webify" it for posting to either a blog or a more traditional website. Look for ways you can include links to additional content, update the story and create a tighter shorter piece for publication. If the story is overly long or complicated, you could break the story down into several smaller pieces and apply the same techniques.

LINKING AND OTHER INTERACTIVE ELEMENTS

Web writers can incorporate interactive elements that will improve a story's clarity, better connect the content to the readers and provide context to the material. **Hyperlinks** allow you to send people to other portions of a site and other places on the web as a part of their reading experience. Understanding how to use these links is important because linking is one of the things that makes the web more than a screen capture of a newspaper or press release.

You should include links in your web pieces to enhance the value of your work. If you are writing a press release about a merger between organizations, you might note,

In a letter sent Wednesday, the companies agreed to certain terms as to how to incorporate company assets. This letter also outlined new management policies and logo options.

As a media professional working on the web, you should think about links you could include and how those links could improve the overall value of the piece. You might want to link "a letter" to a PDF of the letter, which would allow your readers to see the specific terms and language the companies used. You could link "certain terms" to a list of what the companies agreed to, either in the form of a document that already exists or as something you created. You could also link to "management policies," although the companies might not want these to be available to the public. However, a link to "logo options" might give people a sense as to how the companies see their new brand identity moving forward.

Not all of these links will be possible, and you want to avoid overdoing your use of links. Don't just link for the sake of linking. Always think about your readers and what they would want to see as part of the overall reading experience. Here is a list of areas that could lead to quality linking opportunities:

Definitions

Most media professionals would correctly argue that if you need to define a word, you should find a replacement for that word. In the case of direct quotes, however, you can't write around complex terminology or use a more common word. Creating a link to a definition of that word can make things easier on your readers. You can also create links for field-specific terms that require more explanation than you reasonably can provide in your piece.

Background

The information you disseminate at any point in time is related to things that happened earlier. A few paragraphs in a news story or a few lines of copy in a piece of marketing material can help provide basic background information for your readers, but linking can do more for them. You can link to previous pieces on a given topic, a company's "about us" page or anything else you think will help inform your readers.

Original Source Material

The phrase "seeing is believing" can work to your advantage when it comes to gaining audience trust on the web. Your news article could explain that a public official inappropriately used a state email account to proposition female coworkers, but many people might not believe you. However, if you can link to court documents that offer a point-by-point outline of what witnesses said this person did, you can increase your credibility. If you can link to those emails and allow people to read the messages for themselves, you can inspire even more trust. Look for opportunities to link to source documents, such as letters, emails and reports, so you can let your readers see what you have seen and understand what you used to create your own piece of writing.

PROFESSIONAL THOUGHTS
KEN SMITH

In Bryan-College Station, Texas, home of Texas A&M University and a twin-city community of about 200,000 people, information tends to swirl around Ken Smith. A veteran newspaper and digital media practitioner, Smith serves as the city of Bryan's web and emergency communications specialist. In this role, he is responsible for the content, design and development of all the city's web properties, including the city's website, the Bryan Texas Utilities site and the Bryan-College Station Library System site. He also serves as the city's communications liaison to the regional emergency operations center, meaning that he posts web content, disseminates press releases and works with the media in the case of a natural disaster.

Smith said the job pushes him in multiple directions and requires him to remain flexible in his work, even though the core principle behind his work never changes.

"My number one priority for my job, at least what I would consider my number one priority, is public user experience—making sure all of our digital communications and platforms are easy for the public to use, allowing them to find what they need quickly and making sure that they are aware of information they need to know," he said.

Smith started his media career in 2000 as a copy editor and page designer at the St. Petersburg Times in Florida. He also worked as a page-one designer for the Houston Chronicle as well as an assistant news editor and national politics producer for the Washington Post before moving back to Texas. He said much of what he learned in his journalism education and media experience prepared him for his job as the city's webmaster.

"The biggest similarity is that in both worlds, journalism and government/marketing, you're trying to push information out to an audience, and you want that audience to pay attention to what you are saying," Smith said. "Now, at the Washington Post, that audience may be 50 million people, and it may concern the national security of the United States. While at the city of Bryan, that audience might be 2,000 residents of one specific neighborhood, and it may concern the fact that their trash pickup is going to be delayed by one day because of the Fourth of July holiday. But

Ken Smith

the basic premise is the same. You have to write in an engaging, catchy way that is going to make people want to continue reading."

Smith said his site relies on many of the same tools as any other media outlet: social media, search engine optimization and Google analytics. He said these items help drive traffic to the site and keep people aware of what the city is doing on various fronts but that none of these have replaced the importance of working directly with his audience.

"It's very important to be able to communicate through texting, or other modern platforms, but it's just as important to be able to look people in the eye and tell them why you're doing a story, or in my case, why they can't find some piece of information on the city's webpage," he said. "The old fashioned name for this is 'customer service' and it's something that never goes out of style. I happen to be very good at this. But many people are not, and it can mean the difference between being able to land a job, or not, or keep a job, or not."

Through those interpersonal connections as well as his digital discussions, Smith said everyone involved in the city's administration works to better understand what people in Bryan want and how the city can meet those needs.

"As a governmental entity, we really do need to know our residents, because we work for them," he said. "They are the taxpayers. They pay our salaries. They are our ultimate bosses. So we want to know what they like, and don't like. We want to know what they think works, and what they think doesn't."

Knowing his audience also means knowing what they expect from him in terms of interactivity and responsiveness, Smith said.

"More than shaping the content that we create, I think the feedback that we get through our digital platforms (Facebook specifically) reinforces the fact that in today's world, people want instant gratification," he said. "So if someone's power goes out, and they complain about it on the city's Facebook page,

(Continued)

(Continued)

they expect someone to answer their comment. They don't care if it's noon or midnight. If they complain, they expect someone to address it immediately. And so, I think it doesn't necessarily drive 'content' so much as it drives the need for constant 'communication and transparency' between the people and us as the governmental entity."

When it comes to content, however, Smith said he works with video, interactives, charts, graphs, photos, illustrations and more every day, but he still relies heavily on his days as a writer to help tell his stories in a clear and coherent way on the web.

"For me personally, the inverted pyramid style of writing is still the tool that transcends everything," Smith said. "From newspapers news ledes, to 'Top 5' lists, to technical specifications writing, to organizing your departmental budget priorities, the principles of the inverted pyramid have withstood the test of time, and will still be standing long after the next great technology wave hits, and then long after we are all gone."

One Last Thing

Q: If you could tell students anything about media writing or anything you have seen in your time in the field, what would it be?

A: "A few things:

- "Everyone needs an editor. No matter who you are, or what you do, or how high you rise, everyone needs an editor. And, that editor will save you from yourself.

- "Get it right. If you're not sure, don't write it. Your credibility is everything in journalism and in life.

- "Don't ever write something down that you don't want to see splashed all over the internet. This is especially true of social media. Employers do look at your social media accounts. Don't ever think that the disclaimer "opinions are my own, not the company's" will matter to your employer.

- "Learn to code. It can only help you. It will also impress people and raise your profile. You don't have to be a back-end development wizard, but just knowing how to do the basics—and knowing how hard it is—will give you a greater understanding of what can and can't be done, and it will allow you to speak intelligently with developers and other technical persons.

- "Learn everything you can. No matter what it is, never turn down an opportunity to learn some new skills. You never know when you might need them."

ENGAGING READERS

Interactivity goes beyond providing clickable links and opportunities to read what you wrote. The web has made journalism a two-way street, and to get the most out of online writing, you must engage your readers. In the traditional-media areas, advertising professionals have been among the best at soliciting reader reactions and meeting those demands. Advertising has always been a bottom-line business in which success is measured in the number of eyeballs an ad can reach and the amount of business the ad can generate. Writers within this area of the profession became skilled at measuring responses, creating target audiences and focusing on ways to get the most bang for the buck. Public-relations professionals also know how to define their audiences and reach people within them to create well-tailored messages that meet the needs of the readers. In addition, they are skilled at responding to the public's reactions in mutually beneficial ways.

Newspapers and magazines have traditionally limited input to letters to the editor and suggestions for coverage. In most cases, the public was kept on one side of the fence while news journalists served as gatekeepers, who monitored information and determined the value of it. Television journalists also took this approach, relying on predetermined news values to determine content and limiting public input.

On the web, engagement can take many forms: Some choices allow you to bring readers to your site, while other options force you to reach your readers in a realm you do not control. Here are a few interactive opportunities for you:

Contact Options

If you want people to share information with you, it would be a good idea to give them some ways to do that on your site. The standard "contact us" form that appears on a separate page isn't a horrible idea, but it also can make readers feel as though they are dropping a note into a black hole. In addition to one of these options, consider a few other ways to help your readers feel more connected to your site:

- **Staff bios:** If you want people to feel connected to your writers, provide some information about those writers to your audience. A simple mini-bio that includes a photo of the person, some basic content relating to the person's job and maybe a small personal detail ("Jenny has a dog named Pooch that loves to chase squirrels.") can give your readers a human connection with your staff.

- **Email contact:** The ability to email a compliment, complaint or concern directly to the source of the material in question can provide readers with a sense that someone is listening. If you don't want everyone on your staff to have the ability to respond to the general public, consider at least including email addresses for management folks.

- **Social media options:** We will talk in detail about social media in the next chapter, but for now, consider including links to staffers' professional LinkedIn profiles and professional Twitter accounts. This will allow people to reach out via social media, follow your staff members on these platforms and feel a one-on-one connection to people in your organization.

Comments

The comment function most websites provide after each published piece is a great way for your readers to give you instant feedback. The material they read is fresh in their minds, and they have a clear sense of what they think about it. With a few clicks, they can tell you if you made an error, if you missed the bigger picture or if they learned something from you. Readers can also read the thoughts of other people who offered commentary and respond to those people as well. This can lead to a virtual town-hall meeting that will allow all the interested parties to speak their minds.

Commenting among readers can also lead to a series of off-topic screeds and general rants that make people unwilling to read the comments, let alone enter the discussion themselves. As a writer, you should read through the comments on your pieces, even if you think they might be unpleasant or off point. When readers do offer you some important information, it benefits you to reach out to them either via comment or email. This not only establishes trust between you and your readers, but it also helps you develop sources of information for future writing.

The comment function provides your readers with a chance to offer their thoughts on what you have written. It often pays to read what these people have to say so you can better meet their needs.

Live Events

The use of a live chat option through your website or an organized Twitter Q&A can provide your readers with a chance to learn things that matter to them directly from you or an important source. For example, you could create a live web Q&A with the head of your organization after you open a new corporate office or after you announce a large donation. This would allow people to ask questions about how the office will affect the economy in the area or what the donation will actually fund. This approach allows you to filter the questions before answering them and still offer readers important on-message answers. In addition, it provides a humanizing opportunity for your organization as it gives you the chance to put a face and a voice to the company.

Organizations have often relied on additional chat applications, such as Google Hangouts, which allows instant messaging and video chats among multiple participants. These options integrate text functions as well as multimedia options, such as image sharing and emoticons. A live Twitter event (which we will discuss more in the next chapter) has similar benefits, including the ability to draw a wider swath of people to your event. When you use a hashtag approach to your event, you also allow people create a specific stream to follow all the tweets associated with it. You can also have people who participate from a variety of devices and platforms, as opposed to having to route people to your website to participate. The downside, as mentioned elsewhere in this chapter, is that these events can become divisive and caustic, thus undermining the value of the event. When you open yourself to an unregulated pool of consumers and you do so on a medium that can draw innumerable trolls, you run a huge risk. However, if you believe you can run an event like this successfully, it is worth the effort.

THE BIG THREE

Here are the three key things you should take away from this chapter:

1. **Think before you post:** Once you send material out into the digital realm, you can never get it back. A blog post can undermine your readers' confidence and draw negative attention to your organization from all around the world. Whatever you put online has the ability to damage you in ways you never imagined. Always think about what you are doing before you do it.

2. **Embrace interactivity:** Links and comments are just a few of the ways in which you can use the interactivity of the web to your advantage. This platform is truly dynamic and allows you to facilitate two-way communication, thus improving your contact with readers. Don't skip this step in your writing or ignore the feedback you get.

3. **Promote your work:** You have many competitors who can offer content similar to what you are providing, so the difference between being read and being ignored is often your promotional efforts. Get out there and let people know who you are and what you can give them.

KEY TERMS

app 100
blog 96
hyperlink 101

podcast 100
post 93
shiny-object syndrome 100

shovelware 94
vlog 100

DISCUSSION QUESTIONS

1. Of the sites you visit on a daily basis, how many of them have an active blogging presence? Do you read the blogs? Why or why not?

2. When it comes to drawing readers to a website, what do you find to be the content that attracts you the most? What content is of little interest to you or even would repel you from a site? Why is this?

3. What compels you to visit a website? Is it word of mouth, force of habit, connections through social media or some other factor? How can you use this assessment to help you better promote content you would develop for the web or on a specific blog?

WRITE NOW!

1. Find a topic of interest to you and prepare to write a blog on it. Research the topic well enough that you think you could write intelligently on it for at least two weeks, with at least two posts per day. Determine your audience, based on demographic, psychographic and geographic information you can gather. Research any blogs that might compete with you. Determine how you plan to differentiate your work from these competitors. Outline several key features your blog would have and why you think they would serve your readers well. Write this up in a two- to four-page pitch for your instructor.

2. Write a daily blog on the topic you have chosen. Promote the blog on various social network websites as well as through Twitter. Solicit suggestions and comments via these methods as well.

3. Select a piece of media copy (news story, press release, media statement, etc.) and use some of the linking techniques listed in the chapter to digitally enhance it. Determine which words or terms should lead to hyperlinks, and then attach the appropriate content to those elements of the copy. Write a short essay (one to two pages) to explain what you did and why you did it.

NOTES

1. J. Batsell (2015). "Engaged Journalism: Connecting With Digitally Empowered News Audiences." New York: Columbia Journalism Review.

2. E. Butow and R. Bollwitt (2012). "Blogging to Drive Business: Create and Maintain Valuable Customer Connections" (2nd ed.). Indianapolis, Ind.: Que Biz-Tech.

7

SOCIAL MEDIA

LEARNING OBJECTIVES

After completing this chapter, you should be able to:

- Understand the basic benefits of using social media to connect with your readers.

- Determine ways to best cultivate and grow an audience for your social media.

- Evaluate a tweet for accuracy, clarity and appropriateness.

- Compare and contrast social media and traditional media with regard to usage, trust and value.

- Understand potential disasters associated with social media and the ways in which you can avoid them.

How social media is used varies from person to person and from discipline to discipline. Some people use it to share information among like-minded people and keep abreast of important news, while others use it to build brands and market products. Social media often involves the use of to a specific platform or tool, such as Twitter or Facebook, but it often goes beyond that in terms of reach and value.

Much like every other aspect of writing discussed in this book, social media is less about the tools and platforms used to convey information and more about how best to reach your audience. If you have a strong understanding of who is in your audience and what they need, you can use specific social media tools to reach these readers in an effective and helpful way. If you don't understand who is out there or what they want to see, you can fail in a spectacularly ugly and public fashion.

This chapter defines social media in some broad terms and helps you understand how to use various social media tools to connect with your readers. The chapter will also discuss how to reach your readers and build your audience by meeting readers' needs. Finally, the chapter will discuss how things can go wrong on social media and how you can do your best to avoid becoming a cautionary tale.

WHAT IS SOCIAL MEDIA?

Social media relies less on a central focal point of information and more on pockets of interested individuals finding one another on various platforms. Although no pure definition exists for social media, several key concepts and ideas capture the core of what falls into this category:

Many-to-Many Model

The idea behind traditional mass media is a **one-to-many model** in which a main source sends out information to a large, homogenized audience. Newspapers, television stations and magazines all fit this model, in which the publisher disseminates content to subscribers or viewers. The **many-to-many model** allows anyone to be both a sender and a receiver of content, thus placing individuals on par with **legacy media** outlets in terms of potential reach and impact. This new model relies on many people serving as senders as well as receivers, thus leveling the playing field for users and increasing the volume of sources from which people receive information.

Earned Trust and Authority

In a standard media model, the outlet itself becomes the beacon of trust. People tend to trust the newspaper, magazine or television station. In some cases, favored news anchors or columnists become "local celebrities," but overall, the source of the information serves as the authority on the topic. In the case of social media, many individuals serve as the sources of information, and the trust is conveyed on an individual basis. Each reader can decide for himself or herself if that source is worthy of attention. The authority is conveyed by following that source's social media accounts and deciding to share that information with one's own followers. Those "retweets" or shares demonstrate the users' belief in the importance and accuracy of the material they received. Thus, each person who shares content along the way vouches for the credentials of the original sender.

Selective Engagement

Readers "follow" certain Twitter or Instagram accounts to get information from specific individuals. They can decide to follow one reporter from the New York Times but decline to follow a second one. They can choose to follow a specific feed from a publication, such as CNN's national or political feed, but ignore the publication's international feed or sports feed. Users get to pick and choose more, much like a buffet as opposed to just receiving a premade dinner that everyone gets. As the users' interests change or intensify, they can make additional choices to refine their social media selections.

WHY IS SOCIAL MEDIA VALUABLE?

Social media outlets have a great benefit to media professionals in all fields, both as tools to share information and as ways to receive feedback from audience members. Social media gives you direct access to people who have an interest in your content, your products or your causes. In addition, the door swings both ways, allowing readers to offer reporters news tips, give PR practitioners feedback on events and show advertisers what they think of a recent campaign. Here are some of the things that make social media valuable to your audience members and thus important to you:

Access on All Devices

The ubiquity of social media is tied directly to the rise in portable digital devices that are always connected to the internet. Twenty years ago, computers were still giant boxes, strapped to desks, that had limited access to the World Wide Web. People still were forced to carry their email settings from computer to computer on floppy disks. Today, information is stored in the cloud, digital devices can fit in your pocket and you are never out of the loop as long as you have Wi-Fi access or cell service. This makes it much easier to reach people and to meet their needs. Reporters can use these platforms to break news. PR professionals can use them to make announcements. Marketers can use them to create viral campaigns and give followers special discounts. This eliminates the fear of missing out for people who missed a story or a coupon in the paper or who didn't hear about something on the radio or TV news.

Snowballing Audiences

The term "viral" refers to the idea that something can spread quickly within a population from a variety of sources. Much like one person with a cold on the subway, numerous people receive exposure to the content from that contact point. Those people then go in many directions and spread the content to other people. This creates an epidemic of illness when we are talking about colds or the flu, but it when it comes to social media, it can create a wider audience for your original content. For example, if you build a campaign for a local pet shelter that seeks to have animals adopted before they become sick, you would likely target local people who have an interest in animals or who have previously adopted pets from the shelter. However, if you were to share your "Safe Before Sick" campaign on a social media channel, one of your targets might reshare that information to a group of veterinarians, who might raise money for you to get more medicine to treat sick pets. Another person might be an architect, who shares the content with fellow building professionals, with the goal of creating a bigger shelter. Social media can help your messages snowball into areas beyond your target audience, allowing you to reach previously unconsidered readers who can benefit you and your organization.

Shared Benefits

One of the most difficult things in journalism is to develop an audience that views a source as trustworthy and credible. The larger the audience, the harder it is to be all things to all people in terms of trust and credibility. However, one of the benefits of social media is that these elements are inherent in the interpersonal relationships in which sharing occurs. In other words, if Jane trusts Corporation X, she is likely willing to share information about that organization with people who follow her on social media. If Bill follows Jane, he likely trusts her judgment and sees what she has to say as credible. Therefore, he will likely trust whatever she shared from Corporation X, and he might be willing to share it with his followers. This continues to go on as part of that viral pattern we discussed earlier, with more and more people transferring that information and supporting it with their own reputations. This makes it easier to build a brand or a campaign quickly. That said, this idea can cut both ways, with negative information also spreading like wildfire across the internet, so keep that in mind.

PROFESSIONAL THOUGHTS
PATRICK FINLEY

Ever since he and his brother started their own "sports magazine" in first grade, Patrick Finley knew what he wanted to be.

"Sports writing is all I've ever wanted to do," he said. "My dad was a sportswriter for his first 20 years out of college. He'd bring us back stuffed animals from his road trips covering college football and basketball. I thought it was the coolest job in the world."

Finley's passion for sports journalism took him to Naples, Florida, Tucson, Arizona and eventually Chicago, where he now serves as the Bears beat reporter for the Chicago Sun-Times. Although the football season lasts 16 games, plus the playoffs, Finley said his beat is a year-round gig. As part of his beat, he covers the college draft, the NFL combine and the Super Bowl as well as the owners' meetings and the free-agency market. Finley said a lot has changed over the years he has covered sports, particularly in terms of the 24/7 news cycle.

Patrick Finley

"In college, we used to watch the local evening sports news to make sure no one had something we didn't, and then hit the bar," he said. "Today, I can't imagine ever feeling like I was truly 'off the clock.' Social media has changed that, but so has the fact that newspaper web sites are now the printing press that never closes."

To meet the needs of a voracious fan base, Finley said he relies heavily on social media to keep readers

(Continued)

informed about everything happening to the Bears in real time.

Patrick Finley

"Fans want immediate reaction from us on social media every time the Bears do any little thing, and our bosses want a story up—and fast—to maximize the number of page views we get," he said. "The two work hand-in-hand; the fastest and most efficient way to get people to our web site to read the story is to post it on social media."

The issue of personal branding has become crucial in social media across all areas of journalism, and Finley said he notices how important it is when readers follow him on various platforms and interact with him.

"One benefit of social media, particularly Twitter, is that readers become loyal to writers," Finley said. "They're clicking on posts with your face on it, not a corporate logo. If you decide to work elsewhere, you can take that following with you. You can interact with readers with a suddenness that seemed impossible 10 years ago. You can joke with them. It feels more intimate."

Finley found out firsthand the power of social media in July 2017 while he was covering the Bears' training camp. The team's media policy stated that professional journalists could shoot photos and videos only during the first 20 minutes of practice, but fans could shoot and share as much content as they wanted throughout the whole event. In an attempt to

poke fun at this, Finley took to drawing "artist's renderings" of the events he was witnessing, even though he describes his artistic ability as "toddler-esque."

The sketches went viral and became some of his most read tweets, something he said he didn't see coming.

"It taught me that Twitter appreciates something unique, no matter how absolutely silly it might be," Finley said. "I don't pretend to grasp exactly why it went viral—It was intended to be a gentle mocking of a training camp policy where fans could take pictures but media members couldn't—but I imagine it reached beyond my typical football fan followers. My experience with the sketches was a fun one, though Bears PR staffers finally got annoyed by it by the end of camp, I think. It's still weird that some people know me as the guy who sketches stuff, when I'd rather them know me for the job I do."

Still, Finley said social media has become a crucial element of his job and for most jobs within the field because using tools like Twitter and Instagram help media professionals connect with their audiences.

"Social media—in my case, Twitter—is the most efficient, effective way to connect with readers," Finley said. "It helps drive page views, conversation and connection with the audience we serve—and that's absolutely part of my job."

One Last Thing

Q: If you could tell students anything about media writing or anything you have seen in your time in the field, what would it be?

A: Write as much as you can. It's the only way to get better. Read about a wide range of subjects, not just the topic you specialize in. (My Kindle has very few sports books). Treat your coworkers well—some journalists think the cynical worldview that makes them so good at their job gives them a free pass to act that way socially. It doesn't. Respect the copy desk, which will save your butt 100 times a year.

A QUICK LOOK AT SOME SOCIAL MEDIA TOOLS

Social media tools can be scaled or adapted to fit the needs of an audience. They can allow users to select niche topics they want and to filter out content they don't like. In addition, people can use these tools to share information and add to a larger media discussion. This media approach is the digital version of neighborhood chatter, with people gossiping over the back fence or chatting at local restaurants. Social media obviously takes on a broader set of parameters than simple chatter, but these media opportunities are still rooted in that sense of socialization and audience interest.

Social media allows you to weave audio, video, images, graphics and text together as a way to reach an interested audience. Since this book focuses primarily on writing, we won't dig into tools that rely primarily on visuals or audio, such as Facebook Live, Instagram and Snapchat. Instead, we'll focus on a few tools that tend to relate more directly to text and those platforms that require good writing to succeed. At the end of the chapter, however, we will discuss the ways to build good rapport with your audience on social media, a concept that has value for the use of any social media tools.

Twitter: News Anywhere, 280 Characters at a Time

Twitter began as an outgrowth of **Short Message Service (SMS),** in which users could send basic text messages to one another via mobile devices. The SMS approach meant that tweets needed to be no longer than 140 characters. It provided users with an opportunity to transmit their text messages to multiple people in a small group at one time. Initially, the service was viewed as a purely social tool that would limit redundancy in sharing information among friends. In the nearly 10 years since its inception, Twitter has gained more than 200 million users, thus making it a powerful information-sharing tool. Corporations, celebrities and regular people use this tool to reach their audience members with items of interest at any point in time. In November 2017, Twitter doubled the maximum size of a tweet, providing users with a 280-character limit. Reaction to the change was mixed, as many users argued that more useful options would have been more appreciated.[1] As some organizations rewrote their social media policies to accommodate the new limit, others warned users not to waste readers' time with flabby tweets.

Media professionals have embraced Twitter on a professional level in a variety of ways. Public-relations practitioners can use it to promote events and drive traffic to their web work. News reporters use it to provide live coverage of breaking news events. Advertisers can provide followers with exclusive offers, sales information and product-launch awareness. Twitter also allows you to drive traffic to your site through the use of micro-URLs. A tweet can serve as a headline or a teaser for your readers, who can then click the link and head to your website, where you will have more information for them.

Twitter has some drawbacks, many of which are user driven. The quick use of thumb-based keyboards occasionally leads to spelling problems that can come back to haunt you. In 2012, Philip Gilberti, who was wanted in connection with the shooting death of a woman, was found dead at a home near Washington, D.C. Gilberti was believed to be the victim of a self-inflicted gunshot wound, but when ABC7 tweeted out its breaking news alert, it noted that Gilberti "shit and killed himself."[2] The station later corrected the error, but then got the man's name wrong.

It can also be difficult for people to understand more complex topics via Twitter, such as budget initiatives or comprehensive marketing strategies. Even more, writers can have difficulty conveying the proper tone in so few characters, thus angering read-

ers who misunderstand the intent behind the tweets. This can be a difficult platform to master, but it is worth the time, given the large audience that uses it and the way in which viral sharing can dramatically increase your visibility across multiple publics.

Twitter is a great way to provide content to people in short bursts on their digital devices.

© iStockphoto.com/bgwalker

ADAPT
TWITTER IS LEADS AND HEADLINES

Writing a good tweet takes more time and patience than most other forms of writing because you have a limited space in which to express yourself. In many ways, composing a tweet is like building a headline or a lead sentence. The tweet functions like a headline, in that you can use it to draw in readers and then refer them to a bigger piece of copy on your website. It functions like a lead in that you are using it to tell people the most important information first. Here are some key writing tips you can adapt from these writing approaches to create top-notch tweets:

Start With the Noun-Verb Structure

A concrete noun and a vigorous verb will do a world of good for you in any form of writing, but they matter even more in tweets. If you can identify the "who" and the "did what" elements of your tweet, you can give your readers the key information right away. This will keep your focus on the most important elements of what you want to say in the shortest possible space. Once you have those elements, you can build around them with some of the other "W's" and descriptors.

BAD TWEET: *Upon a day's reflection, a story involving CIA torture has additional problematic layers to it, senators argue.* (LINK)

IMPROVED TWEET: *Senators slam CIA torture story, say issues more nuanced than writers indicate.* (LINK)

Make One Point at a Time

Focus is a crucial aspect of Twitter. The better you focus on the main issues associated with the announcement you want to make, the clearer your intent will be to your readers. If you start with the noun-verb structure, your tweet should remain reasonably clear, but always review what you wrote to be certain. The goal of each tweet is to make one good point at a time. If you try to do too much in a tweet, you will confuse your readers. You can send several tweets on an issue if you need to make multiple points.

BAD TWEET: *Fix closets with three simple organizers from @VFhardware; rework basement shelves as well as garden tool storage; Paint on sale too.* (LINK)

IMPROVED TWEET: *Got the spring-cleaning blues? Revitalize your home with paint, organizers from @VFhardware.* (LINK)

Use Smart Substitutions

In headline writing, journalists cram large type into small and odd spaces. To do this, they can break certain style rules within reason to make things fit. On Twitter, you can apply some of the same basic principles to shorten your tweet without making it unnecessarily difficult to read.

Think about using numerals instead of spelling out numbers, even if that goes against your organization's traditional sense of style. Use symbols such as & and % to represent longer words, always taking care not to use the symbols that have a specific meaning in Twitter (#, @, *). Look for shorter words to substitute for longer words as well, such as substituting "hurt" for "injured." The 280-character limit makes it easier to avoid "text speak," such as using letters as words ("U R" for "you are"), but the minimalist nature of Twitter still will push you to think about making smart substitutions.

BAD TWEET: *Federal authorities arrest six in California's largest methamphetamine bust, say ring was responsible for 21 percent of state's supply.*

IMPROVED TWEET: *Feds arrest 6 in Calif. meth bust, say men produced 21% of state's supply.*

Edit and Tighten

Once you write the tweet, go back and edit it in ways that will eliminate extraneous words. This will allow you to sharpen your focus and also help you save space for potential retweets. Look for ways to remove prepositional phrases, redundancies and other wastes of space. Aside from keeping your tweet from getting flabby, you can make sure on spelling, structure and clarity as well. The editing process is crucial to all forms of writing, regardless of how long the piece is. Treat each tweet with the same level of care you treat any major piece of copy you write.

GIVE IT A TRY: Select four or five news stories or press releases and develop tweets that apply the elements listed above. Consider the purpose of the articles and releases in your approach. For example, a tweet for a press release could involve a more persuasive tone, while a news story would likely need more of an objective feel. Compose your tweets so they are no longer than 260 characters, thus saving room for a link and retweet opportunities. Then, see if you can rewrite them to fit the old standard of 140 characters. Compare the tweets for quality, clarity and focus.

The "Storify Approach"

In dealing with live events, journalists often have a wide array of tools at their disposal, including text, photos, video and audio. In addition, social media offers them the tweets and posts of other people as fodder for telling the story more completely. In 2010, **Storify** emerged as a tool that allowed journalists to make sense of all of these elements as they selected content from various social media feeds and added their own information to tell a story. It was acquired by Livefyre in 2013, which was subsequently acquired by Adobe in 2016. Although Adobe announced in late 2017 that it was discontinuing Storify by 2018, the founders of the product said they were proud of their contribution to social media. Xavier Damman told NiemanLab in December 2017 that when Storify launched, most sites didn't allow users to embed tweets, images from Instagram or posts from Facebook. Now, these options are common, and allow journalists to tell stories on other platforms in the way in which only Storify previously could. Thus, even though the tool itself is dead, it is important for you understand the "Storify approach" to telling stories via social media.

Justin Horne
@Justin_Horne

Large road signs down over I-37 near Corpus. #ksatwx #harvey
11:17 PM - Aug 25, 2017

24   803   800

Media professionals used Storify to collect bits of information from multiple digital platforms and tell stories, like this one done in the wake of Hurricane Harvey. Although the tool is being phased out, the "Storify approach" to journalism still has merit as a storytelling option.

This approach gives journalists the ability to weave this content together to tell a well-rounded story as well as the opportunity to continuously update information as the event continues to unfold. Marketing professionals can use the approach to provide a retrospective examination of an event, such as a "Best of the Fair" piece to help promote and recount the most important moments of a state fair. Reporters can use it to provide readers with a timeline to keep people up to date on a developing situation. For example, in August 2017, Hurricane Harvey pounded the state of Texas for several days, creating some horrific flooding. Journalists at Community Impact Newspaper used Storify to gather tweets, video, press release information and other bits of news to track Harvey as it made land and began to wreak havoc on the state.[3] Police Force One used the tool in a similar way, as the writers for this website that serves law enforcement officials gathered tweets, press statements and images of first responders as they helped people who met with Harvey's wrath.[4]

When you use the "Storify approach," you can choose which ever pieces of content you see as helpful from various social media feeds and arrange the pieces of information you gather in whichever way you think will best help readers understand the topic. The biggest thing to keep in mind is that you should gather as much information as you can first and then make choices about what to keep and what to eliminate.

Social networking sites like Facebook and LinkedIn can give you access to important sources of information and help you share content to interested readers.

Facebook and LinkedIn

Social networking websites such as Facebook and LinkedIn provide you with an option to meet people with similar interests and showcase your skills and products. The purpose of these sites is to give you access to a large audience and draw them to your content. Once they arrive, you can promote your stories, your products and your organization, moving readers from these virtual town halls to your own website. These sites also provide you with access to opinion leaders and field experts who can provide you with feedback as well as access to additional audiences that might benefit you.

Creating a post on these sites is not difficult, but you should be aware that you have thousands of competitors on the site who all will vie for the same eyeballs you want. This means you need to keep your posts short, engaging and valuable if you want audience members to embrace your work and read on. The key to posting well is to post frequently over an extended period of time each day. This will draw your readers to your page multiple times during each of their visits to the site. This approach will build readership habits among these audience members and foster a strong tie between you and them.

The posts themselves should include a few lines of text that offer a simple explanation as to the topic, explain the value of the topic and then entice the readers to move deeper into the story with a simple click of a link. Here's an example:

> *With graduation weekend just around the corner, college students face the daunting task of getting a job. According to a recent New York Times article, the biggest stumbling block students face is properly preparing for the in-person interview. Our resident career specialist, Bill Jones, outlines the five biggest blunders people make during the interview process and how best to avoid them in his weekly post, "Big Bill's Big 5." (LINK)*

This post explains what the bigger story will include, what makes it valuable and why you are reading about it now. It then moves you out of the main area of the social networking site and onto either the organization's part of the site or onto the organization's own website. This is a strong example of how to use a few lines of copy to draw readers to a bigger piece.

Facebook is the largest social media platform to date and provides people with opportunities to connect to various people and share important content with anyone they see fit. Most of the outlets discussed in this chapter have crossed paths with Facebook, which metrics indicate has more than 2 billion monthly users.[5]

Facebook often serves as a social media hub for Twitter posts, Instagram images and live videos, as users can opt to have content they share on these platforms simultaneously shared to Facebook as well. In addition, many websites will allow people to use their Facebook profiles to log in or post commentary. This central junction point of information can allow you to see what trends are emerging and learn more about them. You can also use the site to reach out to decision makers and potential sources. The options here are endless in terms of sharing content and finding out what people want from you.

LinkedIn offers you similar opportunities in a more formal setting with a stronger interest in business-based connections. If you think about Facebook being like a local bar, LinkedIn is a cross between a job fair and a breakroom at work. The site, which launched in 2003, provides individuals with the opportunity to create a work-oriented profile, seek jobs and connect with people in fields of interest. Individuals can post content of a work-oriented nature on their own page, which gets shared to the person's connections as part of a timeline. To improve credibility and trust among users, individuals must have an existing relationship before being allowed to connect, and it remains up to the person receiving a connection request to decide if he or she will accept that request.

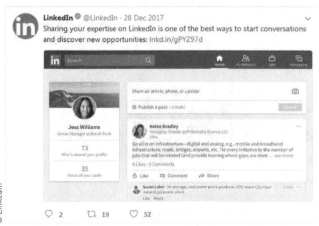

Employers can find potential candidates to fill jobs, post hiring notices and seek connections with like-minded people and organizations. Each user's page contains a timeline of content shared from people the user follows, along with updates as to people who viewed their profile, updates from people within the individual's network and suggestions for people to follow.

This site had more than 500 million members as of April 2017 and provides media practitioners with a great opportunity to seek information from experts, connect with professionals in fields of interest and see what trends are growing within a particular employment area. The site allows organizations to brand build as well as connect with others as part of a grouping function, thus providing both networking and growth opportunities. As is the case with Facebook, LinkedIn allows people to log into third-party platforms with their profile and provide content to people on their own page. It also provides you with an opportunity to connect with people who have a vested interest in your content or who can help you better serve your readership in a variety of ways.

CONNECT
AVOIDING #FAIL WHEN CONNECTING WITH YOUR AUDIENCE

The ability to connect with readers always sounds like a good idea, although using social media to interact with audience members occasionally leads to viral public disasters. You can put in an inordinate amount of time and effort building an audience on social media, only to watch it vanish quickly if you mess up something. Here are some thoughts to help you avoid the big errors that lead to social media misery:

mrlukerobinson Luke Robinson
Susan Boyle has officially the most unfortunate hashtag. Are we all looking forward to Susan Boyle's #susanalbumparty ? http://t.co/H1aW6ViN
About five years ago via web ☆ Favorite ↻ Retweet ↩ Reply

KateRobbins Kate Robbins
Susan Boyle's PR people want sacking! #Susanalbumparty was the hash tag used for her album party!! Oh dear oh dear
About five years ago via Mobile Web ☆ Favorite ↻ Retweet ↩ Reply

@mrlukerobinson via Twitter

Read From the Perspective of a 12-Year-Old Boy

This is a hint for headlines, tweets and anything else that relies on a short burst of text to get a message across. That 12-year-old's mentality helps you avoid double entendres like "Golfer plays round with caddy's balls" or "Six ways to preserve your nuts for the holidays."

The same rule applies to **hashtags**, which have a strong potential to be misread. For example, in 2012, "Britain's Got Talent" star Susan Boyle released a collection of songs, much to the excitement of her fans. To capitalize on this, her public-relations firm started a hashtag campaign to celebrate an album party for Boyle. The problem became clear when people realized #susanalbumparty could be read not as "Susan album party" but as "Sus anal bum party" or "Sus anal bump arty."[6] The firm quickly switched to #SusanBoylesAlbumParty, but the error lives in internet infamy.[7]

A similar "segmentation" problem occurred after the death of former British Prime Minister Margaret Thatcher in 2013. The hashtag #nowthatchersdead began trending as people discussed Thatcher's life and legacy. However, many people read the tag as "Now that Cher's dead," fearing that the longtime singer and actress had died.[8] After a bit of confusion, various celebrities and fans took to Twitter to iron out the confusion regarding the hashtag.

One of the best bits of advice you can receive in journalism is to read something aloud. In many cases, grammar gaffes and awkward wordplay can emerge when you realize that how something sounds in your head won't be exactly how someone else will read it. When you read something aloud, you are able to stress various syllables and contemplate different ways to verbalize words to see if anything can go wrong.

(Continued)

(Continued)

DiGiorno Pizza ✓
@DiGiornoPizza

#WhyIStayed You had pizza.

9/8/14, 11:11 PM

Keosha Varela @K_J_Writes   1h
So many courageous ppl sharing their stories re: #whyistayed and #whyileft. Domestic violence is often a hidden issue, bring it to light!

Adrienne Airhart @craydrienne   1h
I couldn't face the fact that I was a textbook statistic: if (step)daddy hurts you, so will hubby. #whyistayed

Scott Paul
@scottfpaul

Example of a brand using a trending topic without understanding the context #Advertising #SocialMedia #WhyIStayed
10:23 PM - Sep 8, 2014

♡ 37   ↻ 521   ♡ 233

Don't Barge in on a Hashtag

It can be painful for you and your organization if you start an awkward hashtag like #susanalbumparty, but it can be even worse if you misappropriate someone else's campaign. In many cases, people will see a trending hashtag and feel compelled to jump into the mix. This can be problematic for individuals, but for organizations it can be downright dangerous. This is particularly true if the organization doesn't do some research before joining the campaign.

In 2014, thousands of women used the hashtag #WhyIStayed to open up about their experiences with domestic violence. Some people noted that they stayed with an abuser because they felt incapable of leaving or feared what he would do their children. In using the hashtag, readers could share experiences and feel a sense of connectivity to other survivors. However, in the middle of the campaign, DiGiorno Pizza tweeted, "#WhyIStayed You had pizza." The backlash was quick and severe, with DiGiorno quickly apologizing and noting that nobody at the company looked into the purpose of the hashtag before posting.[9]

A hashtag you did not create is like someone else's conversation: Before you chime in, make sure you can

participate appropriately and know what the conversation is about. Hopping onto a viral hashtag for your own gains can be off-putting to the people who are using it for its intended purpose, and they can use that trending tag to make life miserable for you.

Don't Let Robots Run Your Social Media Without Supervision

Like most things in the digital world, you can use an automation system to manage some of your social media efforts. You have the ability to release tweets and postings at certain times of day or to post quickly in response to certain alerts or hashtags. For example, when someone posts a complaint about your company, you can set up an alert to let you know this has happened and automatically offer the person a chance to reach out to you directly for help. This can provide quick and valuable connections to your audience.

However, not every automation goes well when it comes to filtering out problematic social media snafus. In November 2014, the New England Patriots set up a special social media release to commemorate their 1 millionth Twitter follower, complete with an image of the person's Twitter handle on the back of a Patriots jersey and a special message signed by tight end Rob Gronkowski. Unfortunately, the Patriots ran into a problem with their "filter" because the winner's handle included the N-word. The Patriots were forced to apologize for the error.[10]

As columnist Bill Vaughan once noted, "To err is human; to really foul things up requires a computer."[11] If you don't have some sort of human check on your social media, you can put yourself in an unenviable position to apologize for something a computer did without your knowledge.

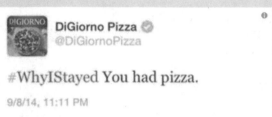

Loyal Poppy 📍 @AniroC_2 · 27 Oct 2017
#AskSeaWorld explain to me in what way is this a natural behaviour and what education is involved? #OpSeaWorld

♡   ↻ 1   ♡ 1

Prepare for the Worst

The ability to connect with readers always sounds like a good idea, but using social media to interact with audience members occasionally leads to viral public disasters. Several recent #Ask campaigns on social media have turned into dumpster fires because the people running them didn't foresee that some people on the Internet might not be polite in their postings.

In 2015, SeaWorld was dealing with negative publicity surrounding animal treatment at its facilities. The organization opened the #AskSeaWorld hashtag to promote a dialogue with social media users and demonstrate transparency. People for the Ethical Treatment of Animals and others interested in animal rights quickly took to social media on that hashtag to shame SeaWorld for its treatment of animals. The campaign went down in flames, as the best SeaWorld could do was complain about having to weed through "a few thousand trolls and bots" to find questions it wanted to answer.[12]

A similar situation occurred at Florida State University when the school's athletic department used its @FSU_Football account to solicit questions for embattled quarterback Jameis Winston. During his career at FSU, Winston was accused of rape, arrested on suspicion of stealing crab legs and associated with other questionable actions.[13] The questions here also got ugly:

> After getting away with a high-profile rape & theft, what crime will you commit to complete your triple crown?

> Are crab legs your favorite seafood?

> Aside from your game, how much has your use/comprehension of the English language improved this offseason?[14]

Before you start a hashtag campaign, you need to assess not just your target audience but also the actual audience you will reach. When you open yourself to the entire public, you run the risk of the discourse becoming disruptive. In addition, you have to assume that there will always be people who dislike or distrust you, even if you believe they shouldn't feel that way. To that end, you should prepare for the worst and then hope for the best.

If you open an "ask" campaign, consider the most likely negative things you will encounter. Then determine if those negatives are worth the positives you believe you will get from this effort.

In addition, before you run a full-on public campaign, you should test it a few times on more controlled platforms. Consider an email option that will allow your readers to submit questions but that provides you with a reviewing and filtering option. This will also help you see any land mines that could emerge in a public campaign.

GIVE IT A TRY: Search the internet to find at least three major "fails" with regard to social media. Give a brief outline of what the person or group was trying to do and what went wrong. Explain what similarities exist between the failures of the campaigns and how you would have reworked these social media efforts to avoid these problems.

BUILDING A SOCIAL MEDIA AUDIENCE

Traditional media had it easy in terms of building an audience: They were usually one of only a few outlets in an area (one or two newspapers or three or four television stations), and they covered everything their audience could possibly want to know about that area. Today, social media audiences are spread around the globe, they have exponentially more choices than previous generations of users and they tend to expect coverage of specific and narrow topics.

Social media requires a lot of work on the part of the media professionals trying to use these tools to reach their audiences. Experts at IMPACT, an award-winning inbound marketing firm, offer the following tips when it comes to building and maintaining a social media audience:

Pick Your Social Media Platform(s) Wisely

Without using the term, IMPACT's Justine Timoteo argues for audience-centric thinking even before you establish your social media presence.[15] She notes that to draw a good audience on social media, you need to find out where people who are interested in your content, cause or product are already and then plant your flag there. It makes little sense to just blitz every social media tool with your content if your audience isn't there to hear or see your content.

Let Users Know You Are Human

Timoteo notes that the "social" part of "social media" can't be overlooked. The audience members crave attention and interaction as much as you do, so look for mutually beneficial ways to connect with them. She suggests adding profile information to your account, including a photo and interesting background information about you. She also notes that you should connect with thought leaders as well as audience members, as you seek to open a dialogue with them. This will let people know you are interested in listening to them, and they will want to stay connected to you.

Produce Valuable Content

People will likely follow you on social media quickly if they think you have something important to tell them. However, if your content doesn't meet their needs or drops off in terms of quality, they will leave you just as quickly. IMPACT's Karisa Egan notes that creativity and visual appeal can help draw people to your content. She also suggests following the "70/20/10 rule," which means that 70 percent of your content should provide a direct benefit to your audience, 20 percent of your content is "shared" from other sources and only 10 percent should outright promote you or your organization.[16] Make sure you are placing an emphasis on quality as well as quantity when it comes to content sharing. One good post is five times more valuable than five weak ones.

Consistently Post at a Comfortable Rate

A sweet spot exists for the amount of content media professionals feel comfortable posting and the amount of material audience members want to consume. Unfortunately, that sweet spot varies greatly based on the platform you are using, the area of the field in which you are working and the topics you are covering. Egan says that nobody enjoys being spammed to death, but few people enjoy being ignored either. The trick to finding the right mix of timely and engaging content is to watch your analytics. If you are posting several times a day and you see a drop in hits or a loss of followers, consider posting less often and placing a higher premium on the quality of your posts. If you see spikes when you post twice a week and then nothing for days when you don't, look for ways to spread the content more evenly across the week. It will take you a while to dial it in properly, but when you do, you will have an engaged and appreciative audience.

THE BIG THREE

Here are the three key things you should take away from this chapter:

1. **Everything moves fast on social media:** Whether it's the dissemination of information or the destruction of your carefully crafted brand thanks to an ugly hashtag, social media does everything at a rapid pace. This can be a blessing or a curse depending on if things are going well or going poorly for you. Once you decide to step onto the social media train, however, you need to understand that there will be little time for course corrections or major fixes.

2. **Anticipate the worst-case scenario:** If the internet has demonstrated one thing repeatedly, it's that

people have an unfettered ability to crush your soul online. With that in mind, you need to play good defense before you decide to make a post, send a tweet or start a campaign. Think about every possible thing that could go wrong, reread your hashtag from the perspective of a 12-year-old boy, plan how you will deal with trolls and hope for the best. If you wander onto social media as innocent as a newborn puppy, you are just asking to get hurt.

3. **Trust is everything:** People on social media will force you to work hard to connect with them, but those readers will ditch you if anything goes wrong. This is why trust matters so much and you need to do everything possible to demonstrate you are a trustworthy and valuable information source. The more trust people place in you, the better off you will be, so put effort into this at every turn.

KEY TERMS

hashtag 117
legacy media 109
many-to-many model 109

micro-URLs 113
one-to-many model 109
Short Message Service (SMS) 113

social media 109
Storify 115
Twitter 113

DISCUSSION QUESTIONS

1. What do you see as some of the benefits of Twitter? What are some of the drawbacks? How do these benefits and drawbacks compare with those of other forms of digital media, such as social networking and blogging?

2. Why do you think social media can lead to negative outcomes, such as the SeaWorld problem and the Jameis Winston situation discussed above? Is it a problem with the platform or the people who use it? How does each contribute to these issues?

WRITE NOW!

1. Select a group or an organization you belong to and analyze it in terms of the audience characteristics we discussed earlier in the book. Then, examine three or four social media platforms that could be used to reach this group. Look up the various statistics associated with the platforms, including who tends to use it, what services it provides and how it reaches people. Which social media tool would be best for you to communicate within the members of the group as well as communicate to audiences of importance for the group? Explain your answers.

2. Find five tweets that are more than 250 characters and try to edit them down to the original 140-character limit. Then, write a few paragraphs in which you explain your edits and how successful you were at trimming the tweets. Also explain if you think the original author needed the additional characters to make his or her point.

3. Look through several news stories, press releases and marketing pieces for a topic that interests you and plan a way to communicate on multiple social media platforms to an audience you think would want to know about the topic. For

example, you could use Twitter to draw people in, a Facebook post to give people some interesting information and a "Storify approach" to tell a longer story. You don't need to limit yourself to

the tools discussed in this chapter if you have experience with others. The goal of the exercise is to see how you would best reach a defined audience with distinct social media tools.

NOTES

1. C. Watson (2017, Nov. 7). "Twitter Users Respond to #280characters Rollout: 'All We Wanted Was an Edit Button.'" The Guardian. Accessed at: https://www.theguardian.com/technology/2017/nov/08/twitter-users-respond-280characters-tweet-limit?utm_term=Autofeed&CMP=twt_b-gdnnews#link_time=1510111791.

2. C. Silverman (2014, Nov. 25). "ABC Station Tweets Unfortunate Typos About Suicide." Accessed at: https://www.poynter.org/news/abc-station-tweets-unfortunate-typos-about-suicide.

3. S. Arrajj (2017, Aug. 26). "Hurricane Harvey: Heavy Rain Expected to Hit Houston Through Saturday Night Into Sunday." Community Impact Newspaper. Accessed at: https://communityimpact.com/houston/news/2017/08/26/hurricane-harvey-flash-flood-warning-extended-centerpoint-restoring-power/.

4. PoliceOne Staff (2017, Aug. 27). "Photos, Videos: First Responders Rush Into Action During Hurricane Harvey." Accessed at: https://www.policeone.com/police-heroes/articles/414231006-Photos-videos-First-responders-rush-into-action-during-Hurricane-Harvey/.

5. J. Constine (2017, June 27). Facebook Now Has 2 Billion Monthly Users...and Responsibility." Tech Crunch. Accessed at: https://techcrunch.com/2017/06/27/facebook-2-billion-users/.

6. B. O'Reilly (2012, Nov. 21). "Twitter Fail—Susan Boyle's Unfortunate Album Launch Hashtag." The Independent. Accessed at: http://www.independent.ie/entertainment/music/twitter-fail-susan-boyles-unfortunate-album-launch-hashtag-28904194.html.

7. K. Brand (2012, Nov. 23). "Twitter Hashtag PR Disaster #Susanalbumparty: I'd Love to Go, Says Katy Brand." The Telegraph. Accessed at: http://www.telegraph.co.uk/women/womens-life/9698831/Twitter-hashtag-PR-disaster-Susanalbumparty-Id-love-to-go-says-Katy-Brand.html.

8. Daily Mail Reporter (2013, April 9). "How Horrified Cher Fans Thought Their Idol Was Dead After Thatcher Critics Started #nowthatcherisdead Hashtag on Twitter." The Daily Mail. Accessed at: http://www.dailymail.co.uk/news/article-2306137/Margaret-Thatcher-dead-Confused-CHER-fans-thought-shed-died-nowthatcherisdead-Twitter-hashtag.html.

9. L. Stampler (2014, Sept. 9). "DiGiorno Used a Hashtag About Domestic Violence to Sell Pizza." Time. Accessed at: http://time.com/3308861/digiorno-social-media-pizza/.

10. J. Molinet (2014, Nov. 13). "Patriots Tweet N-Word in Social Media Fail." The Daily News. Accessed at: http://www.nydailynews.com/sports/football/patriots-tweet-n-word-social-media-fail-article-1.2010665.

11. Quote Investigator. Accessed at: https://quoteinvestigator.com/2010/12/07/foul-computer/.

12. K. Sola (2015, March 27). "#AskSeaWorld Twitter Campaign Pretty Much Goes How You'd Expect." Huffington Post. Accessed at: http://www.huffingtonpost.com/2015/03/27/seaworld-twitter-fail_n_6950902.html.

13. S. Lebron (2014, Aug. 11). "Florida State's #AskJameis Twitter Q&A Backfired Spectacularly." Mic. Accessed at: https://mic.com/articles/95938/florida-state-s-askjameis-twitter-q-a-backfired-spectacularly#.jypjVsAog.

14. C. Wray (2014, Aug. 11). "Best Tweets From FSU's #AskJameis Experiment? Crab Legs, History, the Bama QB Race Are in the Mix." Accessed at: http://www.al.com/sports/index.ssf/2014/08/best_tweets_from_fsus_askjamei.html.

15. J. Timoteo (2017, Jan. 16). "How to Build a Social Media Following in 2017." IMPACT.com.

Accessed at: https://www.impactbnd.com/blog/grow-social-media-following.

16. K. Egan (2016, Sept. 19). "Are You Posting Too Much on social Media?" IMPACT.com. Accessed at: https://www.impactbnd.com/blog/are-you-posting-too-much-on-social-media.

8

LAW AND ETHICS
IN MEDIA WRITING

LEARNING OBJECTIVES

After completing this chapter you should be able to:

- Identify the key protections of the First Amendment and to which forms of media they most directly apply.

- Understand the most common misapplications of the First Amendment and explain why they are incorrect.

- Identify and apply the key elements necessary for proving libel.

- Identify and apply the most prominent defenses against a libel suit.

- Outline the rules associated with copyright protection, including the benefits of it and the ways in which copyrighted content can be legally used.

- Explain the benefits of ethics and how they can vary from media discipline to media discipline.

- Understand the basic areas in which ethical dilemmas are likely to occur and how best to deal with them.

Law and ethics are two important and yet divergent parts of the media world. The law often speaks in absolutes, and the courts offer concrete remedies for specific violations. On the other hand, individual media professionals often compile their own sets of ethics over the course of a career, adjusting and reframing their thoughts based on life experiences.

The purpose of this chapter is not to outline all of the legal decisions or ethical dilemmas you might face over the course of your career in media. Instead, the chapter will provide you with a short look at a few pieces of legal and ethical ground that broadly apply to much of the media landscape. In addition, it is important to understand that technology has often outpaced the law. Recent cases we discuss here will show how social media platforms like Twitter have become flashpoints for legal cases and First Amendment issues.

The chapter will first touch on various aspects of the law, clarifying their intent and debunking a few myths. Then it will examine a broad view of ethical behavior as well as how and why ethics matter to media professionals.

THE FIRST AMENDMENT

The **Bill of Rights** outlines the first 10 amendments to the U.S. Constitution, and it places issues regarding free expression in the very first one. The **First Amendment** is thus often viewed as not only the most important amendment but also the foundation upon which all the rights and responsibilities of the media reside.

What It Says

Congress shall make no law respecting an establishment of religion, or prohibiting the free exercise thereof; or abridging the freedom of speech, or of the press; or the right of the people peaceably to assemble, and to petition the government for a redress of grievances.

Depending on how you view these 45 words, the amendment grants you either five or six freedoms. (Some people count religion twice, as it guarantees you the right to practice as you see fit, and it also explains that you have the right to be free from religion.) Taken collectively, these freedoms of expression and publication provide the underpinnings of what we do and how we can influence the public through our activities as media practitioners.

The Founding Fathers didn't delineate these freedoms because they were printers or because they were heavily religious, although both of these statements are true for many of them. The authors of this document knew that if a country were to thrive, it would need to have an independent media that could inform the citizenry. They also understood that citizens could act in their own best interests and the best interests of society as a whole if those people could get information that was free from government interference.

What It Does and Doesn't Protect

The First Amendment does not protect all forms of expression, despite its broad interpretation by many courts. Ashley Packard, in her book "Digital Media Law," outlines several ways in which speech can be limited[1]:

Categorical Limitations

Courts have found that certain forms of speech have the potential to lead to harm and thus do not get First Amendment protection. These **categorical limitations** include fighting words, threats, false advertising and criminal solicitation. Courts have also noted that things like child pornography are exploitive and thus deserve no protection under the First Amendment.

© WikiCommons

Although the First Amendment provides broad protection for speech and press freedom, it does limit expression through time-place-manner limitations. The right to conduct marches, protests and other public displays are often weighed against the rights of other people who do not wish to be bothered.

Medium-Based Limitations

The initial inclusion of "the press" in the First Amendment covered most media formats available at the time. However, as other forms of media emerged, **medium-based limitations** arrived as well. For example, while newspapers still receive the broadest possible protection, broadcast journalism is governed through the Federal Communications Commission because of its use of the public airwaves. Other media forms, including satellite broadcasts and cable television, fall in between, as do certain forms of public relations and advertising. Current rulings regard the internet as being akin to newspapers in terms of protection.

Time-Place-Manner Limitations

Courts seek to balance the rights of the public against the rights of those who wish to exercise their free speech rights. The **time-place-manner limitations** on expression allow people to express themselves while not impinging upon other people's rights. In 2017, the Illinois Supreme Court stated that a Chicago ordinance banning anyone, including protesters, from spending the night in Grant Park without a permit was constitutional. Protesters argued that closing the park was an attempt to limit free speech, but the courts held that the rules regarding time, place and manner restrictions allowed the city's action.[2] In another case, a court in Wisconsin held that honking a car horn was not a protected form of speech. Azael Brodhead, a state parole agent, drove past Gov. Scott Walker's Wauwatosa home every day as part of a protest. He would honk his horn, extend his middle finger and shout "Recall Walker." Brodhead argued he was exercising his First Amendment rights, but the court disagreed, saying honking was not constitutionally protected. After losing his case, he continued his protest without the use of the horn.[3]

Misconceptions Regarding the Amendment

The First Amendment prevents government intrusion upon free and independent expression. That said, people have long misunderstood what the amendment does for them and what it doesn't do. In the book "The Journalist's Handbook to Online Editing," the authors outline four common misconceptions associated with the First Amendment[4]:

No One Can Stop You From Publishing What You Want

This is where a lot of people get into trouble initially because they erroneously assume speech or the press can't be halted at all. The amendment only mentions Congress, which was later interpreted to mean the government and its agents. In some rare situations, even the government can prevent you from publishing content, including cases of gag orders and national security. Newspaper owners can prevent reporters from publishing information. Companies can limit public-relations practitioners and advertising professionals in terms of the use of social media, as these individuals' statements could reflect a negative corporate image. In addition, many companies of all kinds require employees to sign nondisclosure and noncompete paperwork, which limits their ability to speak freely on certain issues. Violating these contractual obligations can lead to serious problems, which leads us to the next key point:

Freedom Of The Press Protects You From Ramifications

Publishing as you see fit means only that the government cannot suppress your right to publish your thoughts or speak your mind. However, that does not mean you will not face consequences associated with your actions. In 2014, a Los Angeles Superior Court judge refused to dismiss JM Eagle's defamation suit against Phillips & Cohen over a statement made in a press release. In an earlier suit, the court found that JM Eagle sold pipes that didn't comply with the Underwriters Laboratory standards. When the pipe manufacturer affixed the "UL" stamp to these pipes, it violated the False Claims Act, the verdict stated. However, the law firm issued a press release stating that the company had been "selling faulty water system pipes," which prompted the defamation suit. The court initially ruled that defamation had occurred, although an appeals court reversed the ruling in 2016.[5]

Justine Sacco
@JustineSacco

Going to Africa. Hope I don't get AIDS. Just kidding. I'm white!

← Reply ⇄ Retweet ★ Favorite ••• More

3,172 RETWEETS   **1,505** FAVORITES

10:19 AM - 20 Dec 13

Related headlines
❮ And Now, a Funny Holiday Joke from IAC's PR Boss
Kinja @kinja

With a 12-word tweet, PR professional Justine Sacco saw her entire life crumble all around her. Although people are free to express themselves, it doesn't mean consequences will not follow.

© @JustineSacco via Twitter

Even "the court of public opinion" can lead to serious problems for media practitioners. Justine Sacco, a public-relations agent for IAC, tweeted about her impending trip from London to Africa by noting, "Hope I don't get AIDS. Just kidding. I'm white!" Sacco quickly became the number one trending topic on Twitter and was subsequently fired from her job. She told a journalist almost two years later that her life had become a shambles, noting that she couldn't get hired anywhere and that dating was almost impossible because people would Google her and find the tweet.[6] She eventually found another job, but the lesson here is that the amendment protects your right to say what you want without government intrusion, but that doesn't serve as an impenetrable shield to every possible consequence.

The Rights In The First Amendment Are Absolute

Over the years, various court decisions have augmented or diminished the idea that speech and press rights are absolute. As noted within this chapter, courts have ruled against certain forms of speech based on the value of the content. In addition, the courts debated the idea of what kinds of protections the First Amendment affords to commercial speech. In 1942, the Valentine v. Chrestensen case[7] led the Supreme Court to declare that "purely commercial advertising" is not protected under this amendment and thus is not an inalienable right. However, subsequent rulings have eroded or eliminated parts of that finding, with one such decision noting that the government had to find other means of recourse before suppressing commercial speech.

The First Amendment Applies Only To Professional Media

The United States does not license people who wish to disseminate information, and as such, the law makes no demarcation between professional and amateur journalists. Anyone who uses a platform to share information with other people operates under the protections of the First Amendment. Consequently, he or she also assumes the risks associated with publishing material that could defame people.

LIBEL

One of the more misunderstood aspects of law as it pertains to media is the concept of **libel** (not liable, which is something you might be if you libel someone).

As much as you should fear libel and libel suits, you should spend just as much time, if not more, learning what this is, how it works and how you can protect yourself.

One of the more important things to understand with libel is that it's not just a "newspaper concern." You can libel someone in a press release, in an advertisement, on a blog post, through a tweet, on a television report and in many other places. In any situation where you disseminate information to a third party, you run the risk of engaging in libelous behavior. This shouldn't make you paranoid about your work in the field, but it should provide you with a healthy dose of respect for the law and make you judicious regarding what you put into the public sphere.

According to media scholar Chip Stewart, libel requires the following things[8]:

Identification

The individual alleging libel must be clearly identifiable in the potentially libelous material. In most cases, stating a person's name in a piece of writing will establish **identification**, although failing to include a name in something you write does not shield you from libel claims. For example, a political ad could state, "My Democratic challenger has beaten his wife." Although the person isn't named, it is likely the public could ascertain the identity of the individual accused of domestic violence. If the ad noted that "some politicians have engaged in spousal abuse," it would be more difficult to prove identification.

Publication

The information must be sent to someone other than the person who claims to be libeled. In many cases, **publication** occurs when someone disseminates information in a mass media outlet, such as a newspaper or magazine. In the wake of the Boston Marathon bombing in 2013, the New York Post ran a photo of two young men with the headline "Bag Men," noting, "Feds seek these two pictured at the Boston Marathon." The two men, Salaheddin Barhoum and Yassine Zaimi, were not the bombers, nor were they persons of interest, according to authorities. The men sued for **defamation** and eventually settled out of court with the Post.[9] The newspaper has a daily circulation of more than 500,000 copies on weekdays, to say nothing of the digital reach of the paper's website, thus making publication fairly easy to prove.

However, this element has never been limited to professional media workers or legacy-media outlets. Information can be sent via email, social media, blog post or other less traditional ways such as a letter-writing campaign or the creation of billboard advertising. Several people have sued singer and actress Courtney Love, accusing her of posting libelous statements on Twitter. In 2009, Love was accused of defaming fashion designer Dawn Simorangkir on the social media platform. The pair eventually settled out of court for nearly $450,000.[10] However, Love won a separate "**Twibel**" case in which lawyer Rhonda Holmes sued her for $8 million. In a tweet, Love said that while Holmes was looking into missing funds from singer Kurt Cobain's estate, the fraud-litigation attorney was "bought off." Throughout the case, the aspect of publication was not an issue in dispute between the parties. A jury in 2014 sided with Love, and a 2016 appeals court affirmed the ruling.[11] It is also worth mentioning that republication is viewed as publication, so in many cases, you can be held liable for repeating someone else's libelous statements.

Singer Courtney Love has been at the center of two key "Twibel" lawsuits that demonstrated social media's relevance in defamation cases.

Falsity

In the United States, the law dictates that the plaintiff must prove the statement is false in order to win a libel suit. This provides the publisher with a distinct advantage, in that the material can be assumed to be truthful until the plaintiff demonstrates otherwise. In addition, the plaintiff must demonstrate that the substantial elements of the statements in question are false. Minor fact errors or simple grammar mistakes are not enough for a plaintiff to win a libel case.

Defamation

The statements must serve to damage the plaintiff's reputation. Often, this defamation is a case of associating the plaintiff with illegal activities, negative personal conduct or illicit personal affairs. In addition, associating people with socially abhorrent diseases can lower the person's standing within a substantial or respectable group. Falsehoods that hurt a person's business opportunities or standing within the community also fit within these parameters.

ABC settled a defamation case with a meat-processing organization after the news outlet used the term "pink slime" to describe one of the company's products.

In 2017, ABC settled a defamation suit brought by Beef Products Inc. as a result of a series of stories the news agency broadcast and published on its website. The food processing company argued that ABC defamed its company by referring to its "lean finely textured beef" as "pink slime" as well as through other errors and omissions in its reporting. ABC did not retract or apologize for the reporting but noted that "continued litigation of this case is not in the company's interest."[12]

Harm

The plaintiff must show that the statements harm that person's reputation. Stewart notes that these can be **actual damages**, such as the inability to earn an income or emotional suffering. The courts also can award **punitive damages**, which serve to punish publishers for disseminating the material. The greater the irresponsibility on the part of the publisher, the higher the likelihood the court will award punitive damages. In addition, damage amounts are usually related to that level of irresponsibility. In the "pink slime" suit noted above, BPI claimed $1.9 billion in harm, noting the company had to close three of its four processing plants and that it saw an 80 percent drop in revenue after ABC published its stories.[13] It settled for an undisclosed amount.

Fault

To prevent a chilling effect on information exchanges, courts traditionally demand that plaintiffs demonstrate that the publisher either did something or failed to do something that led to the libel. Although the standards of **fault** vary based on a number of variables, private individuals usually must show that the defendant acted in a negligent manner. In the case of public figures, the standard is much higher and usually referred to as **actual malice**. This makes it much harder for politicians, celebrities and other **public figures** to win libel cases, as the plaintiffs must show that the publishers knew the material was false and that they failed to act responsibly. In the Love case noted above, the judge ruled that Holmes was a **limited-purpose public figure**, and thus the standard of actual malice applied in that case.

LEGAL DEFENSES AGAINST LIBEL

The information outlined above demonstrates that libel applies to each area of the media field. Anyone who produces content for distribution runs the risk of engaging in libelous behavior. Below is a list of ways you can best defend yourself against a libel suit if you find yourself on the wrong end of one:

Truth

Truth is the ultimate defense against a libel suit. Without this standard, almost every story involving crime and other misdeeds could lead to a libel suit. A reporter who writes a story saying that Jim Dinkel was arrested on suspicion of burglary would obviously run the risk of defaming Dinkel. However, if the reporter could prove that this information was true, Dinkel would have no ground upon which to stand. This is one of the major reasons this book emphasizes the importance of fact checking. If you put out a press release that said a student on your campus stole money from several rooms on his dorm floor, and that information turned out to be wrong, you could be in a world of legal trouble.

Privilege

Absolute privilege allows officials to speak publicly in their official roles without fear of libel. These statements can include official proclamations city officials make to the media regarding a law or comments judges make while issuing verdicts. In some states, this rule even applies to police officers who make statements about criminal cases. If an official is operating under the blanket of **absolute privilege**, journalists operate under **qualified privilege** in reporting the words of these officials. This traditionally covers reporters who quote sources in the course of their work, but others who engage in this practice through a fair and balanced approach to their work can also find protection against libel here.

Hyperbole and Opinion

In examining any libelous statements, courts must determine whether the statement is fact or opinion. An advertisement that says "Gov. John Gobano is a lousy politician" cannot be proved or disproved and thus would likely fall under the protection of opinion. A press release that notes "Gov. John Gobano is the worst politician in the history of all mankind" also could be protected as a hyperbolic statement. Hyperbole is an instance in which something is so ridiculously overblown as to not be believable by anyone of a reasonable mind. Advertisers can make similar statements about products without fear of being sued through the use of **puffery**. This term applies to advertising that attempts to puff up the value of a product without relying on facts. Thus, when a juice company states, "Our product is the most amazing, super-fantastic juice ever!" the company is engaging in puffery.

Simply referring to a statement as an opinion does not shield you from a libel claim. You can't start every libelous sentence you write with "In my opinion" and expect to get away with it. In terms of hyperbole, the statements must not contain factually provable statements. For example, saying a restaurant's hamburger tasted like "a zombie threw up on it" would probably be hyperbolic. However, if you noted that "this was because the waitress stuck it in her armpit for five minutes before serving it," you have introduced information that could be disproved.

The Communications Decency Act

Section 230 of the **Communications Decency Act of 1996** (see Connect box) protects website owners from libel suits based on the comment sections of their websites. This is why when someone makes a horribly defamatory and false statement against someone else on Facebook, Mark Zuckerberg isn't losing millions of dollars because of it. The CDA is meant to allow publishers to encourage public discussion while not penalizing them if they fail to remove comments that could lead to libel suits. Although publishers who incite commenters to post illegal material or who republish libelous statements themselves can be in trouble, when publishers merely provide an open forum and allow the exchange of ideas, the courts have usually found in their favor.

CONNECT

WORKING WITH YOUR READERS TO MAKE THE WORLD A BETTER PLACE

One of the prominent benefits of the web is the ability for people to share their thoughts and ideas with others. Thanks to the prominence of chat rooms, social networking sites and commenting functions as publishers have moved from a one-way conduit of information to better connect with readers.

Unfortunately, the prominence of anonymous posts and the lack of decorum on some of these sites have led to innumerable angry "flame wars," where libel is all too common and human decency is often discarded.

Before the Communications Decency Act, the law put people who created forums between a rock and a hard place. Publishers who provided the open space for discussion were liable for all content if they monitored the message boards and made choices to eliminate certain posts and statements. However, if publishers didn't monitor the content, they sidestepped liability by allowing people to continue to defame one another.

Thus, Congress introduced Section 230 of the Communications Decency Act, which immunized publishers against liability for comments other people made on the publishers' platforms. It also protected publishers who sought to monitor forums and remove defamatory material.

Although you are legally safe when a couple of posters decide to defame each other, as a media practitioner, you should consider it a better practice to make your site a more inclusive, fair and decent place to share thoughts.

The law has held that you have legal protection to screen and filter comments that could be defamatory. In addition, you have the right to monitor and oversee the content others post to your site. Although the internet is often viewed as a free realm of all expression, it does not necessarily follow that you need to let people turn your site into a giant food fight.

If you host open forums or allow commenting on your website, consider integrating a clear set of expectations for posting. You can also require people to register directly to the site or through a third party like Facebook. Although some people have disdained this approach, it can be helpful in some cases in which posters are particularly out of control.

When people post, you should examine the content and allow spirited discourse but also keep an eye on things to make sure they don't get out of hand. It's like when parents of siblings know when the kids are just roughhousing and when things are getting dangerous. Instead of dropping the hammer on people immediately, use redirection techniques and reminders to help rein in the vitriol.

In the end, if people can't play nice, you can always tell them they can't play at your site. Although you may lose some traffic, you can be comforted to know that the posters who remain will consider you a safe and fair place to offer their thoughts.

GIVE IT A TRY: Pick a blog or news site you frequently visit and select an article with a large number of comments. Review the comments for issues associated with libel and defenses against libel. Make a list of the comments you feel meet the threshold associated with libel and which ones you think are just generally distasteful. Discuss your list with your classmates as part of a broader discussion of where you see a line between the comments on your two lists.

The best way to avoid a lawsuit is to carefully check your facts before you publish your content.

© iStockphotos.com/gpointstudio

How to Avoid a Lawsuit in the First Place

One of the unfortunate truisms of the legal system is that it can be costly to defend yourself against a suit. It can also be time-consuming and emotionally taxing as you work your way through the court system. This is why it is almost always best to avoid being a defendant in the first place. Although you can't always stop people from taking you to court, you can minimize your risk through some of these simple approaches to plying your trade:

Check Your Facts

Since truth is the ultimate defense against a libel suit, the quality of your information gathering will ultimately determine how likely you are to be in trouble. People don't like seeing bad things written about them, but they have less legal ground upon which to stand when the facts are not in their favor.

When one source says something that could lead to a libel concern, check that information with another source. Use official sources and back up their statements with documentation when possible. Also, it never hurts to record conversations when possible, as people often forget what they told you and thus deny they said it. The more concrete your facts, the better chance you have of stopping a suit before it gets started.

Re-Verify Your Information

As you work with multiple sources, you can find that sources you interview later in the process might contradict those you spoke with earlier. For example, in crafting a media statement regarding the departure of a high-ranking company official, a source might tell you the person was fired and that you should check with human resources for a full explanation. However, when you check with human resources, an official there could explain that the person resigned as part of an agreement with the company's board. Clearly these statements can't both be true, and if you pick the wrong one you could either look foolish or engage in libel.

In a case like this, you can go back to the first source and explain your dilemma. The source might provide material to support the statement that the person was fired, or he might reconsider his original statement to you. In either case, it pays to check back and make sure you have the best possible version of the facts.

Do Not Extrapolate

One of the more dangerous things you can do is make statements that go beyond what you know for sure. In some cases, media practitioners want to use language that's more common or smooth out some of the jargon that a source uses. Often, this isn't a major problem, but when dealing with potentially libelous information, it is crucial that you don't go beyond what you can prove or clearly attribute to an official source. For example, if you write a story about a car crash and the investigating officer explains that "alcohol was believed to be involved in the crash," you cannot translate that into "the driver was drunk." One statement is speculative, while the other is definitive. In addition, one is a statement of opinion, while the other makes a legal determination. The same thing is true if you are putting together a media statement for a company that "agreed to a contract termination with an employee who was under investigation." Don't say the person "was fired." Although both statements clearly show the person is no longer working for the organization, the second one demonstrates the company took action and that a preponderance of the fault was with the employee. Only say what you know.

Take Good Notes

In some cases, the only thing between you and the ugly side of a lawsuit is your documentation. Take careful notes on all important events and interviews, recording these exchanges when you can. Find documents to support whatever you write, and then verify the information with independent sources. The more you can show that you were responsible in your writing, the better off you will be.

COPYRIGHT

The concept of **copyright** has become much more important in recent years because of the explosion of media outlets and digital technology. Most people understand that they can't pick up a copy of a novel, scratch out the author's name and then claim authorship. However, many people have no problem copying large sections of text or downloading images from the internet to use them for their own purposes. The widespread access to material and the "copy-and-paste" ease with which people can steal content makes copyright something crucial for media practitioners to understand and appreciate.

Copyright affixes itself upon the creation of material in a fixed form. The minute you create an ad, write a story, take a photo or build a graphic, the work becomes yours, and the copyright of that material goes back to you or your employer, depending on the situation. The purpose of a copyright law is to protect material that cannot be safeguarded in other ways from theft. If your roommate steals your laptop, you can call the police, demonstrate that this was your property and have it returned to you. In the case of intellectual property, this simple remedy isn't available, and thus copyright law fills the gap to give you some recourse. In addition, having these laws in place provides a shield against theft from unscrupulous individuals.

HOW TO AVOID COPYRIGHT INFRINGEMENT

Not every use of copyrighted material is a case of infringement. Every day, news organizations, public-relations firms and advertising agencies use material that falls under copyright law without fear of legal concerns. Here are some of the primary areas in which you can avoid legal problems in this area:

Fair Use

Journalists can legally use copyrighted material without the permission of the copyright holder for educational and informational processes under an area of the law called fair use. In most cases, **fair use** applies to news journalists, although this is not the only area of the field covered in this area of protection. One of the primary factors the courts consider in examining fair use is if the copyrighted work is being used to generate a profit for the user as opposed to the copyright holder. The amount of the work someone is using, the amount of alteration done to the original work and the harm it could create regarding the market for the original are all considerations when a court decides on the outcome of a fair-use case.

Creative Commons

Media practitioners can also use some items licensed through a creative commons process without the approval of the owner. Copyrighted material notes "all rights reserved," which means that unless the material falls under a fair-use area, the copyright owner has the sole right to determine any use of the material. However, some individuals wish to see their work used in other venues without relinquishing their rights under copyright and without having to approve each individual request.

Creative commons licensing provides a halfway point for copyright owners who wish to see their work used but only in certain ways. For example, a person who shot a photograph may allow anyone to use the image in any way for noncommercial uses. A different photographer may require an image to be "passed along unchanged and in whole" but allow all use, including commercial use. This means that you could tweak, change, remix or build upon the first photograph and use it in only noncommercial ways. The second photo could be used in any instance, as long as the image is not altered. For a full list of licenses and explanations, go to creativecommons.org.

Permission

This is perhaps the easiest and simplest way to avoid a problem. If you want to use a chunk of text, a photo, a graphic, a clip of video or anything else, you can identify the owner of the material and ask for permission to use it. In the case of some simple uses, such as a limited distribution flier or a news story, a simple exchange of emails can be effective. In the case of bigger organizations, profit-based enterprises and wider distribution, you should include a formal permission form that outlines usage and rights. That form will include how the owner should be credited, any fees associated with the use and other legal wrangling. The key is that you get formal permission from the person who owns the copyright and that you are honest about your intentions. Misrepresenting your goals or assuming you can do what you want with copyrighted material can lead to serious legal problems.

PROFESSIONAL THOUGHTS
ASHLEY MESSENGER

Ashley Messenger has woven her love of the law and her understanding of media together throughout a 20-year career. She worked as an advertising sales representative and a talk-show host for a radio station in New Mexico and served as an in-house lawyer for a small alternative weekly newspaper. She was an attorney for U.S. News and World Report and now works for National Public Radio. She taught at American University, George Mason University, George Washington University and the University of Michigan. She also literally wrote the book on media law, a textbook titled "A Practical Guide to Media Law."

Messenger said one of the biggest misconceptions media students have pertains to the protections of the First Amendment.

"The first thing to know is that the First Amendment doesn't stop people from suing you or censoring you," she said. "There is no First Amendment Fairy who corrects injustices with a ping of her wand. If someone sues you, even if the case has no merit and you will prevail in the end, you must still incur the expense and stress of defending yourself.

"If you are going to write something that is likely to prompt a harsh response, at least go into the situation fully informed and prepared for the potential consequences," she added. "I say that not to deter anyone from expressing themselves, but only to be appropriately thoughtful about the risks they wish to take."

Ashley Messenger

Messenger said one of the more important things media professionals need to understand is how to clearly and accurately express themselves. When writers fail to think about how an audience might interpret a message, legal problems can emerge, she said.

"There is an ongoing tension between what a writer intends to convey and how an audience might interpret the writing," Messenger said. "We can see this tension in some of the libel and **true threat** cases."

Aside from the First Amendment, one of the biggest issues in media today is copyright, she said. Since everyone now can serve as a publisher, through platforms like Facebook and Twitter, Messenger said people need to understand what is and what is not acceptable to use without permission.

"Photos and music present some of the trickiest and most challenging legal issues, in large part, because the rules aren't necessarily obvious or intuitive to a nonlawyer," she said. "With music in particular, the laws are the result of extensive lobbying by various interest groups, and the process for properly licensing music is obscure, time-consuming, arduous and expensive."

(Continued)

(Continued)

Messenger said all professional media operatives have a responsibility to not only understand the law, but also to think seriously about what they are saying and how they are saying it to their audiences.

"Think rigorously about the 'facts' or ideas that are presented to you or that you may wish to present in your writing," she said. "Being able to think critically can help prevent being misled by others who are not fully honest, or it may help you present a difficult, nuanced issue with more precision."

One Last Thing

Q: If you could tell students anything about media writing or anything you have seen in your time in the field, what would it be?

A: Know the difference between facts and opinions—and particularly between facts and your own opinions. This isn't easy. The Supreme Court has struggled with distinguishing facts and opinions, because sometimes they seem very similar. And the "fact-checking" movement will often try to declare as true or false statements that characterize facts. Remember that statements reflect the motives or beliefs of the speaker and may or may not be directly correlated to the truth. And sometimes the truth is that people believe false things....You may also have to subject your own ideas or beliefs to scrutiny. If you cannot separate your own opinions or beliefs from facts, or if you adhere to a belief in the face of significant contrary evidence, you may harm your own credibility.

ETHICS AND THE MEDIA

Trying to fully grasp ethics is a difficult proposition. Organizations such as the Society for Professional Journalists, the Better Business Bureau, the Institute for Advertising Ethics, the American Association of Advertising Agencies and the National Press Photographers Association have credos that outline what members should aspire to uphold. Businesses, such as public-relations firms, advertising agencies and newsrooms, also create their own codes of ethics that allow them to operate in a fair and equitable manner with members of the public. Individuals within the media field will also come to grips with their own sense of right and wrong and how best to engage their audience members.

In each form of media, ethical guidelines outline the symbiotic nature of the reader-writer relationship. The goal in all forms of media is to provide benefits to the audience members while still benefiting the source of the material. Media disseminate information that audience members can read and use. If that content is an ad, the advertiser gains more business while the user gets a better deal. If that content is a public-relations statement, the practitioner draws attention to an issue and the user learns about an event, a person or an idea. Regardless of the platform or the approach, the relationship has to be win/win.

Ethics provide the mutual understanding upon which these goals are outlined. Consumers understand that advertisers intentionally promote their products in hopes of garnering sales, but ethics determine to what degree these promotional attempts are honest and helpful. Readers understand that news coverage will never be perfectly balanced, but a reporter's ethics help the readers understand that objectivity is the standard to which the reporter is aspiring.

ETHICAL CONCERNS

Each area of media has different levels of concerns with certain aspects of ethics. For example, it is perfectly acceptable for a public-relations practitioner to promote a candidate or an event, but news reporters who do the same thing would be in violation of most newsrooms' ethical codes. This isn't to say one area of the field has better or worse levels of ethical behavior. It is just different because of the expectations associated with each area of the field. Here are some key issues all media professionals need to consider:

Trust and Deceit

The most fragile thing you will deal with on a daily basis in media is trust. No matter how good you have been in the past, if you shatter the trust of your audience members, you will never truly repair this sacred bond. One of the easiest ways to break the bond of trust between you and your readers is to engage in deceptive behavior. When news agencies deceive readers, this often limits the credibility of the reporters and editors involved. In some cases, readers view the media outlet as sloppy or stupid as opposed to nefarious. Although this isn't a good thing, it's a lot better than when advertisers or marketers present material that harms the trust of the audience. In these cases, the "sales" element of the field can lead readers and viewers to accuse the practitioners of willful deception for financial gain. Although it is just as likely that the advertising representative or the PR practitioner merely erred, the public is often less willing to be forgiving. To that end, all media outlets must strive for trust and honesty when dealing with their audiences, even though some outlets may be held to a higher level of scrutiny than others.

Connections

The most valuable commodity in the field of media is connections. When you have an inside source, you can get a crucial story before any other news outlet. When you have a great relationship with a reporter, you can get coverage that puts you ahead of your competition. Any time you have a key connection at a crucial spot, you have a decided advantage over everyone else in your area. That said, this relationship could cut both ways, leading to a conflict of interest.

Conflicts of interest can be anything from a reporter dating a source to an advertising executive awarding a contract to a friend. The closer the relationships between professionals, the deeper the potential entanglements are. One of the hardest things about this field is understanding that you can be close, professional colleagues with other people in the field. However, you aren't friends and that can be a fine line to define.

Plagiarism

Anyone who has written a term paper of any kind has heard of this term and generally knows that it means taking credit for someone else's work. However, **plagiarism** can be a lot more complicated than that. Excerpting large sections of previously published materials without citing the materials directly can lead to allegations of plagiarism. In addition, using similar phrasing or specific chunks of information in multiple published pieces can lead to this problem as well.

At the 2016 Republican National Convention, Melania Trump delivered a speech in support of her husband's candidacy for president that contained several passages reminiscent of some statements Michelle Obama made eight years earlier at the Democratic National Convention. As allegations of plagiarism emerged in the media, the campaign denied that the speech contained any borrowed passages, noting that similar phrases could be found in music and even "My Little Pony."[14] A few days later, a speechwriter stepped forward to take responsibility for the "innocent mistake."[15] When you find yourself writing anything you plan to publish, always make sure you have taken pains to keep the writing in your own words.

Financial Pressure

In financial terms, the Golden Rule has often been reinterpreted to say "He (or she) who has the gold makes the rules." The underlying premise of money being a dominant force in media is not without merit. In many cases, power brokers will plow large amounts of funding into advertising and marketing campaigns to bring their interests to bear. This can lead to a concern regarding how much financial interests outweigh the interests of the audience members.

Newspapers and television stations can fear running afoul of a prominent advertiser and thus shy away from important stories that may undermine their financial interests. Public-relations practitioners and advertising executives must consider their clients' interests when putting forth campaigns, understanding that these clients are footing the bill for their operations. In many cases, the financial interests of these media outlets and their ethical concerns do not run contrary to each other. However, when you feel as though your ethics do not match with what is being asked of you, you should discuss the issues at hand with your boss and your financial backers. In some cases, you can come to a fair and ethical compromise. In other cases, you may need to rethink your role in the organization.

ADAPT
PROMOTION OR PAYOLA?

In the world of advertising, marketing and public relations, the goal is often to connect with the members of the news media in a positive way. To help market movies, promoters often offer junkets, in which they bring in journalists to see a movie, meet with the cast and tour some of the sets. The idea is to help the journalists interact with the individuals associated with the offerings and give these reporters a first look at the material. These junkets also often include free travel, lodging and other gratuities.

Music promoters can offer concert tickets or copies of a band's latest album as an enticement for professional writers to cover the group or review its music. By offering these freebies, the promoters can eliminate concerns of financially strapped publications that might otherwise be unable to cover their clients.

These and dozens of other offerings can be viewed by some as smart business, while others see them as **payola**, an ethical breach of the highest order.

The term "payola" became prevalent in the 1950s, when on-air personalities were paid money to put certain songs into heavy rotation on their disc jockey shows.[16] This helped certain artists gain popularity while others fell by the wayside. In the end, the scandal severely damaged the careers of several prominent music insiders, including legendary disc jockey Alan Freed.

These days, the idea of "pay for play" is clearly out of bounds for all members of the news media, and all paid speech is clearly labeled as such, as is the case with advertising. However, other less overt offerings can lead to conflicts of interest for everyone involved when it isn't clear what is and is not acceptable. For event planners, food and drinks are simply good manners, while to some journalists these freebies are ethical violations waiting to happen.

This is not to say that every hamburger is a bribe or that one group of media professionals has higher ethical standards than do others. However, it is important for all individuals in the profession to understand the rules that govern each branch of media. This will allow them to better interact within a set of shared understandings. In addition, it will prevent embarrassing or awkward moments during these interactions.

HOW TO WORK THROUGH ETHICAL DILEMMAS

As with most ethical codes, ethical dilemmas do not have a "right" or a "wrong" answer. In many cases, whichever way you go, the outcome will make you feel awkward. To help guide you, here are a few things to consider before making any ethical decision:

Assess the Situation

The first thing you need to do before you choose your path is to assess the situation. It's just like everything else we have discussed in the book to this point: Before you write, you have to report. Gathering facts, examining points of view and understanding what is being asked of you will help you make better sense of what you must do. If you feel as though you don't have all the necessary information to make an informed ethical decision, do more reporting. If you think you are missing an angle, do your best to get that angle. If you can't fully see all the ramifications of each choice you need to make, go back through each scenario and take another look. Until you cover all of your bases, don't make a move.

Identify the Values

When you work through an ethical dilemma, you should understand what values you are espousing in each choice you could make. In other words, understand what you're doing and why you're doing it. Are you making a choice to benefit your readers or yourself? Are you seeing this as benefiting your sources or your organization? Are you trying to make someone look good or make someone look bad? In each choice, you will provide a benefit to someone and create a detriment for someone else. Consider the values associated with your choices.

Ethics require you to take an in-depth look at every situation before you act.

Discuss the Issue With Others

One of the hardest things to do is to make an ethical decision on your own. The old adage about failing to see the forest for the trees applies here. You can get so bogged down in the minutiae or feel pulled in so many directions that a logical decision can often elude you. The benefit of working in media organizations is that you can draw from a pool of others who can provide you with some perspective. People in your office might have dealt with a similar situation and can tell you how things worked out for them. People with different backgrounds can provide you with a fresh way to see the issue that you might not have originally considered. At the very least, involving your direct supervisor in your quandary can be helpful. If you have a good boss, you can get some great advice from that person. If you have a great boss, you will find that person backing you up during the decision and in the wake of any backlash.

Pick a Line and Drive

You can twist yourself into knots over every decision you make that has an ethical component to it. However, once you make your choice, you need to stand behind what you do. You might end up facing some pretty grumpy people (or worse), but in the end, if you did the best you could, you can feel satisfied in knowing that you could live with yourself once you made the choice and faced the consequences.

DETERMINING YOUR OWN APPROACH TO ETHICS

You will have to determine on your own what your own ethical code will be and how strongly you will stand by it. In some cases, your ethical standards will be higher or lower than those of the organization for which you work. If you find that you can't handle the disparity between your approach to ethics and the organization's approach, you might need to reconsider your position within the field.

Ethical texts outline the various forms of ethical decision making and ethical standards. Rather than run through every possible approach to ethical reasoning, here are some things to consider as you shape your own approach to ethics:

Embrace Humanity

Although we individually identify with specific sections of the media field, such as advertising, news or public relations, the common thread of basic human decency links us. The nature of humanity is one that we should all seek to embrace as part of our ethical codes. Media professionals who act decently toward one another, treat all people with dignity and create a fair ethical platform are more likely to receive humane treatment in return. Although society often casts people in the roles of "winners" and "losers," a general sense of respect for all people can create a strong ethical baseline upon which we can best plot our own ethical course.

HELPFUL HINTS

A QUICK LOOK AT VARIOUS ETHICAL STANDARDS

Ethics occur on a continuum of human behavior and often lack concrete rules and regulations. As you develop your own ethical codes and standards, you might find it hard to explain exactly how you view your own position in this area. In his book "The Dynamics of Mass Communication," author Joseph R. Dominick outlined several dominant types of ethical typologies[17] that might help you see where you best fit:

The Golden Mean

The underlying assumption in this approach is that the most good happens when people find a middle ground for their choices. News agencies balance the right of people to know against the rights of individuals to be left alone. Advertising practitioners work with clients to find ground between running an ad that might anger some people and pulling the advertisement entirely. This approach seeks compromise and adjustments that create an overall "sweet spot."

The Categorical Imperative

Individuals who espouse this form of ethical behavior use their conscience to determine what is right and what is wrong and then act accordingly. In this approach, every action should be logically based, and people should act in a way that they believe all other people should also act. Thus, if you believe it is OK to lie to someone, it is perfectly acceptable for them to lie to you, under this form

of reasoning. Less nuanced readers of this philosophy equate it to the Golden Rule, in that you should do unto others as you would have them do unto you. However, the philosophy is a bit broader than that because it requires that all people act in the ways in which they would like everyone to act toward everyone else.

The Principle of Utility

This is an ethical code that measures a net benefit that results from the behavior and thus prompts the media professional to act accordingly. This philosophy seeks to maximize the overall gains or limit the overall harm for the most people. Companies use this approach when examining things like automobile recalls. The organization looks at the overall harm that could come to people if the vehicles aren't recalled against other losses, such as diminished consumer confidence or stock-price declines. If the defect is minor, such as the paint on a plastic radio knob wearing off too quickly, the company might not issue the recall. If the problem is severe, such as a failing steering or braking system, the company will likely recall the vehicles.

The Veil of Ignorance

This approach is used to remove qualifiers in negotiations of specific ethical situations. In other words, everyone should be treated the same, regardless of any mitigating circumstances. To that end, if you decide that attack advertisements are an ethically acceptable form of discourse, you would run them against candidates who were Democrats or Republicans. You would also not distinguish among issues of gender, race, age or other similar factors in your choices. As Dominick states in explaining this approach, "Justice is blind."

The Principle of Self-Determination

People who adhere to this ethical standard understand that people have rights that should be respected. In dealing with others, people who espouse the principle of self-determination understand that they can't use other people as a means to their own ends. To that end, the relationship among media professionals as well as between them and the public needs to be mutually beneficial. A reporter can't violate the rights of a source simply to get a story, or a public relations practitioner can't use a reporter to libel a competitor. Everyone's sense of self-determination must be respected.

Experience Is the Best Teacher

Ethical codes are not like luggage: You don't get one set and keep it for life. Instead, throughout your life, you will have a number of experiences that will shape and change the way you see the world. Each experience has the potential to shift your approach to ethics or codify the way you deal with them. For example, you may start out viewing the world totally as a "black or white" proposition, only to find through working in the field that there are many shades of gray. This could embolden you to strengthen your position as someone who believes in right and wrong, or this realization could lead you to decide ethical dilemmas on a case-by-case basis. Do not discount your experiences as you work in this field, and don't miss the chance to see how they might influence your ethical approach to your work.

Understand the Impact of Your Actions

Each choice you make will have a ripple effect on other people and their choices. Understanding how far those ripples reach and what they do to the rest of the pool will help you work more judiciously as an ethical media member. If all you care about is getting the big story or selling the most units, you will see your audience turn on you. If you fail to take a stand on important issues inside and outside of your organization, your audience may view you with a lack of trust. In the end, understanding what will come from each action is crucial to making your best ethical choices.

Examine Codes of Others

When you take words or images from other people, it can be called plagiarism or copyright infringement. However, learning how to create your own ethical code by studying other people's approaches to ethical behavior can lead to some really good outcomes for you. Some people might be older than you and have seen more things than you have. Other people have different life experiences that can provide you with a diverse set of ideas that you could not have found on your own. Look at what these people have to say and see what rationale they offer for their choices.

THE BIG THREE

Here are the three key things you should take away from this chapter:

1. **Embrace law and ethics:** Law and ethics differ regarding their application to the media and various media outlets, but media practitioners should understand the importance of both of them. Remaining on the proper side of the law is crucial, but unethical behavior that skates on the edge of

the law will undermine your ability to build and maintain an interested audience for your content.

2. **Just because you can do something, it doesn't necessarily follow that you should:** In the case of the law, you can easily copy or "borrow" material from the web, but doing so may have you running afoul of the law. Using puffery to sell a product

or shady reporting tactics to get a story may yield short-term results but will cost you in the long run.

3. **Focus on your readers:** The way in which you prioritize your values or conduct yourself legally should keep the focus on the people you serve. The choices you make will directly affect them, and you need to understand how that will occur.

KEY TERMS

absolute privilege 131

actual damages 130

actual malice 130

Bill of Rights 125

categorical limitations 126

Communications Decency Act
     of 1996 131

copyright 133

creative commons 134

defamation 129

fair use 134

fault 130

First Amendment 125

identification 128

libel 128

limited-purpose public figures 130

medium-based limitations 126

payola 138

plagiarism 137

public figures 130

publication 129

puffery 131

punitive damages 130

qualified privilege 131

time-place-manner limitations 126

true threat 135

Twibel 129

DISCUSSION QUESTIONS

1. What do you think is the most difficult ethical challenge you would face during your career in media? Why do you think this is the case? Do you think this is an issue that pertains only to your area, but not to other areas? For example, is this challenge a bigger problem in news than it is in public relations? Why or why not?

2. What are some of the more common misperceptions associated with the First Amendment? What are some of the dangers associated with not fully understanding what the amendment actually does?

3. What is copyright, and why is it crucial to all forms of media? What do you see as the benefits and drawbacks associated with copyright protection?

WRITE NOW!

1. Find a media report in which someone is actively suing someone else for libel. Briefly explain the key elements of the case and then apply the key aspects of successful libel suits as noted by Chip Stewart earlier in the chapter. Then examine the key defenses listed in this chapter and apply each of them to the case. Finally, write a short essay that explains whether you think the person suing

will eventually win, including why you think as you do.

2. Write a two-page essay in which you outline your overall approach to ethical behavior. What kind of ethical code have you adopted in your life, and why do you think it fits who you are? Then explain how you think this might fit with or come into conflict with the area of media in which you most want to

work. How do you think you will manage to shape and grow your ethical paradigm as you become a media professional in that area?

3. Find an ethics code that oversees your media field of choice (advertising, public relations, photography, news, etc.) and compare it with the ethical code used in one other area of the field. Write a two-page essay explaining how they are similar and how they are different. Focus on the key areas of similarity and describe why you think these are important. Also, explain to what degree the differences are important and why you think they exist.

NOTES

1. A. Packard (2012). "Digital Media Law." Hoboken, N.J.: Wiley-Blackwell.

2. J. Bilyk (2017, June 17). "IL Supreme Court: IL Constitution Doesn't Expand Protesters' Assembly Rights Beyond First Amendment." Cook County Record. Accessed at: http://cookcountyrecord.com/stories/511128771-il-supreme-court-il-constitution-doesn-t-expand-protesters-assembly-rights-beyond-first-amendment.

3. Associated Press. (2011, Sept. 12). "Is Horn Honking Protected Free Speech?" Wisconsin Law Journal. Available at: http://wislawjournal.com/2011/09/12/is-horn-honking-protected-free-speech/.

4. K. Rosenauer and V. Filak (2013). "The Journalist's Handbook to Online Editing." New York: Pearson.

5. J-M Manufacturing Co. v. Philips & Cohen. Available at: http://law.justia.com/cases/california/court-of-appeal/2016/b256927.html.

6. J. Ronson (2015, Feb. 12). "How One Stupid Tweet Blew up Justine Sacco's Life." New York Times Magazine. Accessed at: https://www.nytimes.com/2015/02/15/magazine/how-one-stupid-tweet-ruined-justine-saccos-life.html.

7. Valentine v. Chrestensen, 316 U.S. 52 (1942). Available at: http://uscivilliberties.org/cases/4658-valentine-v-chrestensen-316-us-52-1942.html.

8. D. R. "Chip" Stewart (2015). "The Law and Convergent Journalism." In V. Filak (Ed.), "Convergent Journalism: An Introduction" (2nd ed.). Boston, Mass.: Focal.

9. Associated Press. (2014, Oct. 2). "New York Post Settles Lawsuit Over 'Bag Men' Cover Following Boston Marathon Bombing." New York Daily News. Available at: http://www.nydailynews.com/new-york/new-york-post-settles-lawsuit-bag-men-cover-article-1.1960843.

10. S. Frizell (2014, April 8). "Courtney Love's Bittersweet Twitter Update." Time. Available at: http://time.com/54276/courtney-love-twitter-defamation-lawsuits/.

11. E. Gardner (2016, Feb. 1). "Courtney Love's 'Twibel' Win Upheld By Appeals Court." Hollywood Reporter. Accessed at: http://www.hollywoodreporter.com/thr-esq/courtney-loves-twibel-win-upheld-861153.

12. T. McLaughlin (2017, June 28). "ABC TV Settles With Beef Product Maker in "Pink Slime" Defamation Case." Reuters. Accessed at: https://www.reuters.com/article/us-abc-pinkslime-idUSKBN19J1W9.

13. Associated Press (2017, June 28). "ABC, Meat Company Settle $1.9 Billion 'Pink Slime' Suit." Accessed at: https://www.cbsnews.com/news/abc-settles-with-meat-company-in-1-9-billion-pink-slime-suit/.

14. S. Tatum (2016, July 19). "RNC Official Cites 'My Little Pony' to Defend Melania Trump." CNN. Accessed at: http://www.cnn.com/2016/07/19/politics/sean-spicer-melania-trump-my-little-pony/index.html.

15. M. Reston. (2016, July 20). "Trump Campaign Tries to Move on From Plagiarism Controversy." CNN. Accessed at: http://www.cnn.com/2016/07/20/politics/donald-trump-campaign-organization/index.html.

16. D. K. Peneny (2017, May 17). Payola. Accessed at: http://www.history-of-rock.com/payola.htm.

17. J. R. Dominick (2011). "Dynamics of Mass Communication" (11th ed.). New York: McGraw-Hill.

FOCUS ON
NEWS MEDIA

© iStockphoto.com/microgen

9

REPORTING

The Basics and Beyond

LEARNING OBJECTIVES

After completing this chapter you should be able to:

- List several places from which you can gather story ideas that will engage your readers and interest your audience.

- Define and differentiate among the main types of events you might cover.

- Explain why event coverage matters and how each type of event can affect your audience members.

- Show how to gather information in advance of a story to create a story shell.

- Discuss the reasons why certain story types, such as profiles, localizations and obituaries, matter to your readers.

- Explain the value of a news peg and how it can make your story more valuable to your readership.

Reporting will take you through a number of situations that can run the gamut of happy moments and tragic events. As you experience these stories, you will find that certain types of coverage best suit you. If you work for a newspaper or a niche website, you might work on a beat, which is a specialized area of news coverage. In broadcast or in broader based web publications, you could work as a general-assignment reporter, which will have you covering government issues one day and environmental news the next.

This chapter will outline the various types of stories you will see over the course of your reporting career. The list will not be exhaustive, nor will it provide you with the perfect way to cover everything you will see. In some areas of the field, such as crime reporting, experience will be your only true teacher. The chapter will, however, examine ways you can prepare to cover certain basic stories. We will then look at some of the types of stories and areas of coverage you might encounter in your career.

EVENT COVERAGE

An event can be a well-planned announcement that a strong public relations firm creates to disclose an important discovery, the candidacy of an individual running for office or a civic improvement. It can also be a chaotic crime scene, an unpredictable natural disaster or an unfolding crisis. Somewhere in between these extremes are the speeches and meetings that serve as the staple crop of most standard media outlets.

Not every meeting, speech or news conference merits news coverage, so the best way to determine whether you should cover an event comes down to your audience's needs. As you assess the value of the event, you need to figure out why this would matter to the people who are reading what you are writing. Remember to keep the FOCII elements at the front of your mind and see to what degree these will apply to the event. Then decide whether you should attend the event.

Events such as speeches and news conferences often draw a large collection of reporters to a single place to learn about important information.

Types of Events

On some beats, you will cover events such as fires, floods, shootings and other mayhem. On other beats, you need to learn Robert's Rules of Order to fully understand what a board or a committee is doing. Here are a few major types of events you might see during a reporting career:

Breaking News

Anytime something out of the ordinary occurs, reporters need to gather information on it. **Breaking news** comes from crimes and disasters that happen at random times in odd locations. Reporters often head to the scene of the event and gather as much information as possible. Breaking news events are among the most difficult stories for reporters to cover because the events lack structure and don't provide you with much of a chance to prepare. Even more, most of your sources are as uninformed as you are because the event is continuing to unfold.

Speeches

A speech allows someone to talk to a general or specific audience for a set period of time on a topic that matters to both the speaker and the audience. Speeches are often tailored to the audience members, and because they usually involve a singular point of view, they tend to be one-sided affairs. However, these can be good events to cover, as you can help share a person's expertise on a key topic with your readers.

Meetings

A meeting is an event where a governing body of representatives comes together to deal with the business pertaining to that group or the people that the group represents. At this type of event, your job as a reporter is to sit in as a substitute for your readers and distill for them what happened. You don't want to cover any event from the angle of "an event happened," and that is especially true when it comes to a meeting. As we will explain more later in the chapter, you need to choose a specific element of the meeting or a few important items and show your readers why the focus of your story matters to them.

News Conferences

These events help a person or an organization disseminate a single message to multiple media outlets in a single moment. This is a great thing for the media professionals who host the events (see Chapter 12 for a discussion of this), because it allows them to release information all at once instead of sending it out in bits and bites. In addition, it prevents them from having to answer the same questions over and over again during multiple interviews with reporters. From a reporting perspective, you can get a lot of great information because the event is essentially built for you and because sources at the event are usually willing to speak with you. In addition, the practitioners who host the events often have a wide array of background information and other media-release items for you, which can make your reporting job easier.

PREPARING FOR THE EVENT

As noted throughout the book, preparation and accuracy are crucial for success in all aspects of the field. When it comes to covering an event, you need to prepare diligently because you are going to be outside of your comfort zone mentally and outside of your workspace physically. In short, you must be ready for whatever happens. Here are some key aspects of preparation in this area:

Learn What to Expect

If you never attended a speech or meeting before as a journalist, you should spend some time getting acclimated to what will likely happen. This includes understanding the physical layout of the room, who is involved and what will occur at the event. You can get this kind of information from other reporters who have attended events like this one. If you are going somewhere new and no one in your newsroom can help you, consider traveling to the venue before the event. You also should contact the event coordinators to find out what they expect to occur and how long the event will be.

Seek Background

As noted in Chapter 5, the more prepared you are for an interview, the better questions you can ask. The value of preparation is also crucial as you cover meetings, speeches and news conferences. Background research helps you determine what will happen at the event and who is involved. It can also help you feel more confident as you ask questions after the event or during a question-and-answer portion of it. Before you attend an event, gather as much background information as you can.

ADAPT

SHELLING A STORY

One of the things you will face in every area of the media is deadline pressure. You need to perform well when time is not your ally to get your message across. If you need to get a story done in a hurry, you should consider shelling your story. This term refers to typing up a basic set of elements in a story file ahead of time so that all you have to do is add the new material when you get it. Shell information can include some of the background you gathered, any quotes you got from sources before the event and optional lead elements, based on the outcome of the event. Here's an example of a simple meeting **shell**:

> The Springfield City Council (PASSED/REJECTED) a proposal Tuesday night by a X–X vote that would increase property taxes by 2.2 percent to help fund street repair and improvement.

"QUOTE GOES HERE FROM WINNING SIDE"

BACKGROUND: The increase was at the core of a months-long debate between Republicans and Democrats on the council. Several Republicans, including Council President Jane Carleton, ran their recent re-election campaigns on a promise to defeat the measure.

The proposal had come before the council three times already this year, only to be tabled or rejected due to procedural issues. This approach to the tax increase caused several Democrats to lament the ineffective nature of the council.

"We are caught in a cycle of perpetual do-nothing syndrome," First District Alderman Jackie Venash said at last month's meeting. "If this doesn't eventually pass, we'll all need a bunch of pack

(Continued)

(Continued)

mules to traverse our roads, if people don't vote us out first."

At Tuesday's meeting, Venash said SOMETHING GOES HERE

QUOTE FROM VENASH

FINISH STORY

As you can see, the shell allows you to build a lead based on the idea that an important item will either pass or fail. It also allows you to infuse background information and prepare for a transition to the new material. Although the shell isn't long or involved, it prevents you from having to scramble for information at the last minute.

GIVE IT A TRY: Look for a meeting or speech in your area that interests you and create a shell for the event. Research the event, gather relevant documents and reach out to at least one human source for some pre-reporting information. Then, build a shell based on what you have available to you. Feel free to follow up by attending the event and complete the story.

HOW TO COVER THE EVENT

Once you get to an event, you want to assess the situation to determine what might make for interesting and engaging content. Not all events are created equal, and what you expect to happen might not occur. Conversely, sometimes you end up with an incredible story when you didn't expect it. Here are some things to consider when covering an event:

Find the Core

The purpose of any event story is to find the most important aspects of what happened and report them to people who need to know about them. This means that you need to sift through the whole event and determine what matters most instead of simply regurgitating the entire meeting or speech in a chronological format.

As discussed in Chapter 4, the inverted pyramid allows you to focus on the most important element of the story in the lead and then add supporting paragraphs in descending order of importance. To locate those key elements, focus on the FOCII elements noted throughout the book. Then view them through the lens of what you think people would want to know most. This will allow you to zero in on the core of the story and then tell that story effectively.

Look Outside the Lines

What happens when the speaker takes to the microphone or when a group votes on an issue should matter a great deal to your readers. That said, a lot of things that make for interesting content happen "outside the lines" of the event itself. Occasionally, people will stage a protest and draw attention to the concerns they have with the event. In other cases, people will address a board or a council with their concerns during an open-forum portion of an event. Just because you hadn't planned for these things, it doesn't necessarily follow that they don't matter to your readers.

In November 2006, conservative activist David Horowitz came to Ball State University to speak to a group of college Republicans. As he approached the Teachers College building in which he was to speak, he was met by a giant image, projected on the side of the building, noting "Horowitz not welcome." When he entered the building, two protesters attacked him with cream pies, instead striking the police officers who provided

Horowitz with security. When he finally got to his speaking venue, Horowitz was met by a "pizza prank" as someone had called in a pizza order of $230 in his name. Although Horowitz's speech was an event worth covering, the additional elements of his arrival matter, too. You should always look for opportunities to capture the whole event, not just what is happening in the official area of discussion.

David Horowitz speaks to an audience at the CPAC convention. A November 2006 speech Horowitz gave on the campus of Ball State University was more noteworthy for the things that happened outside the lines than what he said from behind the podium.

Post-Event Interviews

Once the event ends, your work is just starting. At many speaking events, people have a predetermined script, which limits their overall spontaneity. Their formal language may not make a lot of sense to your readers, so you should try to meet with the participants after the main event ends. Post-meeting interviews can also be helpful to flesh out the "why" elements of your story. In the earlier example about the property tax increase, you can see how people voted, but they might not fully explain during the meeting why they chose to vote the way they did. When you talk to people after the event, you can delve deeper into their thought process in terms of the vote and what they think might follow after the outcome. You can also ask them to elaborate on any comments they made in the meeting.

Seek Secondary Sources

Just because people weren't at the microphone or voting on an issue, it doesn't mean they shouldn't have a voice in your story. You should look for secondary sources at an event to augment your coverage. These sources can include members of a group that helped arrange a speaker, area residents who protested an event or witnesses to breaking news. They can also include audience members at a speech and citizens who will feel the impact of a policy that a council or board approved. This will help you round out your overall coverage and give your readers a more complete view of what occurred at the event.

Check Your Facts

As noted in Chapter 2, accuracy is crucial to all forms of media writing. In every piece of writing, you should make sure you have proper nouns spelled right, events outlined in their correct sequence and outcomes presented in a clear and coherent way. In the case of an event where someone is passing public policy or at a disaster where people are hurt, accuracy becomes more important than ever.

Many meetings use formal rules, such as **Robert's Rules of Order**, which can be confusing even to some participants. As you watch people second motions, clarify intent or vote on issues, you can get really turned around and feel unsure of what you think you saw. Rather than guess, go ask someone who is involved in the meeting to help you understand what is going on. A quick five-minute check-in can help you avoid a day of confused consumers and painful corrections.

Get Contact Information

Even the best journalists know they will miss something during the reporting process. The reporter might have heard only two of the three key points someone outlined in a speech. After interviewing Politician A, a comment from Politician B might force the reporter to contact Politician A again for a response. Perhaps an editor will raise an issue that the reporter can't answer with the information he or she gathered initially. Regardless of the reason, you always want to have additional access to your sources.

Before you leave an event, check with each person you plan to use in your story, confirm any key elements and then ask how you can reach that person later. This could be a cell phone number, a social media handle or an email address, so long as it is something that will give you the best possible access to that source. Although some people might be reticent to give you their contact information, you can always explain that you might need them to help you clarify something important and you don't want to make a mistake. Most people will then likely give you what you need, as they will appreciate your honesty and your desire to be accurate.

NEWS REPORTING BEYOND THE EVENT

Reporters can't wait around in hopes that a car crash will occur or that a speech will take place every day. They need to go out and find things that matter to their readers beyond simple event coverage. Some reporters will become experts in certain areas of coverage, while others will focus more on "people" stories that help readers get to know about members of the public. The remainder of the chapter will discuss the ways in which you can find things to cover, both in terms of how you seek news and the types of stories you can find. We will begin by exploring those areas of coverage known as beats and then dig into some stories types that are common for newer journalists: features, profiles, localizations and obituaries.

BEATS

Some journalists cover a wide array of topics on a general-assignment desk. From day to day, their lives could include school board coverage and fatality crashes. However, many journalists who work in larger print-style newsrooms or niche publications work on specific areas of coverage called **beats**. A beat approach allows the reporter to become a contact point for people with an interest in a topic area who want to see certain things covered. In addition, a reporter who covers an area repeatedly is more likely to become knowledgeable on that area and also cultivate quality sources.

© iStockphoto.com/paulprescott72

News journalists report specific areas of coverage, known as beats, so they can become experts on the topics and issues in those areas.

Types of Beats

Beats vary based on the types of publications for which you write. In the case of a small-town newspaper, a reporter might be assigned to education or government as a beat, while a much larger paper might have reporters assigned to specific levels of education, such as K–8, high school and college. A government beat might include a reporter who attends to national issues, another who monitors the statehouse and then a few who cover city, county and regional government activities. Beat types tend to break down into three general areas:

Thematic Beats

These are the beats that focus on specific aspects of coverage, such as police news, court coverage, higher education reporting and religious information. **Thematic beats** can involve a wide geographic area or be concentrated in several key areas within the circulation range of a traditional publication. For digital publications, information can be more or less local, based on the target audience it has established. For example, a website that covers entertainment news has the potential to be a global force that touches on movies, music and theater anywhere that news on these topics happen. Conversely, another website that covers entertainment news might focus only on the local music scene of a college town and the theater department associated with that area's university.

Geographic Beats

The beats that fit this area look into specific regions that don't need more than one or two reporters to cover everything going on. A publication might use a single reporter to cover rural areas throughout the state, but a larger newspaper might station one reporter in a town or two and have that person cover everything out there. Some cities are composed of multiple boroughs or zones and reporters are dispatched to these areas. In the case of **geographic beats**, coverage efforts are more about the physical place and what is happening there than any particular aspect of one thematic area.

Conceptual Beats

Beyond the standard beats are things that require a more ethereal approach to beat coverage. **Conceptual beats** focus on things that lack a concrete definition or a central junction point for coverage. Reporters here rely on ideas such as multiculturalism, investigative reporting or data-driven journalism to drill into bigger issues that can arise from investigating with broader concepts or specific tools. Although these issues can come up on any of the other beats discussed, in some news organizations, these reporters receive the opportunity to focus solely on this kind of coverage.

Covering a Beat

The way you cover a beat will largely depend on what beat you get. Certain beats, like sports and city government, will have regularly scheduled events that you need to cover. Other beats, like regional coverage or investigative reporting, will be more free-form. However, consider some of the following items as boilerplate rules for covering a beat:

BEFORE YOU START

Interview your predecessor: You will probably take over your beat from someone who is moving on to something else, be it retirement, another beat or another job. This person is a crucial resource for you as you determine what you need to do first on your beat. Beat work is never really "done," so the person working on the beat before you likely has some great thoughts about what has been going on up until that point.

Ask that person a few simple questions to help you get an idea about the beat. These questions can include:

- What are some big events that will be happening soon on the beat?

- What stories need follow-up work?

- Do you have any of those "I wish I had gotten to that!" pieces that you think should be done on the beat?

If you can pump your predecessor for information, you can have a running start on the topic. You can also learn which sources are helpful and which people you should avoid. Not everything this person says should be taken as gospel, and you are free to form your own opinions, but you want to make sure you get a sense of things before you begin working on your beat.

Read your own publication: Most newsrooms have either an electronic or traditional **morgue** of stories reporters wrote. In some newsrooms, librarians can help you figure out what you need and where it lives. In other cases, you have to do some digging on your own. The more you read, the better sense you will have as to what things are happening in your coverage area.

Talk to your boss: Each boss will expect different things from a beat. Some bosses demand a heavy level of daily stories, such as meeting pieces, "who's who" stories and other day-in, day-out fodder. Other bosses want more complex pieces, such as personality profile stories and investigative reports. Before you start working, make sure you know what your boss wants. Otherwise, it's like going grocery shopping without a list.

Beginning Your Beat

Get out of the office: One of the biggest mistakes new reporters make is to cold-call sources and figure stories will fall from the sky. If you want to call people to set up formal meetings, that's fine, but being someplace is better than being on the phone and hoping news will find you. Go to the main hub of the beat. If you cover the city government beat, head to city hall. If you cover K–12 education, you need to visit the administrative office for the school district. In other words, go someplace and start looking around.

Build sources: Part of what makes a source work for you is if the source knows you and has learned to trust you. Good sources can guide you to important people and big events. As a new reporter in the area, you need to learn what makes for valuable news in the places you cover. In some towns, the local Corn Days Parade might be extremely important, while in other areas, the Annual Sturgeon Spearing Season will lead the news daily. Getting to know sources is a lot like the early stages of a dating relationship: You get to know each other, learn what you can say or do and eventually start a relationship. You also must realize that this will take time. If you're one of a dozen reporters with whom this person interacts, you could get lost in the shuffle. Take your time, be patient and slowly build toward mutual understanding.

Gather documents: Although people can be more or less forthcoming when it comes to information, documents have an uncanny ability to tell the truth in black and white. This makes the process of gathering documents critical to your success on the beat. Look around your beat to figure out what kinds of documents will yield interesting information. They can be as simple as the annual budgets for a school system or the agendas of the monthly school board meetings. They can be as complicated as the retirement pension allocation for teachers and administrators or the contracts associated with the purchase of state vehicles. Many of these are available online, while others can be requested from the official record keepers on your beat. Documents help beat reporters figure out what matters most on that beat.

Continual Beat Work

Follow-up calls: Each time you finish a story, you want to check back with your sources to see if you need to do a follow-up story. In some cases, a story starts and ends in one piece. In most cases, news coverage will lead to an "arc" of story elements that will be part of a continuing dialogue between your news outlet and the community. When you work on a story, you want to check back for continuing developments since the last time you published something. These follow-up efforts will show your sources that you really care about their concerns.

Connect the dots: If you find yourself covering the same stories over and over again, you should see if a bigger trend is present. If you are on the crime beat and you notice that a certain neighborhood has seen an increase in police calls for robberies over the past year, do some digging to see if something has changed recently about that neighborhood. If you are working on an education beat, you might notice that the demographics of the teaching pool remain at about 25 years of age and three years of experience. As time progresses, both should increase, so there might be a massive influx of newer teachers or a spate of retirements. If you dig into this area, you can find a good trend story.

PROFESSIONAL THOUGHTS
ERIC DEUTSCH

Eric Deutsch knew he wanted to be a radio reporter since he was in high school. A veteran of several Midwest and East Coast radio stations, Deutsch said the medium fit his "casual, laidback, quirky style more than the serious suit-and-tie, superficial atmosphere" associated with other fields. However, after his position at WTDY-AM was cut, he found himself looking outside of radio for the next big thing.

"I looked in the nonprofit/government/PR field because I realized I wanted to be on the other side of the business, being the one making the news instead of the one reporting the news," he said. "I had good writing and communication skills and knew how to work with reporters having been one myself."

Today, Deutsch works for the New York City Housing Authority, where he is a writer and editor of standard procedures and manuals. He previously worked for the organization as the publications manager, where he oversaw the NYCHA Journal, a tabloid, bilingual newspaper that is sent to the 400,000-plus residents of public housing in New York City and several other publications. In this realm, Deutsch said he still draws from his radio experience on a daily basis, especially as it pertains to getting people what they want to know quickly.

"When I was a reporter, I would cover long news conferences, or budget announcements, or complicated crime stories that print or TV had the space and

time to explain," he said. "But it was more difficult in radio, because all I had time for were a few sentences and a sound bite. I needed to hit the main one or two points and that's it. This has served me very well in my current field, because that training and experience allows me to excise the extraneous items and make sure to focus on and include the information that really matters to the reader."

It is that approach to audience-centric information that Deutsch says matters most at NYCHA because there are more than 12,000 employees who must understand how the organization's complicated processes operate so they can do their jobs.

"Connecting with and writing for your audience is very important," he said. "At NYCHA, with anything any of us write, our underlying thought is: 'What do the employees responsible for this task care about, what do they want to know?' Of course we need to get our agency's message points out also, but it has to be done in a way that makes our audience want to read about it and care about it."

To get to the heart of these procedures and manuals, Deutsch said his reporting skills come in handy when he speaks with agency department heads, lawyers and subject matter experts.

(Continued)

(Continued)

"Not being afraid is important," he said. "You can't be afraid to ask people the tough questions or to make a live report just using some quickly scribbled notes....In my second career, I can't have fear if I'm going to voice my opinion even if it differs from the head of my agency."

Although radio was his first love, he said his current job is extremely satisfying. In that career, he is able to transfer not only his writing and editing skills, but also other things he learned along the way.

"Non-writing skills can be transferable also," he said. "Having experience on-air means you could be good at leading meetings, making presentations and public speaking. Having layout experience can transfer to making PowerPoint presentations. Interviewing elected officials and newsmakers can help if you work in an intergovernmental affairs office."

One Last Thing

Q: If you could tell students anything about writing or skill acquisition, based on your experiences or anything you've seen, what would it be?

A: People always should look at any skills they acquire as something that can be adapted for use in any job.

FEATURES

As a journalist, you should always look for interesting items that will draw your readers' attention. These kinds of stories can emerge from trends you notice on your beat, interesting people you meet or generally intriguing concepts you encounter in your daily life. Features give you the opportunity to stretch yourself as a reporter and a writer as you learn about things outside of your comfort zone. Here are some of the basic ideas to consider when you look into building feature stories:

Identify the Main Assertion

At the core of every good story is a key point, occasionally referred to as a **main assertion**. One of the better ways of identifying this point is by completing the sentence "This matters because…." In doing this, you might touch on the following questions:

- What makes this story interesting and worth telling?

- Is the story about an individual or a broader concept associated with this person?

- Is this a "small picture" story, where you focus on one instance of something or a "big picture" piece where you see a larger trend?

Other questions will pop up along the way as well, but in each news feature, you need to identify what makes this story important.

Find Competing Stories

See if there are other stories out there on your topic, and determine how this one is going to be different. It isn't easy to create a story that no one has ever written before. However, the more you know about the stories others have written on your topic, the more you can do to make yours special. When you find other stories like the one you want to write, you can see if you can tailor your piece to your audience better. You can also look for angles that went uncovered, updates that the previous story missed and other bits of information that could give you a reason to write your piece.

CONNECT
FIND A NEWS PEG

The question of "Why are you telling this story now?" often comes up with news features. A **news peg** provides the clear answer to this question, as it serves as the rationale for telling your readers a story at a given time. The term refers to the idea that you want to "hang" your story on a timely factor, much like you would hang a coat on a hook or peg on a wall. The better the peg, the better job you will do of connecting with your audience.

The news peg could be something as simple as a trend or a time of year. For example, during hunting season, hunting publications will run pieces on the trends associated with tracking and cleaning certain animals. On the other hand, general news publications run hunter-safety stories and pieces on the overall outcome of the season's harvest.

If you decide to write a retrospective piece, you need to find a reason for why you should write a story on that topic right now. Round numbers are nice, so the 50th anniversary of an incredible sports triumph or important legislation might make for a good story. People like 25th and 75th anniversaries of things as well.

If you're looking for a historic moment, odd anniversaries are usually not a good idea, unless they have a deeper meaning. For example, the 18th anniversary of something is probably not going to fly very well unless it was something like the 18th anniversary of the amendment that gave 18-year-olds the right to vote.

Regardless of your approach to your news peg, you want to make sure that your story connects with the needs of the reader. Don't put a story on how to clean your grill into the winter issue of your magazine. Don't tell people how to avoid stress during finals week in the "Welcome Back to School" issue of your campus newspaper.

When you do some general reporting on a topic, you can usually find a good peg for a story. If you can't find a good news peg, tuck that idea away for a later time when the peg will become more relevant to your readers.

GIVE IT A TRY: Let's reverse the process to make this a bit easier. Here is a list of potential "peg-worthy" elements and ideas that could lead to a good story. Research your audience and your area for potential stories that might match up well with these news pegs. List at least three potential sources for each story as well.

- A silver, gold, diamond or centennial anniversary (25, 50, 75 or 100 years)

- An annual event that brings people from near and far to your area

- An activity that would benefit from a specific "how-to" story

- A health or safety story based on a time of year

- A local look at a nationwide trend

PROFILE WRITING

The **personality profile** helps you explore the life of an interesting person and explain to your readers how this individual arrived at this point in life. A good profile gives you a chance to tell someone's story and that's a powerful thing.

As is the case with everything you've done to this point, reporting will be a key aspect of a good personality profile. That said, profile reporting is harder than normal reporting and will force you to dig deeper into the person's life while picking out small details that will help you tell the story. Profile reporting will take on two specific characteristics: interviewing and observation. Let's start with the interview:

© Bowman Gum

Yogi Berra, the famous former New York Yankee, once noted that, "You can observe a lot by watching." As odd as that sounds, it's good advice if you want to write a great personality profile.

Interviews

You always want to conduct interviews in person, but this is especially important with a subject for a personality profile. You need to do observation (which we'll get to later), but you also want to spend a good amount of time with that person so that you can ask a lot of questions that come from seeing the person interact with others.

In profile reporting, you want to look for ways to generate follow-up questions. Most of the time, you want to focus on the "why?" aspect each time someone reveals a little about himself or herself. So if the source says "I always cry when I hear Johnny Cash's version of 'Get Rhythm,'" you want to find out why. It might remind the source of a special car trip with a long-dead relative or of a traumatic event that really shaped him or her.

As you interview the person, remember that you want to reveal insight about your source, so you should let the source have a little more control over the interview. While you should still get answers to all the key questions you have, you should also listen to what the source is saying and let the person's thoughts guide you as you proceed.

Sources

You want to get back to your source at least one time after an initial interview. The key aspect of the first interview will be to get the bread-and-butter reporting done. Again, you shouldn't ask the source questions you could have gotten answers to through research, but you should view this interview as a wider examination of the person. This is where you learn about your source in several periods of his or her life, the various jobs or moments that shaped this person and so forth. Broad, open-ended questions based on good research should give you a solid base from which to work.

When the source is talking about other people, you should take special note of the names of the people, because these folks will make for great secondary sources. You want to have as many sources as possible, but make sure each one of these sources can add something different to the mix. Think about this in terms of facets of a story. Each person who knows the source in a different way is likely to provide you with different insights that can help you better understand your source. Once you interview the secondary sources, you can go back to your source and conduct another interview with more specific questions.

Observation

The great Yogi Berra once said, "You can observe a lot by watching." If you step away from the obvious nature of the Yogi-ism, you can find some real truth to this. Observations are what make for a great story. The type of observation you do will depend greatly on the type of source you interview. In the majority of cases, you want to be an unobtrusive viewer. You don't want to call attention to yourself, just as you don't want to call attention to yourself in writing the article.

Here are some things you should look for in terms of observation:

Person

You want to describe the person in terms of who they are and why they matter. You can do some of this through physical observation, noting things like the physical stature of the person and the way the person dresses. You will also want to go a bit deeper in terms of an overall persona, including things like values, motives and ideals. This is where you capture the physical and psychological essence of the person.

Environment

What people surround themselves with often reveals a lot about who they are. For some people, their homes are like museums, in that they are filled with precious and elegant things that you aren't allowed to touch. Other people live in giant toy factories of fun and craziness. Issues of organization, cleanliness and more can give you a sense as to what the person lives like and how this reflects who that person is.

Actions

As you examine the interactions your source has with other people, you can learn a great deal about this individual's sense of self. If a person is nice and respectful to a boss or a peer but is cruel to secretaries and custodians, this says something about the person. If a person feels uncomfortable in large crowds but is the life of the party in smaller places, that's insightful information as well. Beyond interaction, simple actions can help you understand what the person values and who they are. Some people can't sit still, regardless of what they are doing. Other people are able to start a single task and not leave until it is accomplished. As you report on your subject, you want to take good notes of these and other types of behaviors.

LOCALIZATIONS

Localizing stories allow you to make a broader topic more locally relevant. These stories usually are about making things more geographically valuable, such as what a national law will mean to the readers of a state newspaper. In other cases, **localizations** are topical, such as what a set of statewide laws regarding lead usage will mean to hunters who use lead-based ammunition.

Here are a few things that will make for a good localization:

A Direct Local Tie

When you have someone local who is participating in a broader event, the localization is simple. If the Miss America competition is happening and the person representing your state comes from your coverage area, you have a great opportunity to localize the pageant. If a plane crashes and people from your area were on board, you have a similarly strong tie that isn't as much fun but is just as important to your readers.

Indirect ties to big stories, like finding an area person who had a relative that fought in World War II, can be valuable in writing localization stories.

© U.S. Coast Guard

An Indirect Local Tie

In some cases, you can find yourself a somewhat solid local tie that can make for a valuable story. When a person who grew up in your coverage area becomes a big celebrity, you can find people who "knew her back in the day" for a good localization story. In other cases, you have familial ties that are local even if the event isn't. A man or woman whose father fought in the D-Day invasion could make for a fascinating look back at the war and the day.

A Microcosm of a Broader Topic

When a large trend begins to emerge, you can see if the trend is present locally. If you have a story on how student loan debt is likely to be the next major drain on the national economy, chances are you have a nearby university with students facing that debt. If small businesses throughout the country are getting tax breaks, you should find out what local businesses feel about it. When you can show how a bigger issue hits home, you have a nice microcosm story.

Not all localization stories are good ideas, however. Here are a few examples of localizations that lead to bad stories:

Big Topic, Weak Reactors

When a big issue takes hold, you can have a chance to do a great reaction story. However, when the people you interview are uninformed or underinformed about the topic at hand, the reactions are really weak. This usually happens when something like a war starts, a nationwide policy begins or a complex set of rules take hold. If you have a lead like "Although the president says continued political and economic sanctions against North Korea are necessary, several high school freshmen disagree," you will have a lousy story.

Big Topic, No Impact

In many cases, local people will be interested in a topic but have little or nothing to say about its overall value. If you write localization stories on people who watch the Grammy Awards or the Oscars, you fit this niche. The local people telling you who deserved the awards won't change who won, nor will it affect the overall voting strategy these groups use. If the best thing a story can say is "local people react to…," you don't have much of a story.

Bad Topic, No Impact

In 2012, the media ran dozens of stories about the potential end of the world, based mainly on the end of the Mayan calendar. These stories often included reactions from local people, asking if they thought the world would end or if they had prepared for it. Similar stories emerge when a zombie movie becomes popular and local reporters see fit to ask local people if they fear a zombie apocalypse. As the world has not ended, nor have zombies attacked, it's a bit of a stretch to say those localizations had much value. Even if these unlikely events were to occur, it's uncertain why reporters would think that the owner of a local diner would be able to provide proper survival techniques.

OBITUARIES

Obituaries are reports of people who have died. This may be the first time they are in the paper, and it will almost certainly be the last. Therefore, being correct and tactful are paramount.

This kind of story can seem problematic or daunting because you intrude upon the grief of others. However, trying to share the stories of people who have died can allow family members to speak and allow readers to learn about a person who mattered to their community. Still, approaching people who are saddened by a loss can seem overwhelming to beginning reporters, leaving them to question the importance of this type of work.

In conducting interviews for these stories, you want to be sensitive, open and sympathetic. In some cases, you have to ask hard questions, such as how the person died, but you can do so in a decent and humane way. You also don't have to worry too much about controlling the conversation. The more you let the person take control, the better the interview will be. That said, you do have a journalistic obligation to fact-check any particular elements of a story along the way. If the person said that "Grandpa Bill" won the Medal of Honor, you should check that against a list of winners, just to make sure it wasn't a tall tale he wove for the grandchildren.

The ability to report for and write on the lives of other people could lead to a broader understanding of why people matter and what they did for the betterment of others. The idea of bothering people can be quite difficult to get past, but in the end, obituaries can be among the most important and meaningful stories you will do in your time as a reporter.

THE BIG THREE

Here are the three key things you should take away from this chapter:

1. **Look for story ideas everywhere:** Reporters who rely solely on event coverage will often run out of good stories to tell or will become bored with their work. From obituaries to news features, you want to find things that are interesting to you and relevant to your readers. If you look at your work as a daily opportunity to find something fun, you will make life better for everyone.

2. **Don't be afraid of a topic:** As Eric Deutsch mentioned, fear shouldn't impede your ability to ask questions and get answers. Some situations are fraught with actual danger, so you do want to be cautious when it comes to covering a forest fire or a police standoff. However, you shouldn't be afraid of asking tough questions or approaching awkward situations during your reporting. Sometimes, those encounters can lead to the best stories.

3. **Reporting requires diligence:** Whether you need to ask tough questions or you need to chase a story, you must remain persistent. Many journalists are accused of "hit-and-run news," where they cover an event but fail to follow up, or they reach out to a source only once for a particular story. When you conduct your reporting, stick with it until you feel you have satisfied your readers. Then get up the next day and do it all over again.

KEY TERMS

beats 152
breaking news 148
conceptual beat 153
geographic beat 153
localization 159

main assertion 156
morgue 154
news peg 157
obituaries 161

personality profile 157
Robert's Rules of Order 151
shell 149
thematic beat 153

DISCUSSION QUESTIONS

1. What do you see as some of the benefits associated with beat coverage? What are some of the drawbacks? What beats do you think are covered too much and which ones do you think don't get enough attention?

2. Of the three types of stories listed in the latter half of the chapter (localizations, profiles and obituaries), which one do you think is the most important to do well? Which one do you think you would have the most difficulty reporting? How do you think you could get past some of your difficulties?

3. What are the benefits and drawbacks associated with each of the events listed in the event coverage part of the chapter? Which ones do you think you would most enjoy covering and why? Which ones would you have the most difficulty covering and why?

WRITE NOW!

1. Walk around your campus, without using any of your digital devices, and see what is going on around you. Listen to other people's conversations or look at the meeting notices on area bulletin boards. See if you notice anything that is actively changing, such as the completion of construction or the addition of a new memorial plaque. Take notes on these topics. Then write up a list of at least five story ideas you found and a list of potential sources for them.

2. Identify at least four beats you think would be germane to the students on your campus. Some of these may overlap with traditional news beats, such as crime or education, while others should be specialized, such as student government or the Greek system. Research those beats and determine several key stories that would come from them. Then list a group of sources for each of those stories.

3. Find a person who you think would make for a good personality profile. Research that individual and then ask for an interview. Identify additional sources who can speak intelligently on the person and interview them as well. Use both interview and observation techniques to help craft your profile. The piece should be at least three pages long, typed, double-spaced, with at least three human sources in it.

10

WRITING FOR TRADITIONAL PRINT NEWS PRODUCTS

LEARNING OBJECTIVES

After completing this chapter you should be able to:

- Explain the differences between the structure of traditional print stories and the standard inverted pyramid.

- Understand why sources form the core of this approach to writing.

- Apply attributions to direct and indirect quotes as needed.

- Define direct quotes, indirect quotes and partial quotes and explain when to use each type of quote.

- Apply the paraphrase-quote structure as you write a standard print story.

- Construct the beginning, the middle and the end of a story based on the structural outline listed in the chapter.

Since the introduction of Publick Occurrences in 1690, the newspaper has been a ubiquitous and important part of American life and culture. The First Amendment to the Constitution lists freedom of the press as a right upon which the government should not infringe. This provided publishers with the opportunity to put ink to paper and express their thoughts and ideas in an arena free from government intrusion.

The value of the press, however, isn't the ink, the paper or even the circulation. It is the way in which good writers organize their thoughts into engaging and valuable prose and use it to reach an interested audience. The writing matters more than anything else involved in newspapers.

This chapter will examine the ways in which print products, here meaning newspaper-style publications, work in terms of their writing. The chapter will also discuss how these stories are structured and how they can be of value to the audience.

NUANCES FOR PRINT WRITING

Print-style writing, which is used in traditional publications and on many journalism-based websites, relies heavily on the inverted-pyramid structure noted in Chapter 4. However, as you will see in this chapter, things such as paragraph length, reliance on **sources** and the use of quoted material will alter your overall approach to writing. Here are some primary aspects of writing that are generally associated with print-style news writing:

Paragraphs

You will find that this type of writing requires you to write in shorter paragraphs than you are used to. This writing approach uses paragraphs of one to two sentences each. Occasionally, paragraphs grow longer, but for the most part, print writers tend to keep their paragraphs short and sweet.

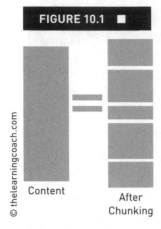

FIGURE 10.1 ■

© thelearningcoach.com

Content   After Chunking

In many English classes, you are directed to write paragraphs that have a main sentence, several supporting sentences and then a concluding sentence. This is meant to create a structure that allows you to offer evidence for each statement you propose in your writing.

In print writing, the same idea is true, in that you need to support your statements with some form of evidence or through the use of sources. However, given the way in which the eye consumes content and the way newspapers use columns of text, you need to think about paragraphs differently in this form of writing.

People don't read word for word and from the left all the way through to the last word on the right of each line. Jakob Nielsen's eye-tracking research shows that people tend to scan material and fixate on certain elements that draw their attention.[1] Additional research demonstrated that people tended to "lock on" to visuals, color and large text before moving on to smaller print.

To improve the readability of smaller text, gaps of white space, created either through indenting or through separation between paragraphs, can help the eye "lock on" to the start of a chunk of text. The more you use shorter paragraphs, the more bits of space you have.

It might help to think of your paragraphs like a rock-climbing wall. A wall that is easier to climb will likely have many more footholds and handholds than a difficult climbing wall. If you have more paragraphs, you will have more indents or spaces between paragraphs (depending on your approach), thus giving your readers more "footholds" for their eyes.

Reliance on Sources

In writing for news publications, you strive to demonstrate **objectivity**. News writers should not take sides on an issue or offer personal opinions in their pieces. This means you need sources to do the hard work for you.

Your readers will come to you with their own thoughts and biases. If they don't believe the president is doing a good job, they will view your story that explains the president is doing a good job with suspicion. To help a reader see why your story makes this claim, you need to use your sources and show your reader from where that information came.

In some cases, information is so well known that your readers will accept it without question. It is when you pair a fact with an opinion that you need to provide your readers the source of your claim. If you could imagine a reader responding to your statement with a "Says who?" rebuttal, you need to rely on a source. For example:

San Francisco is a city in California.

This statement of fact would not have a "Says who?" argument brewing. It's not as if you would need to say, "According to Google Maps, San Francisco is a city in California."

San Francisco is the best city in California.

If you made this statement, you would probably get an argument from people in San Diego, Los Angeles, Sacramento and dozens of other California cities. To make this work, you need to use a source for this information.

Quotes

Most journalists conduct interviews to gather information that will help the readers understand a story. A second and equally valuable reason for conducting interviews is to gather quotes from their sources.

Quotes allow the people in your story, your advertisement or your media release to speak directly to the audience in their own words. While standard information is the staple of all of these forms of writing, quotes can enhance the overall interest level of what you are writing. If you think of the quotes as a cook thinks of a spice, you can see how sprinkling a little here and a little there can do a world of good for the overall dish. However, much like spices, if you use the wrong quotes or you use too many of them for no good reason, you will ruin everything.

The three forms of quotes can be remembered using the mnemonic DIP: direct, indirect and partial.

Direct Quotes

These quotes are taken from the source's mouth, word for word, and placed into your writing. The idealized view of **direct quotes** is that whatever you place between a set of quote marks is sacred: You don't change the words, and you don't play with the phrasing. The words are what they are. It is also generally accepted that you can eliminate utterances such as "um" or "uh" when you write what the person said. Quotes should be word for word, not necessarily grunt for grunt.

You want the quotes to convey valuable information that is germane to a source. In the area of news, your goal is to remain fair and unbiased in what you write. However, you will likely find yourself covering controversial topics that require you to get opposing viewpoints into a story. The quotes allow you to have people say things that you couldn't say.

If one school board member doesn't like the budget plan, he might tell you, "We have created the worst possible budget that will punish at least three generations of students in this district." The source is giving you information that is valuable and should interest your readers. However, if you wrote this in your story without getting it from a source, it would clearly sound biased. This is why direct quotes are valuable.

© Bowman Gum

Again, the wisdom of Yogi Berra emerges: Quotes like his famous "I didn't really say everything I said" show that things said in a unique way can draw readers into your stories.

Direct quotes can also add color or flavor to your story. In many cases, it's not what someone says but how they say it that makes something interesting. For example, New York Yankees great Yogi Berra won three Most Valuable Player awards and 13 World Series titles and was enshrined in the baseball Hall of Fame in 1972. However, it was Berra's mangling of the English language that made him an all-time favorite among sports journalists. He famously noted that a restaurant had become so popular that "no one goes there anymore. It's too crowded." In giving directions to a friend who was visiting Berra's home for the first time, Berra said, "When you come to the fork in the road, take it." You can read these and other Yogi-isms in his book, "The Yogi Book: I Really Didn't Say Everything I Said."[2]

The point is, occasionally the use of a direct quote showcases how people are able to turn a phrase to delight your readers. If the way in which information is said is more engaging than the information itself, a direct quote is a good way to go.

One last thing about direct quotes: In most cases, direct quotes are their own paragraphs, regardless of their length. While you will limit other forms of information to one or two sentences per paragraph, a direct quote will constitute a single paragraph, regardless of its length. That said, you should examine the quote to make sure it's worth whatever number of sentences you include in it.

THE CASES FOR AND AGAINST FIXING QUOTES

For as long as people have been quoted, journalists have grappled with the issue of whether to "clean up" direct quotes for their sources. People don't sound perfect every time they open their mouths and say something. To make life easier on everybody involved, journalists often consider fine-tuning the quotes to fix grammar issues, sentence structure problems or other minor gaffes that are natural during speech.

Some news writers have no problem with these changes, while others consider it an affront to the sacred pact between readers and writers. As you work in various parts of the field, you might be asked to rely solely on the words that come out of a source's mouth, or you might even be asked to create a quote for a source and then have the source approve it. Here are some things to consider:

Clarity

You have a responsibility to your readers to help them understand what is happening in a story and why it matters to them. If you need to use a quote that could be misconstrued because of a poor choice of words or some mangled syntax, some journalists would argue that fixing the quote is the lesser of two evils. Others would argue that it would be best to find a different quote, even if it is less powerful. In either case, clarity should remain a primary consideration as you write.

Fairness

Some sources will have a poor grasp of the English language, and those struggles can lead readers to place less value on those sources. Consider a situation in which a rich corporate executive is on trial for assaulting a poverty-level street vendor. The executive likely has a high level of education and can afford a brilliant, high-priced lawyer to speak on his behalf. The street vendor might have limited legal representation and be less educated. When they speak, they should have equal likelihood of conveying information to your readers. However, if one speaks perfectly and the other doesn't, bias could creep into the minds of your readers. By fixing the quotes, you could level the playing field. On the other hand, you could drastically alter reality.

Digital Media

When reporters were forced to rely on handwritten notes, direct quotes always had some variability to them. Even using old-fashioned shorthand or quick writing tips, reporters would miss a word here or there. However, in the age of digital media, reporters can record a source and replay the quote to guarantee its precise wording. Print journalists who decide to change quotes might find their credibility compromised when digital media outlets present what was actually said. If you cover an event and a source issues a mangled quote, you might choose to clean it up. However, when people see the video or hear the audio from that event, they could see how you changed reality and thus be less likely to trust you.

Meaning

When you decide to make a change to something, you are substituting your judgment for reality. This has the potential to alter the meaning of a statement and provide your readers with an inaccurate view of what was said or intended. When you choose to play God with the words of others, you run the risk of drastically altering what they meant. You should consider this in everything you write, but even more so when you deal with quotes.

Indirect Quotes

People often have trouble getting to the point in a sentence or two when they speak. In other cases, common language is the best way to explain exactly what a source is saying. When the information is vital but the statements your source makes don't merit a word-for-word recounting, consider using **indirect quotes**.

These kinds of quotes, which are often referred to as **paraphrase**, take all the information you want to use from a source and boil it down to the basics for your readers. They help you sift through poor language, jargon and structure issues to create a more succinct version of the facts. They give you the opportunity to restate what the sources told you in the best possible way for your readers.

Here's an example of an interview where you might find the need to paraphrase a source:

Q: *So, you're firing more than 200 people?*

A: *Well not really, you see these people are valued members of the workforce but we are running into a lag time here and we need to readjust to keep our profit margin.*

Q: *But they no longer work here?*

A: *That's true. They are seasonal employees. They help out when we really need the inventory turned around very quickly. Holidays are big for us, as you well know.*

Q: *Will they come back?*

A: *Oh, yes. They are part of a list of people who we call on a seasonal basis. They come and they go.*

Q: *Did they know they were going to be fired?*

A: *Well, I'm sure some knew. Others were probably a little surprised, but those who have been with us for several years know that we do this on occasion. We are very fair and care very much for our employees.*

You can't grab a small chunk of any one of those answers and turn it into a quality quote. To that end, you want to paraphrase the source so that you can boil the answers down to a statement or two:

More than 200 workers at Smitty Co. found themselves without jobs Wednesday morning, as the company laid off a group of seasonal employees.

According to spokesman Bill Smith, the company hires hundreds of extra workers for the holidays, which are traditionally the busiest time of the year for the clothing manufacturer.

As you can see, the use of an indirect quote still allows you to crunch the interview down into a sentence or two and then attribute the information to your source. This helps your readers figure out what is going on and understand who told you this information. It is also a good idea to paraphrase people when they are using ordinary speech.

Partial Quotes

These quotes mix the two aforementioned styles of quoting so you can place emphasis on a key element of a statement a source made. **Partial quotes** work well when someone uses a word or phrase that conveys a precise emotion or when a source says something provocative in a word or two. Here's a good example:

> *The father of a middle school student who was expelled for bringing Ex-Lax brownies to school called the incident "an unfortunate prank" and argued that his daughter should be allowed to continue her education.*

The phrase "an unfortunate prank" provides your readers with a clear sense that this parent doesn't see what his child did as harmful or serious. This clearly conflicts with how the school saw the issue, as the administrators expelled the girl. When someone uses a punchy phrase or an odd word, a partial quote can often be a great tool.

However, you need to use this kind of quote sparingly. In some cases, they can make you look bad as a journalist or make your source look bad. Using only partial quotes can say to your readers, "I'm such a bad reporter, I can't capture more than two words of what this person has to say at any point in an interview." On the other hand, partial quotes can say, "My source is such a terrible speaker, he can only string together two or three decent words at a time." Neither of these outcomes will reflect well on you as a writer, so use partial quotes sparingly.

CONNECT
QUOTING PEOPLE LIKE US

A recurring theme of this book is audience centricity. People always want to know "What's in it for me?"

As we try to answer that question for our readers, we rely heavily on official sources when we write.

You should use official sources in many cases, as outlined in Chapter 8. When you cite officials acting in an official capacity, you receive a certain level of legal protection. However, people usually prefer information if it comes from people like them.

Some textbooks refer to nonofficial sources as "engaged citizens" or "real people," but whatever you call them, they provide important insight to a story.

For example, when officials want to expand a freeway, your story on the issue would likely include city council members, highway planning officials and environmental impact experts. These people all have something important to add to your work.

However, none of these people can really explain at a basic level what this means to "people like us" when it comes to the finished product. A person who uses the freeway to commute to work could explain how bad congestion is now and how this might make life easier on drivers. An area resident could talk about how the expansion would bring noise and pollution to a quiet neighborhood.

When you work on your stories, you can easily find official sources who make a point to converse with the media. However, when you quote "people like us," you will help your readers more fully see how a story affects them and why they should care about it.

GIVE IT A TRY: Interview an official source, acting in an official capacity, on a topic of interest to your readership. Then, interview four or five "people like us" who have a connection to that topic. For example, if you interview a superintendent of schools about a new uniform policy at the district's grade school level, you could interview parents and students and ask what they think of this. Use the information from the first interview to drive your interviews with "people like us." Then, see how those interviews align with the interview with the official source. Does everyone agree on the positives and negatives associated with the topic? Are the "regular people" discussing the same concerns as the official source was? How similar and different are the answers in terms of scope and content?

ATTRIBUTIONS

As noted earlier in the chapter, people want to know where you got your information. **Attributions** should pair with all direct and indirect quotes to provide the answer to that

"Says who?" question. The preferred verb of attribution in this type of writing is "said," as it is nonjudgmental and easy to prove. You can't really tell your readers what someone thinks, believes or feels, but you can tell your readers what someone said.

When someone important is speaking and you want to emphasize that "fame" news element, you can place an attribution at the front of a quote:

> *President Donald Trump said, "America is a sovereign nation, and our first priority is always the safety and security of our citizens."*

When the quote itself has more value than a source or when a source lacks a level of importance, you can place the attribution at the rear of a quote:

> *"I honestly think the school board is just trying to sap my will to live," parent Jane Jones said.*

In a case where you have a quote with multiple sentences, place the attribution after the first full sentence of the quote. This will give your readers a break in the quote and will allow them to understand who said the quote before they get too far into it:

> *"I guess I'm stunned at how fast the jury found my client guilty," attorney Jill Jackman said. "The jurors just really seemed to hate her from the get-go."*

Verbs of Attribution

In English classes, students are often told that "**said**" is a boring word and that more colorful choices, such as "laughed" or "growled" or "argued," are preferable. In journalism classes, news writers learn to be objective, which can be a code word for boring. Thus, "said" (or "says," as Chapter 11 will explain) is the preferred verb of attribution. Other choices that usually make the cut include the following:

- **Testified:** When a source gives a statement as a witness in a legal proceeding, this verb is usually acceptable. *Smith testified that he did not see who shot the bartender.*

- **Stated:** This is often interchanged with "said," particularly if a document is involved. Many journalists view "stated" as the written complement to "said." *The contract stated that the band would arrive at the arena five hours prior to the start of the show.*

- **Announced:** Sources who give formal proclamations often "announce" something, and thus this fits nicely with those situations. *Mayor Frank Thomas announced Wednesday that he would run for a second term.*

- **Asked:** This is the inquisitive form of "said." We say something we know, and we ask for an answer to something we don't. *"So you never saw the shooter, even though he was right in front of you?" attorney James Carlton asked the witness.*

- **According to:** One of the riskier choices among purists, as it can indicate a lack of belief. However, many general news publications allow it in limited doses. *According to Mayor Chip Smithers, alternate-side parking laws will be at the core of this year's campaign.*

Some publications allow the use of "laughed" and "joked" when humor is implied or "yelled" or "warned" when anger is clear. However, in these cases, the writer is asked to serve as an interpreter of meaning, which can lead to problems. If the source comes back the next day and says "I wasn't joking about that issue. I was serious," the writer can look foolish. Writers and editors will often discuss the appropriate nature of attributions and verb choices.

Write attributions verb-noun, and sound like Yoda you will.

Attribution Structure

Grammarians often howl about this issue, given the preferred structure of sentences and the proper ordering of words. The use of a noun-verb structure would dictate that attributions place the "who" before the "what," leading to attributions of "Smith said," or "she said." Editors and writers often argue that long titles and writing pace should allow the use of verb-noun structure when necessary: "said Smith, who runs a shelter for homeless children." Or "said Barb Gibson, the vice president in charge of regional programming for WZZZ-TV."

Each side has merit. Grammarians are correct in that noun-verb structure is preferred and that rarely would you write other forms of sentences with the verb first. You wouldn't say "Ran I" or "Fought did Smith" unless you were mimicking Yoda from the "Star Wars" franchise. Writers and editors are also correct that when grammar impedes flow and structure, it can do more harm than good. If someone were involved in a bar fight, he might yell, "Do you know who you're messing with?" Rarely could you imagine such rage coming across in a grammatically correct fashion: "Do you know with whom you are messing?" Keep both angles in mind, although when possible, you should write in a way that reflects correct grammar.

Repetition of Attributions

Attributions can seem like a pain for writers, especially when it appears that every single thing needs to be attributed. Writers who ascribe to a strict attribution philosophy will argue that each sentence in a story needs to be attributed to the source to avoid confusion and limit the writer's liability. Writers who see attributions as a disruption to the flow and structure of a story often attribute at key points of a story and allow the reader to mentally "carry" that attribution forward until another source is introduced.

Each approach can have problems. In 1996, an explosion at Centennial Park during the Olympics killed two people and injured more than 100 others. Just before the bomb detonated, security guard Richard Jewell spotted the package, alerted authorities and helped move people away from the area. In the weeks that followed, the media turned its attention to Jewell as the most likely bombing suspect.[3]

In the ESPN film "Judging Jewell," Bert Roughton of the Atlanta Journal-Constitution discussed several statements the paper made in print regarding Jewell, including one unattributed statement that said Jewell "fits the profile of the lone bomber." Roughton said that the statement reflected the attitude of law enforcement officials the reporters had interviewed but that without the attribution, the statement sounded like something the newspaper was reporting because it knew it to be true.[4] After 88 days of investigation, the FBI stated that Jewell was no longer a suspect, and in 2005, Eric Rudolph confessed to the bombing.[5] The stigma of this intense scrutiny stuck with Jewell for the rest of his life. It would be unfair to blame the lack of attribution for all of this, but it remains an example of a statement that demanded a "Says who?" answer.

Conversely, in less newsy pieces, attributions can feel like a blockade to flow and pace. If you wrote a piece on a family that ran a restaurant, you could end up with sentences like this:

Mary Johnson said her husband, Bert Johnson, was the first person to ask Jimmy Johnson and Jane Johnson to be part of the business. Jimmy Johnson said it was actually his cousin Johnny Johnson who came up with the restaurant idea.

Although style for news dictates the attribution of each sentence and the use of first and last names to avoid confusion and an overly familiar tone, the attributions here make these sentences almost unreadable.

You will find that many of these issues lack an absolute right and an absolute wrong. It is always best to consult with your editor before making a final call on when and where to attribute and how best to do it.

PROFESSIONAL THOUGHTS

JON SEIDEL

As a federal courts reporter for the Chicago Sun-Times, Jon Seidel says the key to writing for the news is to be able to translate complex concepts into reader-friendly copy.

"Young writers are easy to spot because they get caught up in technical jargon," he said. "I was no different. They find themselves covering government machinations they don't understand, and the news cycle leaves them little time to learn. Ultimately, a lawyer winds up offering an explanation to the young reporter, and that reporter repeats that explanation in the newspaper. Problem is, the reporter fails to translate the legalese."

Seidel said his goal in covering the ins and outs of the legal system is to explain stories to his readers in the easiest way possible.

"Be plain," he said. "Write in a language the reader understands. This rule stands no matter the medium. And once you write your story, sit back and think about how well you've done. Take the time to edit yourself. And don't write for the lawyers. Write for your readers."

Seidel spends most of his time covering public corruption, terrorism cases and organized crime, but said every now and then he has to learn something new to help his readers connect with his work.

"You never know what will pop up in court," he said. "Recently we had a teen YouTube sensation arrested on child porn charges. I had never heard of him before and I had to learn pretty quickly."

Even though he has spent his entire career in the newspaper field, Seidel said he has to write across platforms, including the web and social media. Whether he is writing a 2,800-word story or a 280-character tweet, he said he strives to keep the writing clear and free of errors.

"No one is obligated to read what we write, so we want to give people something interesting to read,"

Jon Seidel

he said. "If they don't care—or can't even comprehend what you wrote—they'll go elsewhere. Write clearly. And use proper grammar and style. Readers expect it."

As the industry evolves, Seidel said his job continues to grow and change. As it does, the underlying tenets of good writing and solid storytelling will help him find a place in the new media world.

"My college diploma was 3 years old when I first heard of the iPhone," he said. "Yeah, I'm old. But what transformative technology will come along after you've graduated? Will you be ready? You should be if you can write a story in plain language without getting bogged down in jargon and fluff. I've worked for newspapers my entire career, but I've also dabbled in other forms of media. Storytelling is the key skill that translates. It will help you move from job to job as the industry evolves."

One Last Thing

Q: If you could tell students anything about media writing or anything you have seen in your time in the field, what would it be?

A: College is the time to pick up every skill you can. This is a tough, tough business, and it is changing rapidly. You might not care about a particular concept, but the person reading your resume could. So explore them. Experiment. Try picking up new pieces of technology. And practice writing well today. That way you'll be ready when the big story breaks at your first job.

EXPANDING THE INVERTED PYRAMID

The inverted pyramid is great for organizing your thoughts and for quickly writing information in a short, tight fashion. However, the inverted pyramid can come across as somewhat boring or even lacking in crucial details.

In the field of print, journalists have often reshaped the inverted pyramid to infuse more source material and background elements to help upgrade this tried-and-true method of writing. Let's look at the beginning, middle and end of a print story in a more expanded inverted pyramid:

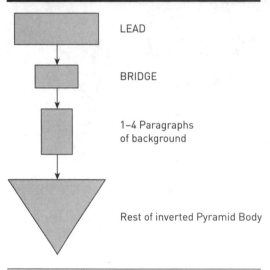

FIGURE 10.2 ■ **The expanded inverted pyramid provides you with more options for storytelling and gives you the opportunity to infuse background information into your pieces.**

LEAD

BRIDGE

1–4 Paragraphs of background

Rest of inverted Pyramid Body

The Beginning

Instead of thinking of just the first paragraph of the story, as noted in Chapter 4, you should consider the first third of the story as the beginning. At this stage, you will outline enough information to help engage the reader with information, entice the reader with some interesting flavor and then explain any background the reader might need to fully understand the story.

Lead

The lead of the expanded inverted-pyramid story should continue to be a single sentence of 25 to 35 words that captures as many of the 5W's and 1H as possible. You also want to emphasize some of the FOCII points explained earlier in the book:

Despite overwhelming support from community members, a five-block stretch of Ohio Avenue will not be renamed for slain civil rights leader Martin Luther King, Jr., the Springfield City Council decided Monday.

This lead explains who did what, when and where. It also touches on some of the news points, including fame, conflict and immediacy. It sets the stage for a story that will detail what the council did and why the council members voted the way they did.

Bridge

The second paragraph is where to decide how best to move your readers from the lead into the rest of the story. This paragraph is called a **bridge**, and like an actual bridge, it is used to transition people from one place to another smoothly.

A bridge can be one of a number of things. It can be a direct quote that advances the story. It can identify any of the W's or the H that don't show up in the lead but that need immediate attention. It can also be an indirect quote that adds to the theme of the piece.

Choose your bridge based on what would matter most to your readers. If you have to do some heavy explaining regarding why or how something happened, sum up what people need to know in simple paraphrase. If a direct quote can provide clarity or strongly support the lead, use it.

"We aren't saying Dr. King isn't important," council member Pat Jones said. "We just don't think the city is best served by confusing travelers or upsetting business owners."

The direct quote adds some emotion to the issue while addressing one of the W's (the why), regarding the council's decision.

Background

At this point, you want to make sure everyone reading your story has the same level of understanding regarding the topic. This is a great point to infuse a few paragraphs of background. Here you can sum up any information that gives readers a glimpse into what has happened to this point and then move them forward into the current story:

> *Monday was the third time in the past two years the Street for King Coalition brought the issue before the council.*

> *Proponents of the change noted Ohio Avenue's importance to the city's own civil rights efforts and said the change would show progress in how the city deals with race.*

> *The largest opponents to the change was the Ohio Avenue Merchants Association, who said the change would confuse shoppers and lower their bottom lines. Several storeowners also cited research that found many people associated streets named after King with being in "the bad part of town."*

The background here allows you to explain how the city got to this point with this issue. It also helps establish the sources you are likely to quote throughout the remainder of the piece. The partial quote adds feel and will likely need some attribution later in the story when the issue comes to the surface again.

The Middle

The core of a good story will continue to develop using the material you gathered from your sources, including facts and quotes. How you order the material will remain based on the importance of the information. The pieces you include will continue down the story in descending order of importance for the most part. However, to improve the overall flow and structure of your middle, you will need to find ways to transition between these bits of information

Paraphrase-Quote Pairings

In most cases, you need to create a structure that pairs indirect and direct quotes to tell your story. You can paraphrase a source to introduce a direct quote and then move into that quote. As you write your paraphrase, you want to look for ways to provide value in that indirect quote without stepping on the direct quote that will follow. Here's an example of a bad paraphrase and quote pairing that does just that:

> *Council member Bill Babcock said he said he opposed the renaming of Ohio Avenue because it would make life difficult on merchants and not because he was racist.*

> *"I am not a racist," he said. "I just oppose this proposal because it would make life difficult on storeowners in this area."*

In this pairing, you see both a repeating of the language in the paragraphs and a repeating of the underlying theme. Instead of this, you want to make your paraphrase strong and informative and then smoothly transition into the quote:

Council member Bill Babcock said some constituents told him only a racist would reject the proposal but noted that several merchants said they feared the impact the change would have for them.

"I am not a racist," he said. "I just oppose this proposal because it would make life difficult on storeowners in this area."

This leads to a less repetitive pairing that will provide your readers with some additional background as to why this person voted this way.

The middle can be constructed almost entirely out of these pairing of indirect and direct quotes. In some cases you will need additional material to transition between opposing viewpoints, thus requiring an indirect-direct-indirect quote structure.

Make Sure The Middle Matters

The most important thing about your middle is that you need to make sure it matters. In many cases, writers have a great lead and a wonderful closing, but they view the middle as a dumping ground for generic information. A well-written middle will keep the readers engaged from that great lead to the final paragraph, so don't just write for the sake of writing. Go back through the middle once you finish writing and tighten it up. A quality middle will have readers attached to the story until they reach the end.

The End

In June 2007, nearly 12 million people crowded around their television sets to see the finale of the TV show "The Sopranos."[6] The question was whether reputed mob boss Tony Soprano would live or die and what would become of the rest of his underworld family. As the show creeps toward its conclusion, Tony is sitting in a diner with his family as suspicious characters come and go. As the show reaches its final minute, someone enters the restaurant and suddenly the screen goes black. A moment later, the credits roll.

A decade later, fans remained irate and hounded creator David Chase for an answer: "What happened?"[7] Over the years, Chase has reacted in a number of ways to these questions, but in the end, he refused to give the audience members what they desperately wanted: closure.

Stories that fail to end can leave people with a sense of confusion or anxiety. Although most of the news stories you write will never truly have a conclusion, you can create an ending for your readers that is more satisfying than Chase's "cut to black." Here are a few ways you can seal the deal:

A Look Forward

In most situations, a story you are writing will be just a slice of a larger whole. When this is the case, you want to give your readers the understanding of what will come next in the situation. This could be as simple as telling them, "The city council will revisit this issue at its July 10 meeting." That is enough to bring a piece to a close while still looking forward. Other similar uses of the look forward include "The election will take place Nov. 4." and "All the money raised at the game will go to the Smith family."

An Encapsulating Quote

One of the harder things to do when closing a story is to avoid injecting yourself or your opinions into that final paragraph. Instead of using your thoughts to come to a conclusion, look at what your sources have given you that might nicely sum up the piece.

A good quote that encapsulates the feeling of the piece often works best to bring closure to the story. In a story like the one used as an example above, with the renaming of a city street, a closing quote could be something like this from one of the people involved:

"We understand the council has concerns, but we are undeterred," Smith said. "This issue isn't over by a long shot."

This gives you the sense that the people who want to see the street renamed will likely be back to ask the council to reconsider its position. It both looks forward and brings closure.

ADAPT
PARROTING YOUR SOURCES

Sources matter a great deal to reporters, and capturing their exact words can make the difference between a great story and a lousy one. However, as you saw earlier in the chapter, not everything a source says should be transmitted from the source to the audience in word-for-word fashion. In many cases, sources rely on jargon, corporate-speak or "legal-ese" as they answer your questions, leaving you in an odd position.

In some cases, you want to use the exact words a source uses to avoid any legal problems. For example, if a police officer tells you, "Alcohol contributed to the crash," you don't want to translate that to, "Officer John Smith said the driver was drunk." The officer merely stated alcohol was involved but didn't say the person was legally intoxicated. That might seem like hair-splitting to you, but legal distinctions exist between those two statements.

However, this doesn't mean you need to act like a parrot and simply repeat everything your source says, clinging to jargon as if it were a lifeboat in a sea of verbiage. When a source says, "We will see some involuntary separations in our workforce," you need to figure out what that means: Are people being laid off or fired? Don't let the jargon smooth over real consequences for people in your audience.

Don't let words like "cutting-edge solution" or "revolutionary restructuring" go unchecked as they find their way into your copy. How is something a "cutting-edge solution," or what makes something "revolutionary" in its approach to restructuring? When someone tells you about a "paradigm" or "paradigm shift," ask if they actually know what that means. If not, don't use it. If so, make them explain it to you in plain English.

GIVE IT A TRY: Here are general euphemisms and jargon used in a variety of press releases, news conferences and source interviews. Read each one and translate it to something you think readers would more likely understand if you used it in a news story:

a. Bob was transported to a nearby medical facility.

b. The armed perpetrators fled the bank with an undisclosed amount of cash.

c. Carl cited a diminution of morale as a key driver in his relocation to a new corporate entity.

d. Jane likely perpetrated an illegal activity.

e. More than 180 workers will be permanently decoupled from their positions within the company.

f. Sue engaged in waste removal as a sanitation engineer.

THE BIG THREE

Here are the three key things you should take away from this chapter:

1. **Rely on sources:** Whether you use direct quotes, indirect quotes or any other form of information, back up what you are saying so your readers know they can trust you. Rely on sources to tell the stories and remain a neutral observer. Attribute your information to those sources so you can demonstrate that the thoughts and opinions are based on the words of others.

2. **Avoid repetition:** When you create paraphrase to introduce your quotes, you don't want to say exactly what the quote will say. When you craft the middle of your story, you don't want to include three quotes that all say the same thing. As you write, you want to tighten your structure and your verbiage to make sure your readers are getting the best information in the least amount of space.

3. **Flavor with care:** Quotes matter a lot in print writing, but when they are altered or overused, they can do more harm than good. Use quotes properly and efficiently. When you select your quotes, keep clarity, accuracy and fairness in mind.

KEY TERMS

attribution 170
bridge 174
direct quotes 167

indirect quotes 169
objectivity 166
paraphrase 169

said 171
sources 165

DISCUSSION QUESTIONS

1. When you see information in a print-style product, do you pay attention to the source of the information? Do you care whether the source is an official or a regular person? If you do notice these things, whom do you trust more and why?

2. Compare and contrast the benefits of direct and indirect quotes. What makes each of them good in certain circumstances and what are some of the drawbacks of each?

3. Do you prefer a strict inverted-pyramid style or do you prefer the expanded version here? What are some of the reasons to use each? What are some of the drawbacks of each form?

WRITE NOW!

1. Conduct an interview with a person of interest to you. It can be a classmate, a teacher, a politician or anyone else. Make sure you capture direct quotes, even if you need to record the entire interview. Then write a one- to two-page piece that shows your ability to use direct and indirect quotes. The piece doesn't need an exotic lead, but it should tell your readers what the piece will cover. (Bill Smith works as a janitor at the school and says teachers are the messiest people in the building.) Then use

paraphrases and quotes to create a smooth-flowing piece that has a solid middle and a good ending.

2. Cover a meeting, speech or news conference and then write an expanded inverted-pyramid story. Remember to have a strong lead that engages the readers and focuses on the key aspects of what makes the event important and that moves seamlessly into the bridge. Add a proper amount of background and then build the rest of the story as

outlined in the chapter. Keep the middle tight, and then come up with a strong closing quote.

3. Review a news article regarding a local issue that you find either in a local newspaper or on a news-based website. (Avoid TV or radio sites, as we'll get to those later in the book.) Analyze the article for overall structure, including the beginning, the middle and the end of the piece. Does the lead grab you and make you want to read on? Is the middle tight or flabby? Does the piece end well or does it look as though the writer just stopped writing? Does the piece have flow or is it choppy? Also, review the quotes in terms of value and structure. Are the direct quotes set up well or do they repeat the paraphrase that introduces them? Are they intriguing and interesting or are they something that a writer should have paraphrased? Write a short essay that analyzes the story and discusses these key issues.

NOTES

1. J. Nielsen (2006, April 17). "F-Shaped Pattern of Reading on the Web: Misunderstood, but Still Relevant (Even on Mobile)." Nielsen Norman Group. Accessed at: http://www.nngroup.com/articles/f-shaped-pattern-reading-web-content/.

2. Y. Berra (1998). "The Yogi Book: I Really Didn't Say Everything I Said." New York: Workman.

3. R. Ostrow (2000). "Richard Jewell Case Study." Accessed at: http://www.columbia.edu/itc/journalism/j6075/edit/readings/jewell.html.

4. "30 for 30 Shorts: Judging Jewell." Accessed at: http://www.espn.com/30for30/film?page=judgingjewell.

5. E. Barry (2005, Aug. 23). "Atlanta Olympics Bomber Apologizes to His Victims." Los Angeles Times. Accessed at: http://articles.latimes.com/2005/aug/23/nation/na-rudolph23.

6. J. Dempsey (2007, June 12). "Nearly 12 Million for 'Sopranos.'" Variety. Accessed at: http://variety.com.

7. S. Evans (2016, May 22). "'The Sopranos' Ending Still Makes Creator David Chase 'Want to Cry.'" Accessed at: http://www.hollywoodreporter.com/live-feed/sopranos-ending-still-makes-david-896532.

11

WRITING FOR BROADCAST

Journalists who write text for broadcast stories must meet certain challenges not present in most other forms of media writing. Broadcasters must cope with how best to integrate audio and video elements into their storytelling. Their writing must roll off the tongues of the anchors and reporters. They must construct their stories so that audience members can understand them as they hear them. If you work in broadcast, these and other concerns will become part of your daily routine.

This chapter will outline how broadcast writing is similar to and yet different from the other forms of writing discussed within this book. As this is not a production book, the elements of video and audio will be part of this chapter only as they relate to broadcast writing. (A number of other books you can find online will provide you with excellent instruction on editing video and audio.)

The chapter will examine the underlying premises of writing for this medium as well as the physical ways in which scripts differ from other written content. Finally, the chapter will outline the types of pieces you will write and to what degree they integrate visual and audio elements.

NUANCES FOR BROADCAST WRITING

Broadcast writers often use the acronym **KISS** as a guiding principle for their work. This stands for either "Keep it short and simple" or "Keep it simple, stupid," depending on your interpretation. This reliance on simplicity is often why broadcast journalism gets a bad rap as being simplistic. However, any good writer will tell you it is a lot harder to write concisely and simply than to write long, complicated sentences.

Here are a few things broadcasters need to consider when putting their stories together:

Writing Concisely

In broadcast, the idea of keeping things simple is about using the right word in the right place at the right time. Concise writing means sticking firmly to the noun-verb or noun-verb-object sentence structure discussed earlier in the book. Broadcasters must find concrete nouns and vigorous verbs that can convey meaning on their own, thus limiting the need for adverbs and adjectives. Broadcast sentences range from eight to 15 words each, so broadcasters should trim prepositional phrases and superfluous articles. If the other forms of writing in this book can be described as "lean," broadcast writing needs to be downright skinny while still doing the job as well, or better than, writing other forms.

HELPFUL HINTS

THE EYES AND EARS OF WRITING

The majority of the nuances listed in this chapter help you write for the ear, meaning that the words tell the story in a way that listeners can easily understand it. Here are two easy ways to translate from work written for the eye to content written for the ear:

Simplify and Minimize

If someone in your house asks you to head to the grocery store for one item, chances are pretty good that you will return with the right thing. However, the more items that person adds to the list, the worse your odds become if you just hear those items and don't write them down. Use this principle in writing for the ear, as you cut down on extraneous items and focus on the key aspects of the material in a concise fashion:

Eye sentence: Congressman Jim Johnson was arrested Thursday on suspicion of six counts of fraud, four counts of embezzlement and 14 misdemeanors associated with his campaign's mismanagement of funds.

Ear sentence: Congressman Jim Johnson was arrested Thursday after he was accused of misusing campaign funds.

Cater to the Mind's Eye

A script written for the ear should appeal to the senses. Even when video can provide visuals, the text should help readers see the news in their own mind's eye. The more you choose words that accentuate aspects of sight, sound, taste and feel, the better you are:

Eye sentence: With one swing of the bat, centerfielder Bill Amway earned a 5–4 win for the Red Sox as he hit a three-run home run over the left-field wall at Fenway Park.

Ear sentence: With the crack of the bat, centerfielder Bill Amway crushed a three-run homer over the Green Monster, giving the Red Sox a 5–4 win.

Other words can play to smell (odor, stench, fragrance), taste (bitter, sweet, salty) and touch (cool, cold, frigid) as well. Think about how each word you use could be more descriptive in etching an idea into the mental picture you want your audience members to have. Go back through each word choice you make and look for better choices that play to each sense. This will help your stories stick more strongly in the minds of your listeners and viewers.

Writing to Be Heard

The biggest difference between writing for text-based products and writing for broadcast comes in how the material is received. In newspapers, web stories, press releases, print ads and more, the information is transmitted in a written form. People read the content with their eyes and then think about what they just read. If the readers are confused, they can read the content a second time. If they still aren't sure, which is never a good sign, they can put the paper away, save the digital link or hold on to the advertisement until they can look up confusing words or review perplexing concepts.

In broadcast, people use their ears to consume the content and then process what they just heard before they think about it. The audience members get only one chance to hear what the reporter said. They don't get a chance to stop and think about what they heard before the next bit of content arrives. They can't rewind that moment in time easily and get a second chance to understand the news.

To make things easy on your audience members, you need to write to be heard. Choose common words that are used in their most familiar ways. Write in short sentences that contain one idea each. Pick words that have an auditory component to them as opposed to words that don't.

Writing to Be Spoken

Broadcast expert Robert Papper notes that broadcast writing is meant to be spoken on one end and heard on the other. He also explains that the writing structure isn't exactly conversational, as conversations tend to have too many grammatical and structural problems. Instead, the form is more akin to how we wish we would speak if we were to stop and collect our thoughts before saying each sentence.[1]

If you write broadcast copy well, any broadcaster can pick it up and read it properly with very little practice. Obviously, practice will improve the read, but the goal is to make the writing as universal as possible for the journalist. To do this, you can exchange words like "children" for "kids" and complex numbers for accurate approximations.

The writing also needs to build in spaces for the person reading the news to breathe in an unobtrusive fashion. Journalists who write in this format often use short sentences and a conversational structure so that breathing becomes a natural part of the delivery. When done well, the reader shouldn't run out of air or be forced to gasp while reading.

Writing for the Distracted

During the advent of broadcast, radios and televisions were rare and fascinating devices. In the 1920s, people would gather around the radio and actively listen to their favorite programs. In the 1940s, families and friends would crowd near a screen that was smaller than the iPhone 8 to watch sporting events and see news programs. This heavy dose of attention allowed broadcast journalists to write in a way that more directly matched the print writing of the time. These writers didn't have to worry as much that people weren't always aware of what was happening on the airwaves.

Today, people are constantly distracted while they listen to radios or watch TV. Radio consumption happens primarily in vehicles, where people are likely chatting with friends, talking on a mobile phone or attempting to drive safely.[2] Television has become a ubiquitous member of most households and is often turned on for background noise or companionship. Broadcast journalists understand this constant state of distraction among viewers and listeners and write in a way that first attracts attention and then delivers information. This approach of orienting the audience to the content and then delivering it prevents the consumers from missing key information on important stories.

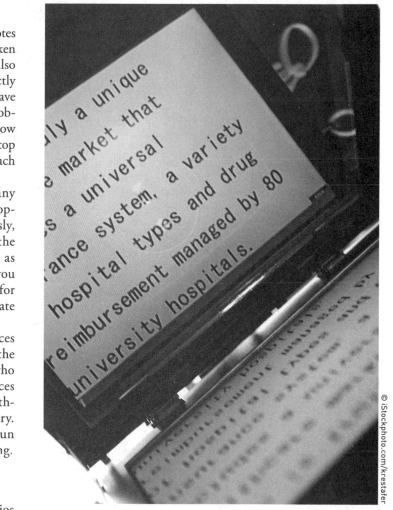

Broadcasters read content aloud from scripts and teleprompters, which means journalists who write for this medium must consider this issue when building stories.

© iStockphoto.com/krestafer

Broadcast is a mass medium in that it starts at a single source and reaches a large audience. However, unlike the other media used to disseminate content, broadcast has a face-to-face component to it that gives it a more personal feel for the audience members.

Viewers basically "invite" broadcast journalists into their homes each night to share information about the day's events. This interpersonal connection, even if it is really a one-way relationship, is something that broadcasters can use to connect with audience members.

One of the ways in which broadcasters connect is through the use of first- and second-person language. Broadcast journalists often direct information to audience members by explaining how "you" can get involved in a story or what a story means to "you." This gives the listener a stronger sense of personal empowerment while the statement remains genuine, thanks to that interpersonal tie between the sender and the receiver.

In addition, reporters often become part of the story in a variety of ways. In simple news stories, reporters include stand-up segments, where they appear on camera and infuse themselves into the news. In most cases, the reporter remains neutral on the topic, but that injection of a personal touch allows the viewers to associate a real person with the storytelling. In live segments (discussed later in the chapter), the reporter will often banter with the anchor from a personal perspective.

For example, during a story about a political scandal, an anchor might ask, "Did the mayor tell you if he planned to quit?" The reporter would then answer in first person, noting, "I did ask the mayor if he planned to resign, and he told me that was not even an option in his mind." This use of interaction can give the audience members a feeling of being on the inside of a story alongside the journalists.

In other cases, broadcasters can become part of the story through personal participation. Morning-show anchors often take part in on-set segments, whereas nightly news reporters can allow viewers to live vicariously through their own participation in an event.

Use the opportunities available to you as you write scripts and pitch stories to take advantage of this unique aspect of your medium. This can help you feel more connected to your audience and allow them to feel the same way about you.

GIVE IT A TRY: Select a traditional inverted-pyramid story from a newspaper or a website and rework it to include more interpersonal engagement. Look for ways in which you can directly or indirectly reach out to your readers through the use of first and second person or through potential stand-up ideas. Not every story will lend itself to this type of interpersonal engagement, so select your topic carefully and apply your use of these techniques judiciously.

STRUCTURE

Broadcast writing tends to follow less of an inverted-pyramid structure than print or web writing, primarily because of the way in which audience members consume the content. Audience members who are told stories are used to chronological stories instead of those written in descending order of importance. Most "tales" we tell start at the beginning and move through the resolution of the issue. Broadcast mirrors that chronology while still relying on the interest elements outlined in Chapter 1. It also tends to take on a "circle" approach, in which the content is provided to the viewers in a way that alerts them to important content, grabs their attention with the material and then brings the story full circle at the end.

The Lead

In an inverted-pyramid story, the lead tries to jam as much information into the first sentence as possible. In broadcast, the writers assume that the audience members aren't fully paying attention to the story. The writers know that the viewers need a heads-up before the 5W's and 1H show up.

The lead of a broadcast story is akin to a print or web headline. The first sentence serves to alert the audience members about something that might interest them. The purpose of the lead sentence is to mentally "poke" the audience before getting into the details of the story.

Here's a standard print story lead:

Northwestern State University's Board of Governors voted Tuesday to increase tuition by 5.5 percent for undergraduate students and 10.5 percent for graduate students.

For a print story, this works well because it gives the readers all the important information right away. In broadcast, however, by the time the listeners catch on to that first sentence and start paying attention, they missed what happened and what it means to them. This is why a broadcast lead has to alert the audience to the topic before getting into the specifics:

Students at Northwestern State University will be paying more for school this year.

The broadcast lead alerts the listeners who should care (students, people involved in Northwestern State University) without getting into the specifics (tuition increase, specific percentages for each type of student). With this type of lead, interested audience members can orient themselves to the news story quickly and avoid missing important information.

The Body

If a print story is a pyramid, a broadcast story is more of a circular story; it will introduce the most important thing in the story and then move forward in a direction that will "close the loop." The first sentence of the body will look like a print lead, although still not as detailed:

The school's board of governors voted today to increase undergraduate tuition by 5.5 percent. Graduate students will see a 10.5 percent increase to their tuition bills.

What comes next will be the various elements of the story that help tell a story in a chronological format:

Board members agreed in July that tuition should be raised but did not note an amount.

An audit of the school in August found that tuition needed at least a 5 percent hike across the board.

During today's meeting, the trustees settled on the approved amounts, saying they thought the increases were appropriate. Members also said they didn't want to have to raise tuition again next year.

In this case, the body walks the audience members through the various stages of the story, including when the issue came up, when the board settled on an amount and why board members believe this approach works. The chronological approach puts the story into a format that listeners and viewers can easily digest.

You will also notice that each sentence has a single information point in it. If you write sentences that have too many things going on in them or that have overly complex construction, you will lose the listeners. The body should be a few simple sentences like these, especially if video is not involved.

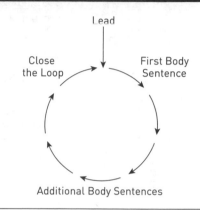

FIGURE 11.1 ■ While print and web stories use an inverted-pyramid structure, broadcast stories use a circular model, with a lead that works like a print headline. The rest of the sentences providing content in an easy-to-consume fashion.

Lead

Close the Loop

First Body Sentence

Additional Body Sentences

The Close

A closing for a broadcast story should seal the deal in some way. In the case of reporter-driven stories that use video, the reporter can provide a personal **sign-off** that includes the station's call letters:

For W-X-X-X-T-V, I'm James Simon.

This lets the audience know that the story package is over and that it is time to move on to the next story. Since the reporter a part of the story from its beginning, this is a simple way to close up.

In other situations, the final sentence of the story can bring the story full circle and close the loop. To do this, you want to look forward on the story or revisit the main issue of the story in a simple conclusion:

The board will revisit the tuition issue next year.

Your final sentence also could provide the audience with options to act. You can tell listeners or viewers to visit a website, call a phone number or participate in an event. In these cases, television reporters often state the information during the closing and rely on a graphic to reinforce the point:

For more information on the tuition increase, visit the university's website at N-W-S-U-dot-E-D-U/tuition.

ADAPT
SCRIPT BASICS

The purpose of a **script** is to make the story easy for the anchor or reporter to read aloud. This means you will need to adapt some of the basics of writing to fit the needs of someone speaking the words out loud if you want the piece to work well.

Here are a few things that you need to keep in mind as you write your scripts:
Balcony Toss VO/SOT
Glenn Hubbard
3-24-08

Video	Audio
	(EDDIE)
ON CAM TAKE VO SHOTS OF BAR	An Alabama college student is still in the hospital—after being thrown from a hotel balcony in Panama City last week.
SUPER: Sandpiper Resort, Panama City, Florida	Police say the student was at a bar Thursday night when a security guard kidnapped her and later raped her.
SHOTS OF BALCONY	The two then struggled and the student fell from the hotel's sixth floor.
SHOTS OF HOSPITAL	She suffered broken bones and a concussion but is expected to make a full recovery.
PICTURE OF SUSPECT	Officers say it didn't take long to solve the crime.
SOT [MCU JONES]	(SOT: DETECTIVE JOHN JONES)
SUPER: Detective John Jones, Panama City Police	YEAH—THE GUY WAS JUST STANDING THERE AND WE ARRESTED HIM, AND THAT WAS ABOUT IT.
	(EDDIE)
ON CAM	Her assailant is in jail on a million-dollar bond.

Typed Copy

Just as in all the other forms of media writing, readability is the primary goal. However, because the copy has to be read aloud smoothly, the script is often double or triple spaced. Some experts prefer a formatting approach that places the copy in all capital letters, while others prefer a standard approach.

In some newsrooms, the page is split, with the information that needs be read on the right half of the page and the information regarding any video graphics on the left.

In other newsrooms, the video information is less detailed and is merely noted at the top of each section, as you will see with examples later in the chapter. Both approaches help the reader know when the video will be on the screen and when to pause so that people on the video can be heard.

Verb Tense

Broadcast is an immediate medium that often takes people to events as they unfold. Even when material is gathered prior to air, broadcasters use the present tense as much as possible. When you type your script, look for opportunities to recast your verbs in present tense, including the use of "says" instead of "said" for attributions.

Pronunciation

In copy written for a text-based consumer, words need to be spelled properly. In broadcast, the reader must also know how the word should sound when spoken. Reporters or anchors who stumble over pronunciations will look foolish and lack credibility. To that end, scripts often include phonetic elements called **pronouncers**.

In most cases, you would avoid complicated words in favor of simpler ones, but that doesn't always work. For example, when a crime happens in Nevada, Missouri, it's in NEE-vay-da, but if it happens in Las Vegas, Nevada, it's in neh-VA-da. The pronouncer should break the word into syllables and show where the emphasis should take place. It's best to include both the word itself and the pronouncer in parentheses so the reader can rely on either prior knowledge or your phonetic help to say the word properly. For example, Wisconsin natives are more likely to get tripped up when reading o-CON-o-mo-wok than if you simply gave them the city's name, Oconomowoc.

Abbreviations

Some abbreviations, such as St. and Dr., have multiple meanings and can trip up a reader. You could have a meeting at St. Paul's Church on Mulberry Dr. or you could meet Dr. Paul Church on Mulberry St. In broadcast writing, we avoid shortening things that could lead to a flustered anchor or reporter.

When you need to use abbreviations, you can use hyphens and spacing to dictate how you want someone to pronounce something. For example, if you were to write about acquired immune deficiency syndrome, you would use the acronym "AIDS," which is pronounced as a single word. If you did a story on the Federal Bureau of Investigation, you need to make sure the anchor doesn't call the FBI "the fibbie." Hyphenate the letters to fix this: F-B-I. You can perform similar fixes on telephone numbers ("Call one-800-four-eight-two, two-one-two-seven.").

Numbers and Symbols

Broadcast audience members have trouble retaining and understanding numbers, especially if the numbers are large or complex. Printed copy tends to use the exact numbers ("The principal will make $50,152 this year"), but broadcasters usually round those numbers to something less cumbersome. Broadcast writing pushes you to write the copy the way you would say it ("The principal will make about 50 thousand dollars this year") to avoid confusion. Numbers less than 10 are spelled out, as single digits might get lost on a page ("The president will send one plane with two negotiators to the meeting"). Symbols are also spelled out ("Join our Twitter conversation at hash-tag W-R-T-V cares"; "Using your telephone, dial pound sign five-four-three to make a payment").

GIVE IT A TRY: Take a standard print story or press release from a source you trust and turn it into a simple script. (Look at the example above and the section on creating a "reader" later in the chapter for some guidance in how to format the script.) Apply the basic tenets of lead writing, body copy formation and story ending you learned here to the piece. Be sure to pay attention to verb tense, pronunciation help and other items mentioned here that could trip you up as a broadcast journalist. Don't worry too much about timing the script at this point, but you can keep it to 20 or 30 seconds if you want a target.

INTEGRATING ADDITIONAL ELEMENTS

As noted earlier, one of the bigger challenges broadcasters face is pairing the script with video and audio elements. Video can tell stories when used well, and it can distract viewers when the text and pictures don't match up. Audio segments, known as **soundbites** or **actualities**, can lend credibility to a report or they can lead to confused listeners. Here are some ways to properly integrate these important elements into your broadcast pieces:

Writing to Video

When journalists create stories for broadcast, the goal is to use the video and the spoken words to augment and support each other. **Writing to video** allows audience members to more fully engage the content without confusion. When the video and the words don't go together, the viewers can feel disoriented and thus miss key news elements in the story.

Video that adds no value to a story, such as photos of the backs of people or random crowd shots, is referred to as wallpaper.

For example, if a reporter is talking about a bright and sunny day while the video is showing gray skies and rainy conditions, this disconnect can leave the audience members puzzled. However, when the video of a beautiful day is paired with a matching description, the audience members can better understand what's going on and thus engage the story. When you write your stories for broadcast, you need to know what kind of video is available that will pair with the text. If you want to talk about a large crowd at an event, you need to make sure that you have video that will support that idea.

When you don't have supporting video, you run into a familiar broadcast journalism problem called **wallpaper** video. The term refers to the use of generic visual elements that don't enhance the storytelling elements of the spoken word. An example of this would be a story on school truancy where the reporter shows the feet of children walking through the halls of a school or video of the exterior of the school building. In cases like these, the text is literally being "wallpapered" over by video just to cover the story.

Writing Into and Out of Soundbites

As explained in Chapter 10, print journalists rely heavily on quotes to add flavor and allow sources to speak directly to audience members. Broadcast journalists have a similar opportunity when they record interviews with sources and take small clips of them to include in the stories. These small portions of the interviews are called soundbites or actualities. They create the opportunity to infuse not only the words but also the voice and emotion of the source into the stories.

As is the case with direct quotes, broadcast journalists need to write copy that introduces the soundbites, thus preparing the audience members for who will speak and what the person will say. The **lead-in** needs to inform the listener as to the source and content without repeating the soundbite or giving the soundbite a weak open:

Horrible lead-in: In responding to the budget crisis, University System President Nate Craft had this to say:

"The loss of more than 20 percent of our revenue over the next biennium is more than our campuses can withstand without cutting faculty and staff positions."

Bad lead-in: University System President Nate Craft says a 20 percent loss in revenue would force campuses to cut faculty and staff positions.

"The loss of more than 20 percent of our revenue over the next biennium is more than our campuses can withstand without cutting faculty and staff positions."

Better lead-in: University System President Nate Craft says the budget cuts the governor proposed would substantially weaken all of the campuses across the state.

"The loss of more than 20 percent of our revenue over the next biennium is more than our campuses can withstand without cutting faculty and staff positions."

In addition, you must transition from the soundbite back into your script. (During the scripting process, soundbites aren't written out in full. In most cases, they simply include an "out," which is a typewritten chunk of information that includes the last few words the source will say. This shows the reporter when to resume reading the script.) Journalists often refer to this as writing out of a soundbite, and it is a crucial skill that allows you to continue the flow of your story. If you need to add information to clarify the soundbite, the "out" can be a good place to do it:

Craft also says the cuts would force the faculty who remain to teach one extra class per semester.

If you need to transition to another aspect of the story or lead into a different source, the out can create a transition between the pieces.

Although he sees Craft's concerns, Governor James Bold says the university system needs to find creative ways to fix its finances.

You will rarely place soundbites back to back, just as you will rarely place quotes together with no transition, so consider the "out" in your script a chance to buffer between soundbites.

TYPES OF STORIES

Broadcasters use a variety of approaches to cover news. When pieced together, this array of stories will create a cohesive newscast. The types of stories broadcast journalists create vary based on length and the integration of video and audio elements. Here is a list of the stories and how complex they are:

Reader

This is the simplest form of storytelling in broadcast, as it involves nothing but a script and the anchor or reporter. The **reader** contains no video or soundbites and just has the journalist reading the story aloud. These traditionally last 10 to 20 seconds each and contain about four or five sentences of copy. In television, an over-the-shoulder graphic may augment the storytelling. This could include a visual of a police badge for a crime story or a photo of the mayor for a story involving his or her office.

Voice-Over

The **voice-over**, or VO, adds the element of video to the story but remains a fairly simple storytelling tool. The voice-over story starts with the journalist reading the first sentence from the story while on camera. As the story moves into the second sentence, the video associated with the story begins to roll on the screen, allowing the viewers to hear the reporter's voice over the video. The journalist will reappear on the screen to finish the final sentence of the story before transitioning to the next story in the newscast.

VO/SOT

VO/SOT stands for "voice-over/sound on tape" and integrates the use of a soundbite or two into a story. The story begins the way a VO does, with the journalist on camera for the first sentence before the video rolls and the voice continues. However, at some point in the story, the journalist integrates a soundbite from a source. Once the soundbite has aired, the journalist continues reading the script as the rest of the video airs. Most VO/SOTs include one or two soundbites and run for about 35 to 40 seconds.

AN EXAMPLE OF A VO/SOT

{REPORTER On Camera}
POLICE ARE LOOKING FOR A SUSPECT IN CONNECTION WITH A BANK ROBBERY ON GREENVILLE BOULEVARD THIS AFTERNOON.
{Take VO }
{Super: "Greenville Boulevard"}
OFFICERS SAY A MAN WALKED INTO THIS BB&T BRANCH AT AROUND 4:30…SHOWED THE TELLER A GUN AND GOT AWAY WITH AN UNDISCLOSED AMOUNT OF MONEY. PUBLIC INFORMATION OFFICER JANE DOE SAYS IT'S THE THIRD BANK ROBBERY IN GREENVILLE THIS MONTH.

{SOT}
{Super: "Jane Doe, Greenville Police Public Information Officer"}
{Doe :08 outcue: "…not acceptable."}
{VO Cont.}
THE OTHER TWO ROBBERIES HAPPENED LAST WEEK AT THIS WELLS FARGO BRANCH ON FIRETOWER ROAD AND AT ANOTHER BB&T BRANCH ON MEMORIAL DRIVE.
{REPORTER On Cam}
POLICE ARE ASKING YOU TO CALL CRIMESTOPPERS IF YOU HAVE INFORMATION ON THESE ROBBERIES.

Source: Courtesy of Glenn Hubbard.

Package

This is the traditional news-story format that people are used to seeing on broadcast television. Reporters edit the video and voice their script in advance so that the entire story is ready to plug into the newscast as a **package** of content. In other words, the story has been preassembled and requires no live efforts from anyone aside from a brief introduction and a concluding statement from the anchor. These stories contain soundbites from at least two sources and will likely include a standup. The standup works like a soundbite but shows the reporter in the field offering information on the topic. Package stories usually run between 1:30 and 2 minutes each and are the staple of most newscasts.

AN EXAMPLE OF A PACKAGE

Video	Audio
SOT: Nick Floyd	"It doesn't matter what time of year it is, if the lights are on at night or if they see guys running around out there, trust me, somebody drops by to see what's going on".
B-Roll	The East Carolina Baseball program holds an annual World Series to conclude its fall practice regimen. Assistant coach Ben Sanderson says the games are always an exciting event for the community.
SOT: Ben Sanderson	"Probably the last 15 years at least it's been going on. It dates back into Coach Leclair's time and continued into Coach Godwin's tenure and it's always been an exciting event."
B-Roll	The three-game series consists of intersquad competition that allows the coaches and fans to get an idea what to expect in the spring.
SOT: Ben Sanderson	"It gives our fans and the community kind of a first glimpse at our team in that competitive atmosphere"
SOT: Ben Fultz	"We've been working all fall and it's our chance to prove ourselves every year".
B-Roll	Sanderson says East Carolina has always had a successful turnout at the event.
SOT: Ben Sanderson	"We have more fans at our fall world series that a lot of schools in the country have at their regular season games".
B-Roll	Senior outfielder Ben Fultz says the community support always puts an added sense of excitement on the event.
SOT: Ben Fultz	"Playing baseball it's awesome to see fans in the stands. It motivates you more, it gets people pumped and gets you motivated".
B-Roll	Keely Warren...Pirate News Network

Source: Courtesy of Glenn Hubbard.

LOS

LOS stands for "live on set" or "live on scene" and involves integrating interaction between the reporter and the anchor during a live newscast. The anchor will start to talk about the story before introducing the reporter who is covering the story. The reporter, who will either be live in the studio or reporting live from a location associated with the story, will say a line or two about the topic before the prepackaged story goes on air. Once the story is complete, the live portion of the newscast returns with the reporter offering some summary statements or conducting a brief question and answer session with the anchor to wrap up the piece. In most cases, these stories run longer than a traditional package and do not include a stand up within the package.

AN EXAMPLE OF AN LOS

Slug: Fablehaven
Correspondent: Emily Valla
Air date: 04/4 6 p.m.
Run time: 2:01

Video	Audio
In studio Readers: Jay Hildebrandt and Karole Honas	**LEAD IN** **JAY:** "FABLEHAVEN" AUTHOR BRANDON MULL VISITED LOCAL SCHOOLS TODAY. **KAROLE:** OFTEN THESE ASSEMBLIES COST SCHOOL DISTRICTS UP TO $1,500, BUT MULL'S VISIT TO IDAHO FALLS TODAY WAS FREE BECAUSE THIS AREA SELLS SO MANY OF HIS BOOKS. **JAY:** LOCAL NEWS 8'S EMILY VALLA WAS AT TODAY'S ASSEMBLIES WHERE IT WAS OBVIOUS HOW MUCH THE KIDS LOVE HIM.
b-roll (assembly, children laughing)	**Nat/VO – EMILY:** FOR THE 45 MINUTES BRANDON MULL TALKED TO LINDON PARK ELEMENTARY SCHOOL, THESE KIDS PRETTY MUCH NEVER STOPPED LAUGHING. THE BEST-SELLING AUTHOR TOOK STUDENTS THROUGH AN IMAGINATION GAME.
Sage interview Super: Sage/6th Grade Student	**SOT – Sage:** "They made up the Cheez-It as a big monster."
b-roll (pulling book off shelf)	**VO – EMILY:** AND THAT'S THE KIND OF IMAGINATION THAT MULL BRINGS TO HIS BOOKS, LIKE "FABELHAVEN." (MORE)
2-2-2 Mull interview Super: Brandon Mull/Children's Author	**SOT – Brandon Mull:** "It's the story of Kendra and Seth who discover their grandparents are the caretakers of a secret wildlife park for magical creatures."
Emily stand up Super: Emily Valla/Local People Local News	**SOT – EMILY:** FABLEHAVEN IS BRANDON MULL'S MOST POPULAR SERIES. NOW THIS BOOK IS CLEARLY WELL LOVED IN THIS LIBRARY, AND THIS BOOK ALONE IS OVER 500 PAGES. AND THERE'S FIVE OF THEM IN THIS SERIES.
b-roll (panning books, book open with pages sticking up)	**VO –** THE BOOKS ARE NEW YORK TIMES BEST SELLERS AND ARE TRANSLATED INTO MANY LANGUAGES ALL OVER THE WORLD.
b-roll (Mull talking to students at assembly)	**VO –** SO MULL DOESN'T HAVE TO DO THINGS LIKE SCHOOL TOURS, BUT HE LOVES THEM.
Mull interview	**SOT – Brandon Mull:** "I spend a lot of my year alone in a room typing. So it's nice to sometimes get out of my office and get around the kids who are actually reading my stories and be able to talk to them and listen to them."

Video	Audio
Strait interview Super: Ginger Strait/ Teacher, Lindon Park Elementary	**SOT – Ginger Strait:** "This is real life literacy. It's relevant. The kids care. They are so excited to hear from an author who's written a book."
Dylan interview Super: Dylan/6th Grade Student	**SOT – Dylan:** "I try to get as much books as I can so I can read at home."
b-roll (panning school library)	**VO – EMILY:** FOR DYLAN, THAT INCLUDES MANY OF MULL'S BOOKS. (MORE)
3-3-3 Mull interview	**SOT – Mull:** "A parent came up to me and told me that my books, the Fablehaven series, were the books that made her kid into a reader. And that's always the best thing I can hear."
b-roll (more of assembly)	**Out cue VO – EMILY:** IN IDAHO FALLS, I'M EMILY VALLA.
In studio	**Lead out VO graphic – JAY:** MULL IS SIGNING NEW AND WELL-LOVED BOOKS AT BARNES AND NOBLE IN IDAHO FALLS TONIGHT AT 6:30.
In studio	**KAROLE:** CHAD MORRIS, THE AUTHOR OF "CRAGBRIDGE HALL," ALSO VISITED IDAHO FALLS SCHOOLS TODAY.
In studio	**JAY AND KAROLE AD LIB.** ###

Source: Courtesy of Glenn Hubbard.

PROFESSIONAL THOUGHTS
LUCHA RAMEY

Lucha Ramey has worked for PBS, Warner Bros, NASA-TV and local news markets in Lexington, Kentucky, Pittsburgh and NBC O&O WTVJ in Miami. As a local TV news producer, she covered the 2000 presidential election; the terrorist attacks of Sept. 11, 2001; and the anthrax scares that followed. For the past 15 years, Ramey has built upon the lessons learned in her journalistic career, adding corporate communications, executive counseling, advertising and strategic marketing to her portfolio.

She's used her skills in a variety of industries, from nuclear power generation at the Tennessee Valley Authority (Knoxville, Tennessee) to health care at the University of Louisville Hospital in Kentucky and James Graham Brown Cancer Center to higher education at St. Mary's University in San Antonio, Texas. She is currently the Director of Communications for Penn-Harris-Madison School Corporation, a top ranked Indiana suburban school

Lucha Ramey

(Continued)

(Continued)

district outside of South Bend that serves nearly 11,000 students in 15 schools.

Through each phase of her career, she has thought of herself as a reporter of sorts, gathering information and telling stories.

As a student at Northwestern University, Ramey learned various aspects of journalism, ranging from magazine and newspaper writing to radio and television news. She said that the model the Medill School of Journalism used kept the focus on telling stories clearly, regardless of the platform.

"It was clear that good writing is the foundation for *all* forms of journalism," Ramey said. "I had to write and report in magazine and newspaper style first before I could progress to broadcast, where we studied both radio and TV."

Ramey said this approach to training helped her make a fairly simple transition from news to public relations.

"The transition to PR was relatively smooth because my first job out of TV news [was] as a producer for NASA-TV as a federal contractor," she said. "I was still using my same skill set. It was still [a] producing job but in a less stressful working environment."

In her role with NASA, she produced video news releases for local and national television stations and coordinated news conferences for the NASA-TV satellite feed. She said her goal was to provide key messages in a succinct fashion for the media outlets that sought her help.

"I've found over the years that I have to be the reporter on the inside of the organization gathering the facts in order to sort everything out and figure out what is the most important information," she said. "Also, if I can't understand the story, I can't pitch the story. The reporters have to understand the story in order for their readers and viewers to understand it."

Even as a broadcast journalist, Ramey said she found that she was using a lot of skills that are often thought of as being more akin to public relations practitioners or advertising professionals.

"The biggest thing that my years in TV news taught me and helped me in the transition and since was marketing," she said. "In Pittsburgh, I learned how to produce to the rating meters, hitting certain segments at a certain time in order to gain the Nielsen rating credit for that quarter hour....We went

to seminars and training sessions all the time to get the latest reports so that we could seek out and report the types of stories our viewers, down to their neighborhood, had indicated they wanted to see. So it's always been a part of my 'pitch' during a job interview that marketing/communications is about selling an organization's brand/image. I know how to 'sell' and deliver."

At each stop along her career, she said, the one constant was figuring out who was in the audience, what those people wanted to know and how best to give it to them.

"Good writing is key to making a connection to your audience and this is true for all forms of media, even social media for personal use," she said. "Think about it: Which spam emails do you open? The ones with the catchy and relevant subject lines. Which links or videos do you click on Facebook? Those that have intrigued you and you want to read or see more of. Which tweets do you retweet? Again, those that have piqued your interest. So these same principles apply to marketing, even more so in the digital age where PR professionals have to now write and manage print, video, online and digital forms of communication."

One Last Thing

Q: If you could tell students anything about media writing or anything you have seen in your time in the field, what would it be?

A: If you're a journalism student, always look for a person who's being affected by the story. Tell the story from their point of view and interview the opposing sides and officials. But don't be quick to always paint the officials as the uncaring, removed "suits." Sometimes a story can work being told from their point of view. Your writing should be clear and understandable so your audience can make their own decision. Do your best to present all the facts. If they won't fit into your story space, there are now other ways to get the information out there: sidebars, website, social media, etc. Always be fair and objective.

POLISHING YOUR FINAL PIECE FOR DELIVERY

As mentioned earlier, broadcast writing serves the ear more than the eye. To make sure your work does the job, you can't just have content that is "good on paper." It has to sound right, read well and feel natural as you deliver it. Once you are finished writing everything down and you think the story is ready for production, apply these tips as you read the piece aloud:

- **Check your time:** Time is a big issue in broadcast journalism, especially if your piece is part of a larger broadcast segment. Every second you are long or short is a second someone else has to deal with. You should find out how long your piece is expected to be and how close you are to that mark. If you are long or short by a couple seconds, look for simple fixes, such as changing out words or tightening sentence structure. If you are short or long by a lot, consider where you need to cut or add to make the story fit the time without undermining the value of the piece.

- **Check your pace:** Adrenaline is a wonderful thing in some cases, but not in broadcast. If you feel you are getting really jacked up and you are reading a 1:30 story in 14 seconds, you probably need to calm down and work on your pace. You should pace your story in such a way that you aren't going so fast as to lose or confuse readers, but also not so slowly that you leave seconds of dead air between sentences. A decent pace is usually your standard conversational approach, dialed back to be just a bit slower. You are always speaking a bit more quickly than you think you are.

- **Check your enunciation:** When you read aloud, open your mouth so that you fully form the words you are speaking. This will prevent you from sounding like you're mumbling through a mouthful of marbles. Proper enunciation comes from all parts of your mouth, including your tongue, cheeks, lips and soft palate. Use all of these as you form words and speak audibly. If you find yourself saying words like "gonna" or "wanna," chances are you aren't focusing on forming the words properly.

- **Check your pronunciation:** The pronouncers in your script should help you feel confident in saying unfamiliar words out loud. That said, you still have to say them, so take a couple practice swings at some of these. Check with other people who have a working knowledge of your topic to see if your pronunciation sounds accurate. If you aren't saying a word correctly, you will lose credibility, so practice saying unfamiliar words until you are confident in your approach to them.

Once you go through these steps, make the proper edits to your piece and give it another read. When you feel you have addressed all of these issues, you can feel confident your writing has met the standards your viewers have come to expect of you.

THE BIG THREE

Here are the three key things you should take away from this chapter:

1. **Write for the ear:** Broadcast is transmitted aurally and requires you to consider how something will sound when it is spoken and how it will sound when it is heard. This means that you need to look at your word choices, your sentence length and your overall clarity both in terms of information and also in terms of audio and video transmission. "Crack" or "snap" sounds a lot better than "broken" or "in pieces."

2. **Play to the strengths of the platform:** You have the ability to use audio and video elements to augment your content, so you should consider them as you write. Write in a way that allows your video to pair well with your script. Consider your options and try them out loud as you create your script.

3. **Connect with your audience:** Broadcast journalists have the opportunity to reach out to viewers and put a face on their news stories in ways that other journalists can't. Take advantage of these opportunities to form bonds with your audience members through the use of personal pronouns, audience-centric story approaches and other similar touches in your writing. This bond will sponsor trust from your audience and allow you to serve these people better.

KEY TERMS

actuality 188	pronouncer 187	voice-over 189
KISS 181	reader 189	VO/SOT 190
lead-in 188	script 186	wallpaper 188
LOS 191	sign-off 186	writing to video 188
package 190	soundbite 188	

DISCUSSION QUESTIONS

1. What are some of the benefits and drawbacks associated with writing to video? What does video improve in your storytelling and how does video limit your writing?

2. What are some of the similarities and differences between text-based quotes and broadcast soundbites? What are the benefits and drawbacks of each from the perspectives of the journalists who use them and the audience members who receive them?

3. How does writing for the ear differ from the other forms of writing you do in the field of journalism? What things do you need to do for the journalist reading the story to make it work well? What things do you need to do to help your audience understand the information as they hear and see the news?

WRITE NOW!

1. Find a story in a newspaper and rewrite it in broadcast format. Follow the rules associated with broadcast leads, style and sentence structure. You can do this multiple times, starting with writing a simple reader and then working into a script for a VO/SOT or a package.

2. Look at a story on a website that is associated with a television station and locate a story that is done in both text and video format. Compare and contrast the ways in which these stories are done. Did the writer rework the story to accentuate the values of each medium, or did the script just become

"shovelware" online? What are some things that could be done better in each version to improve the overall storytelling?

3. Look through a small handful of print or web stories for elements that can be problematic for broadcast. For words that are too complicated, suggest replacements that are easier for the audience to understand. For words that are difficult to pronounce, suggest replacements or create pronouncers for them. For awkward abbreviations or complex numbers, rework these key elements to make things easier on the journalist and the audience members.

NOTES

1. R. Papper (2005). "Broadcast Writing and Speaking." In S. Quinn and V. Filak (Eds.), "Convergent Journalism: An Introduction." Burlington, MA: Focal.

2. E. Shearer (2017, June 16). "Audio and Podcasting Fact Sheet." Accessed at: http://www.journalism.org/fact-sheet/audio-and-podcasting/.

FOCUS ON MARKETING MEDIA

© iStockphoto.com/Cecilie_Arcurs

12

PUBLIC RELATIONS

LEARNING OBJECTIVES

After completing this chapter you should be able to:

- Understand the key aspects of public relations and how they relate to your work as a media professional.

- Explain the concept of transparency and why it has value in the field of public relations.

- Identify the key elements to providing the best possible message to your readers.

- Create properly formatted public-relations material, including a standard press release.

- Understand the various forms of information you will release and how to work with the media to meet their needs as you release content.

Public relations is an exceptionally rewarding field within media, even though many people outside of journalism don't know how PR works or what professionals in this field do.

Other areas of media have tangible products that most members of the public can see. In the case of print products and websites, the identity of the journalist is attached to the content through a **byline** or other identifying feature. In addition, the work is easy to see: Online journalists post their work to the web, while print reporters produce newspapers and magazines.

Broadcast journalists are usually at the forefront of the news, either as field reporters or anchors. The names and faces of the journalists make them local or national celebrities in the minds of their viewers. Even those people behind the scenes can point to the newscast and explain their roles in the broadcast.

Advertising professionals have glossy spreads in magazines, newspaper ads, billboards and television commercials to help explain their jobs. Unlike news journalists, people at advertising agencies don't get their names on their work, but the content remains tangible. The ad that just popped up on your Facebook feed came from somewhere, and people in advertising can explain their role in its creation and dissemination.

Public-relations practitioners' work is often filtered through multiple media outlets, and thus the public rarely sees it in its purest form. A reporter will use a bit of information from a **press release**, leaving the public unable to see the practitioner's work. A short interview on the nightly news with a CEO can require a great deal of work on the part of a PR firm, but the public rarely considers the practitioner's role in all of this.

In many cases, the work of the practitioner comes to the public eye only when something goes horribly awry. In addition, popular culture has led the public to erroneously view PR practitioners as slick operators who constantly find a way to **spin** bad news into good news. In fact, the goals, ethics and tactics of PR are akin to those in every other area of the field, as you will see throughout the chapter.

This chapter will examine the basic elements of public relations and how they meet the needs of the general public. In addition, we will see how PR differs from some of the other forms of writing we have discussed, as well as the ways it is similar to writing for news and advertising. Finally, the chapter will address several keys to creating good copy as a public-relations practitioner.

DEFINING PR

In 1995, a block party in a university town got out of hand. After a day of drinking, the partygoers attempted to keep the party going with a bonfire they set in the middle of the street, fueling it with alcohol and broken furniture. When firefighters attempted to extinguish the blaze, they were repelled with a hail of rocks, bottles and cans.

A small cadre of police officers then attempted to quell the crowd and met the same fate. During this time, the partiers started more bonfires down the street, broke into several homes and even lit a car on fire.

Police dressed in riot gear then entered the area to make it safe for fire officials. With chemical sprays, batons and fire hoses, police and fire officials finally got control of the area, with dozens of people being injured and arrested in the process.

A journalist called the police the next day for information on the incident, asking if police responded properly to the riot. The officer in charge rebuked the journalist, arguing that it was not a riot and it should not be viewed as such.

Calling a riot a "large, prolonged disturbance" is an example of the kind of public relations and messaging you don't want to use.

After recounting the chaos and destruction, as well as the police response, the journalist asked how the police officials would frame this incident, if they weren't willing to call it a riot.

"It was a large, prolonged disturbance," the officer replied before ending the interview.

This situation illustrates the difference between trying to use verbal gymnastics to alter reality and the nature of properly constructed public-relations efforts.

PR practitioners communicate valuable and engaging information from an organization, company or group to a target audience in a clear and coherent manner. To this end, they are no different from news journalists or advertising professionals. Attempts to define public relations have often failed because it is a large field that involves a number of duties, opportunities and dissemination platforms. However, here are a few terms and concepts that appear in many good definitions of PR:

Deliberate

Public-relations workers take action that is intentional. In other words, the practitioners act with the hope of creating a specific result. Some practitioners attempt to gain understanding as they connect an unknown political candidate or unfamiliar topic with people who need to know this person or idea. In other cases, these professionals will solicit feedback to see how well an idea fared or whether people enjoyed an event. In every case, however, the action is deliberate in the sense that practitioners want to create influence within the target audience.

Prepared

Off-the-cuff comments and quick-witted jabs tend to get the most attention in this field, but overall, public relations is an organized attempt to create action or reaction. Events associated with campaigns require high levels of preparation and a lot of work during the execution phase. Speeches require heavy editing and numerous revisions. Good practitioners will make sure they properly prepare spokespeople before news conferences. They will also have extensive amounts of information available to reporters at these events. Research and planning are key components of everything professionals do in this field.

© iStockphoto.com/bgwalker

PROFESSIONAL THOUGHTS
ERIN WHITE

Erin White's career path has led her to the center of some of the most hotly debated topics in the United States. As deputy communications director for New York City Mayor Bill de Blasio and former communications manager for reproductive rights at the American Civil Liberties Union, White said she finds herself working to convey messages and advocate for policies that affect the lives of 8.5 million New Yorkers.

"Informing and educating is the foundational purpose of journalism," she said. "While PR does often educate and inform, it does so with a purpose: to drive change. That change might mean encouraging consumers to buy Pepsi instead of Coke or convincing women in Alabama to tell their legislators to stop restricting reproductive health care, but the work always sets its sights on change."

Before moving into communications, White worked at two regional daily newspapers. She said media writing, interviewing and other journalistic skills have helped her succeed in communications.

"While I often apply the skills differently, I still use the skills I learned in journalism daily," White said.

"As a communications professional, I separate good information from bad information. I channel my reporting experience to spot potential policy holes. And I use the skills I developed refining stories to refine messages and connect with New Yorkers.

"When I regularly pitched reporters, the ability to find and apply data and ensure accuracy by fact checking and solid sourcing meant that reporters felt they could trust me. When I worked for the ACLU, I often found myself literally doing the reporting to help journalists grasp important concepts, uncover important statistics or to provide critical background. Did that work provide information that supported my arguments? Yes. But it also often vastly improved reporters' final stories. That's not spin—it's course correction."

One of the key differences she found between news journalism and public relations is that of action. White said that the best PR is advocacy that seeks to drive change. In order to do that, she said, she often works with news professionals to get her message out to a larger audience.

"I speak reporters' language, but my end goal is to help them speak mine," White said. "My solid ground-

Erin White

ing in journalism means I can serve as 'translator,' filtering the information, ideas and framing necessary to my cause through a journalist, to the public. Given that writing makes up large majorities of the communications I have with reporters—emails, press releases, statements, fact sheets, backgrounders—that 'translation' either happens in writing or it doesn't happen at all."

In using the skills she gained in her various stops, White said, she can train newer practitioners to communicate important information effectively and clearly.

"The most relevant skill that news writing develops is the ability to quickly and concisely communicate the most important facts or ideas," she said. "In fact, when I'm training young PR coworkers, I often ask them to study writing in news stories so that they can internalize the concept of a 'lede.' Being able to give a two-sentence version of your pitch—whether it's about a new beauty brand or the need to take climate change seriously—will make or break you in the PR business. The ability to pluck the most important and relevant pieces of information will breed success in any field related to communication (and in many that are not). Applying that one step further and organizing that important information in a way that audiences can quickly and easily understand will guarantee success in any field related to communication. Journalistic writing provides an incredible training ground for acquiring these skills."

One Last Thing

Q: If you could tell students anything about media writing or anything you have seen in your time in the field, what would it be?

A: Journalism is an incredible training ground, but don't be afraid to take those skills out into the world in a new way. Influence takes many forms.

Well-Performed

Legendary baseball pitcher and pitching coach Johnny Sain used to tell his pitchers, "Nobody wants to hear about the labor pains. They just want to see the baby." His point was that regardless of how well his players tried, the only thing that mattered was how well they pitched in the game. Fair or not, PR work is often judged in the same way. How well practitioners execute their work will determine how they are judged. A well-planned and well-polished press release can miss the audience or contain an egregious error. An outstanding event can be doomed if weather interferes or a key participant doesn't appear. Often what people see is all they can judge, and in most cases, that is the performance itself.

Mutually Beneficial

Communication within the sphere of PR must serve the sender and the receiver. If the practitioners' work benefits only their clients, the public will become distrustful, making whatever benefits the practitioners receive from the public short-lived. In most cases, PR professionals want to foster a strong, long-term relationship between their clients and the public, so all communication must benefit both groups. In creating mutually beneficial messages, practitioners can ensure that both sides will see positive gains over time.

Responsive

As noted throughout the book, the audience matters a great deal to all media professionals. In public relations, good practitioners understand that sending a message is important, but receiving feedback from the recipients of that message also matters. As the flow of information moves from sender to receiver and then back from the receiver to the sender, the practitioners can gain insight as to what is working and what isn't in terms of the message and the communication medium.

These terms make it clear that public relations is a complicated field that requires people to communicate effectively, gather facts and provide clear information. PR also requires its practitioners to engage in effective critical thinking and problem solving.

TYPES OF PR WRITING

Public-relations practitioners should expect to write for all major platforms and outlets, including newspapers, magazines, websites, television, radio and social media channels. Throughout this book, you can see how the type of writing varies from platform to platform.

Below are the various pieces practitioners create on a daily basis and what needs each one of them meets. Practitioners adapt these pieces to fit the needs of the media outlets that will receive them. For example, an **announcement** about the hiring of a CEO can be written in a four-paragraph brief format for a newspaper and then rewritten as a 20-second piece for a local radio station. The key here is to understand what each tool does and why you need to master it.

News Release

This is the practitioner's most common tool. The purpose of the **news release** is to inform the media about an important topic that deserves public attention. A news release, or press release as it is often called, can create awareness, draw attention or inspire action. It outlines the core elements of an event at a local museum. For a full examination of the various elements of a release, look at the breakout box later in the chapter.

According to author Dennis Wilcox,[1] news releases fall into several basic categories:

Announcements

These releases allow you to notify the media and the public about things such as changes in personnel, product launches, employment opportunities and legal actions. These are also useful to inform the public about charitable acts, big contracts and other positive outcomes your organization has experienced. Later in the chapter is an example of an announcement used to highlight an organization's name change and mission statement. It presents both the current and previous names of the group as well as some strong rationalization behind its changes. In addition, the standard information listed in the breakout box below is here as well.

Spot Announcements

This form of release alerts the media to breaking news items that affect the company or organization, such as a fire at a job site or a power outage at a stadium. When something happens out of the ordinary and the media might have an interest in it, a **spot announcement** has value.

Reaction Releases

These releases allow you to respond to newsworthy events and statements that affect your audience. For example, if your client is a candidate for public office and her opponent releases a negative ad or a nonpartisan group releases a poll, the media would likely want to know what your client thinks about the recent development. A **reaction release** allows you to issue a statement that states your client's position in the wake of the news.

Bad News

Crisis communication is one of the fastest growing areas of public relations, so knowing how to get important information out to the public when bad news strikes is crucial to doing your job as a practitioner. These types of releases allow you to explain issues related to bad news and make statements regarding what will happen next from your end.

Localization

In some cases, you have a local interest in putting information out to the public about a broader issue. If you worked for a local farming co-op, a national law that would ban a certain fertilizer or a court case that cuts back on farming subsidies would require you to offer a local perspective. Localization releases allow you to bring the broader issue to your readers in a local way.

Fact Sheets

These pieces provide the basic information about a topic, a company, a group, an event or an idea. The items in here are often simple chunks of information that allow the readers to digest key points in a simple and straightforward way. These sheets help reporters who need to quickly understand the background associated with topic. **Fact sheets** can also list key sources the reporters can contact, important historical moments that can inform on a current situation or time-date-place elements for an upcoming event. The abbreviated version of the Fox Cities Marathon's press kit outlines the various aspects noted here. You can see how the various elements of the kit provide facts, contact information and other quick-hit data to help reporters get a firm grasp on the topic at hand.

Media Alerts

This form of writing blends the lead-writing approach associated with the inverted pyramid and the bulleted approach common to fact sheets. **Media alerts** typically use many of the 5W's and 1H as a starting point for the bullets. Practitioners then fill in the information associated

Example Of A Standard News Release

Contact: Pamela Williams-Lime President
920.733.4089
pwilliams-lime@troutmuseum.org

The Trout Museum of Art plans programs to "SPARK!" imaginations of those with memory loss

History Museum at the Castle, The Building for Kids Children's Museum join The Trout Museum of Art to provide cultural programming for people with memory loss

APPLETON, Wis. (Sept. 15, 2014) – This fall, The Trout Museum of Art, History Museum at the Castle and The Building for Kids Children's Museum will launch a series of programs for people with memory loss called SPARK! The first of the three pilot programs will take place at The Trout Museum on Monday, Oct. 13 from 2–3:30 p.m.

"SPARK! is an exciting new program for caregivers and loved ones living with memory loss," said Pamela Williams-Lime, president of The Trout Museum of Art. "We are proud to partner with other local museums to expand our program offerings to serve a growing population in our community."

This program is made possible through funding from the Helen Bader Foundation, a philanthropic organization that launched the SPARK! initiative to help museums in the Midwest create meaningful experiences for adults with memory loss and their caregivers. Supplemental funding for the local program was provided through the Community Foundation of the Fox Valley Region.

The Trout Museum of Art, History Museum at the Castle and The Building for Kids Children's Museum are among several Wisconsin museums awarded funding by the Helen Bader Foundation to create programming inspired by the "Meet me at MOMA" program at the Museum of Modern Art. Both programs encourage participants to engage in lively discussions, art-making and other multi-sensory activities.

Each one-hour SPARK! program will be led by a specially trained museum educator who will engage participants in interactive exhibit experiences. The programs will also include opportunities for important social interactions among individuals living with memory loss and their caregivers. SPARK! events will also be held at History Museum at the Castle on Nov. 10, 2014, and at The Building for Kids Children's Museum on Jan. 12, 2015.

As space for this free-of-charge program is limited, registration is requested at least one week in advance of each program. Those interested in attending can register for one or more events by contacting The Trout Museum of Art at 920-733-4089.

###

About The Trout Museum of Art

The Trout Museum of Art's mission is to excite the community about the visual arts. The activities which allow the museum to fulfill its mission include: exhibitions, educational programming, a biennial exhibit for local artists, and special events, such as the annual Art at the Park artist exhibitor festival, lectures, workshops, family fun days and the Jazz at the Trout series.

About the Fox Cities Building for the Arts

The Fox Cities Building for the Arts serves as a collaborative business enterprise designed to empower nonprofit arts organizations to better serve the community through program partnerships, increased visibility and more efficient operations for years to come. In addition to The Trout Museum of Art which is operated by the Fox Cities Building for the Arts, five other area arts organizations currently reside in the building: the Fox Valley Symphony Orchestra, new Voices (formerly the White Heron Chorale), the Makaroff Youth Ballet and the Appleton Boychoir. Most recently, the building became a beacon of the downtown Appleton skyline with a LED light installation by nationally recognized artist Sandy Garnett.

Source: Courtesy of Red Shoes PR.

Example Of An Announcement News Release

Media contact:
Karen Smith
Karen@redshoespr.com
(920) 574-3253

New brand, same mission: the Emergency Shelter of the Fox Valley changes name to Homeless Connections

Appleton, Wis. *(Nov. 11, 2014)* – In an effort to fully represent its available services, the Emergency Shelter of the Fox Valley will officially change its name to Homeless Connections on Nov. 11, 2014. The move comes after the organization assessed that its existing name did not fully convey all of its programs offered to clients and the community.

"At the root of it all, our goal remains focused on improving the quality of living for those we serve and for the community as a whole," said Jerome Martin, executive director of Homeless Connections. "This updated name and look will provide better positioning as we collaborate and partner with other local agencies or organizations to invest in our clients' futures and success."

Homeless Connections serves approximately 3,000 individuals and families each year who are facing or at-risk of facing homelessness and provides temporary shelter and guidance to help prevent future homeless episodes and promote self-sufficiency. In 2013, Homeless Connections served 80,541 meals and provided 26,847 nights of shelter across its client base. The average stay of clients in the last year was 34 nights, and the staff is assisted by more than 1,000 volunteers.

Homeless Connections provides four program areas: shelter for men, women and children; case management, which includes assistance for transportation, clothing or work equipment; street outreach, which serves individuals who are homeless but do not typically seek shelter services; and a high-risk prevention program. The high-risk prevention program—through direct financial assistance, case management and follow-up services—currently holds a 98 percent success rate of preventing individuals and families who are at high risk of losing their community housing from becoming homeless.

The re-branding process was completed through research and a task force made up of staff, clients, volunteers and other members of the community. This change comes just ahead of National Hunger & Homelessness Awareness Week, which takes place from Nov. 15–23 this year.

Secura Insurance and Homeless Connections partner to raise awareness

SECURA Insurance and Homeless Connections are partnering to raise awareness and funds during National Hunger & Homelessness Awareness Week. SECURA Insurance, through their fund at the Community Foundation for the Fox Valley Region. The goal is to raise $15,000 in 15 days.

(Continued)

(Continued)

SECURA will match all donations, up to $15,000, contributed from November 16 to November 30. Checks can be sent to: Homeless Connections, 400 N Division Street, Appleton, Wisconsin 54911, or donations can be made online at www.homelessconnections.net. For more information about how you can contribute to the challenge, contact Community Relations Director Jennifer Dieter at (920) 734-9603 or jennifer@homelessconnections.net.

###

About Homeless Connections (formerly Emergency Shelter of the Fox Valley)

As a leading organization fighting homelessness in the Fox Valley community, the mission of Homeless Connections is to end homelessness by connecting individuals and families to resources that promote self-sufficiency and prevent future homeless episodes. Homeless Connections serves approximately 3,000 individuals each year to meet basic needs through four core areas of impact: Shelter, Case Management, Street Outreach and Prevention. It is the only homeless shelter in northeast Wisconsin that serves families regardless of cause of homelessness and collaborates with other like-minded organizations to provide case management to its clients and improve the quality of living for those we serve and for the community as a whole.

Source: Courtesy of Red Shoes PR.

HELPFUL HINTS

THE COMPONENTS OF A STANDARD NEWS RELEASE

As is the case with other forms of journalism highlighted throughout the book, public-relations writing requires you to format your work in a certain way to meet the needs of your readers. The goal of a good press release is to have it draw the attention of news media professionals, inform them about an important topic and compel them to engage the topic, either by writing on the topic or by contacting you for more information.

Robert S. "Pritch" Pritchard, who spent 25 years as a public affairs officer in the U.S. Navy, has spent the past decade-plus working with students in various university-based public relations agencies with the goal of helping them craft writing that meets these needs. Currently, he serves as an adviser at the Lindsey + Asp public-relations agency at the University of Oklahoma, where he uses a standard approach to press releases that meets professional standards as he emphasizes both information and formatting. Here is a standard release, with some key commentary from Pritchard:

LINDSEY + ASP
THE GAYLORD COLLEGE OF JOURNALISM AND MASS COMMUNICATION
ADVERTISING AND PUBLIC RELATIONS

(1) Contact:
Lauren Reed (xxx) xxx-xxxx
or Megan Snowbarger (xxx) xxx-xxxx
xxxxx@gmail.com

FOR IMMEDIATE RELEASE (2)

(3) LINDSEY + ASP LANDS $77,500 CONTRACT WITH FORT SILL

(4) NORMAN, OKLAHOMA (Sept. 30, 2011) – The University of Oklahoma's student-operated advertising and public relations agency, Lindsey + Asp, landed its largest contract to date in the amount of $77,500.

The one-year contract for the Office of Strategic Communication for the U.S. Army Fires Center of Excellence at Fort Sill in Lawton, Okla. runs from Sept. 28, 2011 through Sept. 27, 2012. The contract also includes options to extend through four additional years.

(5)(6) Lindsey + Asp Agency will produce a variety of collateral materials to promote Team Sill and the museums at Fort Sill. The agency will also plan and execute a number

(7) -more-

(8) Fort Sill — Reed

of communication campaigns and edit and produce several videos and public service announcements.

One initiative on which the student-operated agency will focus includes a Guide by Cell® system, which will allow museum visitors to take interactive, self-guided tours using their personal smartphones.

(9) Fort Sill has been a client of Lindsey + Asp since the fall semester of 2010. So far, the agency has produced posters as part of a vehicle safety campaign, redesigned Fort Sill museum brochures, conducted research on similar museums nationally and held focus groups to discern attitudes and beliefs with regard to military museums.

"I think it's huge that in only our third year of operation, we have been able to land a contract like this," said Bob "Pritch" Pritchard, Faculty Adviser of Lindsey + Asp. "It shows the professionalism and talent of our young professionals and gives them a real edge as they enter the business world."

(10) Lindsey + Asp was founded in August 2009 and is the premiere learning laboratory for advertising and public relations in the Gaylord College of Journalism and Mass Communication at the University of Oklahoma. The agency employs more than 50 students in service to more than a dozen clients.

(11) ###

Source: Courtesy of Lindsey + Asp public-relations agency.

1. All of the information included in the slug or identification block is essential and must be single-spaced. It appears near the top and on the right side of the release. This should include the name and title of the contact person for the release as well as any contact information for people seeking additional information.

2. When the information should be released is noted in the line, which appears in all capitals, directly across from and to the left of the slug. In many cases, the information is ready for release upon receipt, although certain situations can lead you to request an embargo until a specific date and time.

3. The story headline goes here, centered in a larger and bolded font to draw the attention of the readers, and it should be single-spaced and placed three lines below the contact information.

4. Three lines below the headline, a dateline should start the story. The dateline includes the name of the city in capital letters and the state's name in lowercase letters, which should be abbreviated or spelled out according to Associated Press style. After the city and the state comes the date the event took place. The date should appear in parentheses. This emphasizes the immediacy aspect of the information as well as the geographic base from where that information originated.

5. Each margin should be approximately one inch.

6. The body copy is double-spaced so it makes it easier for editors to make copy changes, if necessary.

7. If a story is longer than one page, **-more-** should appear centered at the bottom of all pages except the last page. Never split the last word on a line.

8. The author's name (line one) and a one-to-three word slug line (line two, single-spaced) should appear at the top left of the second (and subsequent) pages.

9. All paragraphs should be indented, including the first paragraph.

10. With the exception of feature stories, the last paragraph usually is the boilerplate or corporate tag, which is a standard statement about the company or organization generating the news release. Because it is a standard statement, some groups single-space the boilerplate and place it after the end-of-story symbol.

11. An end-of-story symbol of ### or –30– must appear centered on the next line after the last paragraph. This signals to the readers that the release is finished.

PRESS SERVICES AVAILABLE

Operational Services:

> The Media Tent on race day will have power and Wi-Fi capabilities for computer Internet access. Table space will be set aside for working media and a separate interview area will be set up for winner debriefings.

MEDIA CONTACTS

For media inquiries, please contact:
Sara Montonati, Red Shoes PR xxx-xxx-xxxx
xxxxx@redshoespr.com

Events:
Saturday, Sept. 20, 2014

- Affinity Medical Group Orthopedic & Sports Medicine 5K Run/Walk

Riverside Park
500 E. Wisconsin Ave., Neenah
9 a.m. start

Sunday, Sept. 21, 2014

- All events start: UWFox

1478 Midway Road, Menasha (Outside Barlow Planetarium)
7:00 a.m.: ThedaCare Half Marathon
Community First Fox Cities Marathon and Orthopedic & Sports Institute Relay Marathon
All events finish: Riverside Park, 500 E. Wisconsin Ave., Neenah

Quick Facts

- Up to 8,000 total runners and walkers expected in five races
- 2,300 volunteers throughout race weekend
- It is the event's 24th year — the first year was 1991
- 32 turns on full marathon course
- 38 streets on full marathon course
- Number of medical personnel: Approx. 150
    - o On-course medical stations – 4 stations, 10 people per station
    - o Moped/Bike teams – 10 teams, two people per team
    - o On-course medical vans – 3 vans, 2 people per van
    - o Ambulances – 10 ambulances, 2 people per van
    - o 40 student nurses and medical staff at finish line

FUN FACTS

Fox Cities Marathon Participants

Since 1991 (including this year), participants total:

    Marathon – over 24,000 participants

    Half Marathon – over 37,000 participants

    Relay Marathon – nearly 9,000 participants

    5K Run/Walk – over 16,000 participants

Why 26.2 miles?

Most people assume that the Marathon distance of 26.2 miles represents the distance between the battlefields of Marathon and Athens that Pheidippides supposedly ran to announce a Greek victory of the Persian army, but that's not exactly true. When the Marathon was first introduced in the Olympic Games by Baron Pierre de Coubertin in 1896, the race was 40 kilometers — the actual distance between the two cities. However, the distance was changed in 1908 when the Olympics were held in London, England. Race organizers originally set the start in downtown Windsor but subsequently moved it to the lawn of Windsor Castle so the royal family could watch the start from their front porch. The finish line, however, remained the same so the race became 26 miles and 285 yards, the distance from the royal lawn to the finish line in Olympic Stadium.

How long is 26.2 miles?

- A basketball player would have to go baseline to baseline 1,471 times in a game to run a marathon distance

- A major league baseball player would have to hit 385 home runs to cover the distance of a marathon

- An NFL quarterback would have had to string together 231 200-yard passing games to reach the distance

Source: Courtesy of Red Shoes PR.

---

with each element. This approach gives your readers the basic "who will do what, when, where and why" information with the promise of getting more value if they attend the event. An alert outlines the visual elements available for video and photography journalists as well as the standard time-date-place information associated with the event.

Pitches

Story **pitches** are common throughout the various aspects of journalism. In newsrooms, reporters often research areas that interest them and then suggest to an editor that the topic merits a story. Public-relations pitches mimic this approach, as practitioners suggest ideas for stories to news outlets. Practitioners write "pitch letters" or "pitch emails" to reporters, in which they outline the topic and provide facts on it. The pitches also contain potential sources and contact information.

Social Media

Prior to the digital media era, public-relations practitioners were at the mercy of news reporters and editors when it came to reaching an audience. The journalists at TV stations and newspapers could ignore their events or promotions if they felt the ideas weren't interesting or if something more "important" came about during the day. PR firms didn't own television transmitters or printing presses, so they could be shut out easily.

As we discussed in Chapter 7, social media and web publications have democratized information dissemination in a big way, as interested publics and engaging sources can skip past traditional media organizations and connect on their own. Organizations and individuals

All media professionals must use their moral compass to guide them toward truth telling.

© iStockphoto.com/olm26250

maintain their own Twitter accounts, Facebook profiles and corporate websites, where they can provide information whenever and however they see fit. People who want to know what these people have to say can "opt in" by following them on Twitter, liking a page on Facebook or choosing to receive updates from a website.

PR professionals should also find potential connections through these media platforms. When a person or organization engages you on social media, consider how that individual can provide value to you and your company. Following others who have shown an interest in you can help you build relationships and learn about developments within fields of interest. It is also a way to build a brand, develop clout and alert other like-minded people to your social media presence.

As also noted in Chapter 7, potential disasters lurk around every corner for people who use these platforms poorly, so relying on key writing and information-sharing skills outlined throughout the book will help you as you use these tools. In addition, we will discuss why you shouldn't forsake your relationship with traditional media outlets just because you opened a Twitter account for your latest project.

KEYS TO PR

Public relations has several key elements that all good practitioners should embrace. Some of these concepts might seem either counterintuitive or overly simplistic, given the public's misperception of how PR works. That said, they remain the bedrock of what good practitioners do.

Transparency

The idea behind **transparency** is to lay bare all of the issues associated with a topic, regardless of how good or bad they are, in a clear and immediate way. This allows everyone within your audience to see what has happened, why it happened and everything else that is known about the issue. Transparency says, "Here is what we know. We have nothing to hide."

This approach seems like a bad idea. Transparency lets everyone see everything that went wrong in the time of crisis, outlines all of the faults associated with an idea and provides people with information you would just as soon they not have. On its face, transparency appears to undermine PR efforts, but it doesn't. Here's why:

The More You Hide, The Worse It Is

The instinct for most people when something goes bad is to try to hide the problem, and that approach starts at an early age. Little kids will stick bad report cards in their sock drawers, flip over couch cushions they spilled juice on and pretend that someone else in the house ate all the cookies before dinner. In most cases, parents figure out what happened, punish the child more severely and wonder what else the kids have been hiding.

This isn't that far of a cry from what happens when a crisis strikes an organization. Most people instinctively want to "close ranks" and keep outsiders from getting a look at the situation. The instinct to keep as much information private as possible is a logical one. If people don't know that something bad is going on, they can't be angry about it. However, once people find out, the backlash will be much worse and lead to even greater levels of mistrust.

The "Bandage" Approach

When you have to pull off a bandage, it usually hurts, especially if you try to rip it off a little bit at a time. The best advice for getting the bandage off is to grab a corner and pull quickly. For some reason, this solves the problem and makes for a less painful experience. Transparency within public relations allows the same thing: a quick yank that solves the problem.

Good public-relations practitioners will espouse the benefits of transparency. They push for a full accounting of what happened and a public display of that information. This will allow the information to become available all at once, be dealt with in a shorter period of time and then let people move on with life. If things come out in drips and drops, the problem will remain in the public eye longer and the public will be more suspicious of the organization. Losing the trust of the audience is the worst thing that can happen, and hiding things will essentially guarantee this result.

Craft the Best Possible Message

Your goal in PR is to create the best possible message and disseminate it in a way that your audience can accept and understand it. Here are the keys to crafting a quality message:

Support Your Claims

As stated throughout this book, preparation is the key to everything you do. Conduct enough research on your topic to make intelligent statements in your message. Gather enough information so you can explain the claims you make. If you send out a press release that calls your charity event "the biggest charity event in the organization's history," you need to back up that statement. Is it the biggest based on the amount of money you raised? The length of the event? The number of people who attended? Don't say it just because it sounds good. Make sure you can support what you write.

Also, don't be afraid to tell people you don't know something. No matter how well you research or how informed you are, you will run into questions that stump you. Trying to fake your way around these questions will only draw suspicion and undermine your credibility. If someone asks you something you don't know that answer to, simply say "I don't know, but I will find out for you." Then go get the answer.

Present Information Clearly

Clarity is the gold standard for writing across all media forms. The goal in public-relations writing is to reach your readers on their level. In many cases, this means translating corporate jargon or organizational slang into everyday language. Look for simple ways to explain complex topics, especially when you write for a general audience that lacks your level of insight.

When it comes time to write, simply say what you mean and say it to the best of your ability. You need to find common terms to explain organization jargon. You also need to use wording that best matches the reading level of your audience. In many cases, we over-write to make something sound more important or more valuable. In other cases, we write with big words and long sentences because we think these things make us look smarter. If you know what you are talking about and you have confidence in your skills, you can use simple and direct language to deliver a clear message.

© iStockphoto.com/peshkov

A good public relations practitioner understands the various audiences a message must reach and how best to craft specific messages to meet the needs of each group.

Have a Heart

In crafting a message, you have to understand that being right and being accurate sometimes take a backseat to the need to be humane. In the wake of a disaster, the now-threadbare phrase "Our thoughts and prayers tonight go out to..." may seem hollow, but at least it recognizes that something bad has happened. When you try to ignore something bad that has happened or make it seem less problematic than it is, you create the sense that you don't care.

For example, an explosion and fire at a Turkish coal mine in 2014 left more than 230 people dead and hundreds others injured. In the wake of the disaster, Turkish Prime Minister Recep Tayyip Erdoğan attempted to address citizens in the town of Soma, where families were still coming to grips with the devastation. According to an article in The Guardian, the prime minister delivered a speech that was insensitive and attempted to deflect responsibility for the disaster. He was said to tell the family members of miners, "These types of incidents are ordinary things." He then went on to list a series of serious mining disasters that had occurred around the world since the 1800s.[2]

Erdoğan had done research on the topic, and he delivered a truthful statement about the coal industry. However, that wasn't what people needed to hear at that point. They needed a sensitive and caring approach instead of a history lesson on the dangers of mining. When it comes to putting forth statements in situations like this, humanity should be your guiding principle and your primary purpose.

Understand Your Audience

Practitioners in this field often have multiple audiences they need to appease, and therefore they must fashion multiple messages. A spokeswoman for a corporation that just posted record losses will have to craft several messages for a wide array of anxious people. Although the core of the message might be the same (don't panic), the approach she takes and the facts she emphasizes will differ substantially.

Chapter 1 discussed the importance of understanding your readers and finding the best ways to get your message to them. A number of the factors outlined there should resonate for you here, including figuring out who is in your audience, what they need to know and how to get the information to them. Below are some additional aspects of understanding your audience:

Internal Versus External Audiences

In news and advertising, the goal is to craft a message that reaches out to a segment of the general public. Public-relations practitioners also have to reach beyond the borders of their companies or organizations to inform, engage and inspire audience members, but they do have a second audience: people within their own organizations.

When changes occur within a company or group, the idea of self-interest kicks in for everyone involved: What does this mean to me? While a news report can do its job as it explains that Company X has filed for bankruptcy, a PR practitioner has to explain that issue to various constituencies, both inside and outside of the company. Workers wonder if this means they will lose their jobs. Stockholders worry about their investment. Customers think about the products they bought and the warranties associated with them. In each case, a practitioner must craft a message that accurately addresses the concerns.

The practitioner will examine each audience and determine what those readers will need to know. Her message to the stockholders will discuss financial reorganization and projected earnings. Her message to customers will explain product guarantees and future purchase options. Her message to workers will outline the employment approach the company will take next. These messages will satisfy the needs of each group of readers and help each reader answer the "What's in it for me?" question.

What People Need To Know And How To Get It To Them

Public-relations practitioners often control not just what information gets out, but who gets it first and how they get it. They must determine who needs to know what, in what order and how best to get them that information. This is most important in the case of a large change or a crisis.

For example, if the legendary head basketball coach at your university decides to quit, you have several publics you need to address: The players who might decide to stay or leave; the coaching staff that might wonder about their jobs; the season-ticket holders who are financially valuable to you; the campus community who will likely be shocked and the media who will wonder if there is more to this story than just a case of a coach wanting to leave.

If you tell the media first, a lot of your other publics will be upset that they didn't get this information firsthand. If you tell the players before the staff, some of the coaches may wonder why they were kept out of the loop. If you hold off on telling the media for too long, the players and coaches might use social media and leak the information, thus stoking the fires of suspicion among the news practitioners.

In addition, how you announce the information is important. An email to wider publics like the student body and the season-ticket holders might make sense, but emailing the players and coaches may come across as cold and distant. A face-to-face meeting with key team personnel might work so that those people can forward the information to others more quickly. However, people who found out secondhand might feel slighted or the message might be lost or mistranslated along the way.

You need to be able to address these concerns before crafting your message and as you disseminate it. This will allow you to make sure the information doesn't get lost in the process.

Vary The Points Without Contradiction

Critics of public relations often say that practitioners just tell people whatever they want to hear. Practitioners do want to focus on what people need to know, but that doesn't mean they

CONNECT
HOMETOWN NEWS RELEASE

When it comes to connecting with your audience, you need to focus on things that the audience will want to see. In the case of news releases, this can seem daunting as you target a nebulous "media" audience with your work. However, if you speak the media's language, you can make your information appealing to them.

Here is what is called a "hometown news release," which is issued by a public-relations practitioner at the University of Wisconsin–Oshkosh in hopes of appealing to the Sheboygan Press, a cross-state newspaper. The release is issued to note the success of a UWO student who comes from Sheboygan. Note the following key elements that make this work:

1. The release starts with a geographic tie between the publication and the subject. In using the phrase "Sheboygan South 2007 graduate," the author alerts the paper's editor to a clear local tie.

2. The author mimics the writing style of the publication, relying on paraphrase-quote pairings and strong direct quotes. The author uses one-sentence paragraphs, which is normal in newspapers, and makes the quotes their own paragraphs.

3. This part of the release provides the editor with background on the award, allowing him or her to see how important this honor is. This helps stimulate the editor's interest in the award-winning student.

4. The author brings the piece to a conclusion with a "look forward" at what this student hopes to accomplish next. The closing also touches on the local angle, noting the student hopes to move back home to Sheboygan. The quote provides a clear conclusion for the piece.

The release does a solid job of presenting information in descending order of importance, providing value in each paragraph and creating clear flow from point to point. It also mimics a standard story, complete with an important beginning, a middle that matters and an end that brings finality.

(Continued)

(Continued)

Special to: Sheboygan Press

By: Linda Derber

Contact: email xxxxx@uwosh.edu cell xxx-xxx-xxxx

For Immediate Release

(1) (Oshkosh)—Sheboygan South 2007 graduate, Jonathan Delray, received the Chancellor's Award during spring commencement from University of Wisconsin-Oshkosh in May.

Delray graduated with degrees in music education and vocal performance.

(2) No stranger to the performance world, Delray was inspired to start his musical career in high school with his choral director, Dr. Linda Jacobs.

"She showed me how tremendously influential a choral director can be on students who are facing the pitfalls of adolescence," Delray said.

During his time at Sheboygan South, Delray was an active member of the Concert Choir as well as the show choir, "The South High Singers."

When the time came for Delray to choose a college to attend, he and his wife decided UW Oshkosh was the best fit because of their desire to become educators.

Never losing his passion for music, Delray served as the president of the Chamber Choir for four years, tutored piano students, served as an assistant conductor for the University Choir and was president of Students for Music.

(3) The Chancellor's Award is meant to recognize students for their achievements in academics, university service and community activities. Delray strived to receive the Chancellor's Award for a few years, and now that he has won, he considers it one of his highest honors.

"It's validation to me that my collegiate career has really had the impact that I always dreamt it could," Delray said. "A few years ago, I attended my first [UW Oshkosh] commencement ceremony. Once there, I noticed all the stories of accomplished graduating seniors and I immediately circled the name of this award in the program. Since then, it's been my aspiration to be granted this award. I consider this honor to be one of the crowning achievements of my undergraduate collegiate career, but I understand that my real work is just beginning."

Delray was also the founder, conductor and music director for the Oshkosh Correctional Facility's Second Chance Choir. Second Chance Choir developed from Delray's original idea to start a musical program at the Oshkosh Correctional Facility. It is comprised of approximately 40 inmates at the facility.

Delray said Second Chance Choir completed a collection of 10 songs, six choral pieces and four instrumental projects that became one of the keynote events at the Martin Luther King Jr. Day Ceremony sponsored by the Oshkosh Esther group in January.

Delray recalls a rehearsal held the day before Thanksgiving 2013, when each member said what he or she was thankful for. To Delray that was a heart-warming bonding experience.

"It was an incredibly meaningful day where we all became part of a community, not just a choir," Delray said.

(4) Delray and his wife will be moving back to Sheboygan to be closer to family. His ideal career would be a high school choral director, but Delray is not going to pass up any opportunity.

"Ideally, I will become a high school choral director, but any job in this field is a career worth having and will bring tremendous satisfaction," Delray said.

Source: Courtesy of Linda Derber.

GIVE IT A TRY: Select a standard press release, media alert or other similar item and rewrite it to fit the "hometown news release" format. You might need to conduct an interview to do this or you might decide to rely on the material available to you. Research the person on whom this release will center as well as the media outlets in that person's "hometown" area so you can make a targeted pitch to the local journalism community. Be sure to emphasize the connection between the community and your subject in the lead of your release.

can lie to audience members to make them happy. However, practitioners can focus on various angles to provide each group of readers specific aspects of a story.

A news release to a group of stockholders might emphasize that a bad financial quarter will result in some "belt-tightening efforts" in your company. This should assuage their fears that your company is performing poorly and show them you want to fix the problems. A companywide email might emphasize that despite a poor quarter, no one will be fired, and no layoffs are planned. This information should ease the workers' anxiety and allow them to get back to work. This variation on the theme is both acceptable and valuable as you communicate effectively with varied publics.

What you cannot do, however, is contradict yourself as you explain a situation. You cannot, for example, write to your stockholders and tell them that you will cut the workforce by 10 percent to fix financial deficits and simultaneously tell the workers that no one will be fired or laid off. These messages might be exactly what each group wants to hear, but these moves are mutually exclusive. Eventually, you will have to go back on one of your promises and nothing good can come of that.

Public relations practitioners use multiple social media tools and work with news outlets to help reach additional audiences.

WHY THE MEDIA MATTERS

Stereotyping places public-relations practitioners and news reporters on opposing sides of every issue. Practitioners put things in the best light, while reporters dig for dirt. News seeks the truth, while PR seeks to hide it. Every stereotype has a grain of truth to it, but in most cases, the practitioners need the reporters and the reporters need the practitioners. It is not a perfectly symbiotic relationship, but it is a valuable one that everyone in PR should look to cultivate.

The web has democratized the process of information dissemination in many ways. In years past, to get a message out to a broader audience, you needed access to a TV network, a radio station or a newspaper. In most cases, these delivery mechanisms were beyond the reach of most public-relations organizations, and thus they were at the mercy of what editors and producers thought should be aired or printed. The web allows you to reach interested audiences via corporate websites, email newsletters, opt-in social media accounts and other digital platforms. Your organization can now bypass gatekeepers and present your message directly to your audience.

These changes in media seem to make it counterintuitive that you would need to cater to news organizations. However, the news outlets serve as both an audience and a megaphone of sorts that helps you reach a broader array of people. Here are a few of the benefits you can reap if you work with, as opposed to against, the news media:

Their Audiences Can Become Your Audiences

Although you can both exist on the same digital plane, websites associated with traditional media powers have a much bigger reach. They have readers with interests in a variety of topics. The news sites also focus on specific physical areas, which can help you target your readers geographically.

Although some people might check your client's website or Twitter feed daily, more people will probably visit the sites associated with local news outlets. In addition, broadcast and print news operations maintain a presence on those traditional media platforms, allowing them to reach out to people who consider the morning paper and the nightly news crucial sources of information.

Their Credibility Can Become Your Credibility

The explosion of websites over the past decade has created an information overload for the general public. In this sea of content, audience members need someone to them make sense of what matters and why. News journalists have traditionally assumed this role, and they continue to help people understand the world around them.

Although people distrust certain news channels, they generally trust the news media more than they do corporations. Like it or not, the stigma associated with corporations and public-relations practitioners remains in the minds of many people. If you work with the media to put forth your messages, you can piggyback on their credibility as predominantly fair and objective purveyors of content. The more the news media can serve as a conduit of information for you, the more the credible your content will be.

Your Understanding Can Become Their Understanding

As you work with news media professionals, you will find that speaking their language will benefit you. However, as Erin White points out (see her interview in this chapter), when she speaks the media's language, her goal is to get the reporters to speak hers. Public-relations practitioners attempt to persuade audiences to see a topic or a situation in a particular way.

If you work with the media, you can find ways to help them understand what your organization is all about, why your group is taking a certain position or how your way of thinking works best for their readers and viewers. In other words, you can help reporters understand what you think and why you think it in hopes that they can understand you and convey your message to a larger group.

ADAPT
WRITING LIKE THE NEWS JOURNALISTS

Given the importance of the news media in disseminating your message, you need to find ways to adapt your approach to writing to fit their approach to writing. A "one-size-fits-all" press release that you toss into the body of an email and pump out to a predefined list of addresses isn't going to cut it.

You need to see how the news journalists in each medium tend to write and then craft specific pitches and releases that fit those specifications. The chapters on news outline specific ways in which print media differ from broadcast media in terms of writing style. However, here are some other things to consider in terms of writing for your media audience:

Length

In broadcast, time is a crucial element, and brevity is valued above almost everything else. Stories that anchors read without video run between 10 and 15 seconds each. Stories that reporters put together with video and several quoted sources run between 1:30 and 2 minutes, depending on the topic's importance. Sources who appear on screen, offering their thoughts in what is called a "soundbite" or an "actuality," get only about 10 seconds to make their point.

In print, quotes are usually short as well, ranging from two to three sentences. Briefs like those anchor-read stories in broadcast run about four or five sentences. Short news stories can be anywhere from 12 to 15 sentences as well.

Structure

Get your most important information up to the top of your pitches and news releases. In general, the inverted pyramid and the "circle" approach to writing dictate that you tell a story in a short and value-driven way, and you should use those formats for that reason.

In addition, you can write your piece in a way that mimics news stories' structure. For example, using one-sentence paragraphs, keeping quotes as their own paragraphs and telling the story in descending order of importance will draw the attention of your print media reporters. Using words that reflect action, constructing your sentences in the present tense and building various forms of a story to account for time-based needs will impress broadcast reporters.

Medium-Specific Needs

If you study stories in the newspaper, you will find that longer stories have multiple sources and contain direct quotes from these sources. Putting these elements into your news releases will help the journalists complete their stories. This will also improve the likelihood of having your information included in the pieces they write.

Broadcast tends to rely on audio and video to tell stories. The visual elements are key for television journalists and can lead to an improved presence for your content on the air. Thus, a few video quotes (soundbites or actualities) sent via email or linked to on a media-only portion of your website will help you connect with

the reporters. Access to video clips of your organization doing things that showcase your value will also give you a leg up. Better yet, a promise of a one-on-one, on-camera interview with an important source can lead to even better coverage.

If you think of the media as an important audience to serve, you can see this form of adapting as just another case of telling a story in a way that reaches a valuable public.

GIVE IT A TRY: Find a standard press release on a topic of interest to you and write it for three basic platforms: print, broadcast and online. For the print piece, write a four- to six-paragraph inverted-pyramid brief that provides the reader with key information on the topic while placing emphasis on your organization's role in the news. For the broadcast piece, write a 20-second reader that follows the broadcast format outlined in Chapter 11. Make sure to read the piece aloud to avoid overly long sentences, word stumbles or other similar problems. For the web piece, write a 250- to 350-word blog post that provides an appropriate tone and feel for the material as well as accentuating the value for the readers. Include at least two hyperlinks to meaningful content.

THE BIG THREE

Here are the three key things you should take away from the chapter:

1. **PR is not spin:** Public-relations practitioners must take a deliberate and well-planned approach to conveying important information to audience members in a clear and concise fashion. Then they must listen to the public's response to determine how well their audience received the message. This field is not about telling people what they want to hear. It's about telling people what they need to know.

2. **Approach your message based on your audience:** When you need to reach an audience, you should analyze the group, determine what the people in it need to know and then craft your

message to meet those needs. Each person in an audience has a clear self-interest. Your goal is to determine what those people need to know and then tell it to them in a way that touches on that interest. Messages can vary from audience to audience, as long as the underlying facts aren't mutually exclusive.

3. **Connect with the news media:** Although stereotypes have news people and PR people at odds with each other, the reality is that they need each other. Learn how to speak the language of news people and you can help them understand yours. Work to make their job easier and you will gain ground in your own field. The relationship will never be perfect, but a symbiotic pairing can lead to some beneficial outcomes.

KEY TERMS

announcement 204	news release 205	spin 201
byline 201	pitch 211	spot announcement 207
fact sheet 210	press release 201	transparency 212
media alert 211	reaction release 207	

DISCUSSION QUESTIONS

1. What is the value of transparency in public relations? Why should practitioners admit when bad things happen to their organization or talk to reporters in the time of a crisis? Why do you feel this way?

2. What are the benefits of working with the news media? How can news outlets benefit you as a public-relations practitioner?

WRITE NOW!

1. For this essay, you are a public-relations practitioner for a publicly traded computer company that will report a huge financial loss for the year. First, determine four specific groups of people that this financial loss could affect. Second, explain what you think their primary concerns will be and why you think their concerns should matter to you as a PR practitioner. Finally, outline what information you would highlight in a message to each of those groups and why it would meet each group's interests.

2. Find a press release online and review its content and approach to its message. Using the key elements of PR listed in this chapter (transparency, message clarity and audience centricity), write a short essay that explains how well or how poorly you think this release does in addressing those elements. Also, analyze the structure of the piece. Is it organized in an inverted-pyramid structure, chronological structure or some other format? Is this approach effective in conveying the important aspects of the material?

3. Select a topic for a persuasive argument. First, make a statement of opinion that you want to persuade others to believe. Second, write two or three sentences to explain the audience for this message and why you chose this audience. Finally, write a one to two-page essay that uses facts and opinion to persuade that audience to think as you do on this topic. Make sure to include at least one strong statement of fact that supports your claim and at least one counterargument that you will address and defeat in your writing.

4. Pick a topic of interest and craft a press release using the formula outlined in the book. Pay particular attention to both the formatting nuances as well as the informational approach you take in creating this work.

NOTES

1. D. Wilcox (2009). "Public Relations Writing and Media Techniques" (6th ed.). Boston, Mass.: Allyn & Bacon.

2. A. Scott (2014, May 15). "Erdoğan's Self-Defence Over Soma's Mining Disaster Was Badly Misjudged." The Guardian. Accessed at: https://www.theguardian.com/commentisfree/2014/may/15/erdogan-turkey-mining-disaster-turkish-prime-minister.

13

ADVERTISING

LEARNING OBJECTIVES

After completing this chapter you should be able to:

- Define advertising in terms of its transmission methods, content, purpose and audience.

- Comprehend the way in which advertisements target audience members' needs, using product benefits and product characteristics to persuade customers to purchase goods and services.

- Understand how to craft a solid three-step creative brief that will dictate how to approach an advertising campaign.

- Create basic advertising copy that provides interest, information and suggestions for action to the audience.

- Understand ways to determine if an advertisement or an advertising campaign was successful.

Advertising is about more than telling people what to buy and where to buy it. It is a communication format that mixes information and persuasion elements in an attempt to convince audience members to act. The desired action can take many forms, including purchasing a product, supporting a candidate or forming an opinion. In addition, some advertising is geared toward preventing action, such as buying some other company's product, supporting a different candidate or changing an opinion.

Writing for advertising is about more than finding the next catchphrase or big marketing campaign. For every three-word slogan, such as "Just Do It" or "I'm Lovin' It," advertising professionals write thousands upon thousands of words in the form of creative briefs, marketing strategies, audience surveys and more. Without a firm grasp of the fundamentals of writing, you will fail to get your advertising career off the ground.

Visual issues, including color choices and the use of art elements, play a large part in how advertising works, and with that in mind, you will want to read some design books to learn about them. For this book, however, the majority of the focus will be on the writing of advertising copy and how the text can help draw in readers.

This chapter will outline the basics of advertising, giving you a definition of the field and a sense of how it works. In addition, it will show you the things you must understand to create quality messages and how you can help clients see why those messages have value. Finally, it will walk through basic message formation and communication in a way that will help you achieve success in writing for your audience.

DEFINING ADVERTISING

Advertising does not have a definition upon which all people can agree. This issue arises because, in many cases, good advertising is in the eye of the beholder. For some, if the product sells, that's all that matters. For others, advertising should serve as a bridge between senders and receivers that leads to a long-standing, mutually beneficial relationship.

Advertisers like Red Bull pay to have their messages placed in the public eye in hopes of drawing viewers who will become consumers of their products.

As we saw in Chapter 12 with public relations, advertising has several words or terms that tend to occur in most good definitions of this form of communication. These terms include some of the following items:

Paid Communication

One thing that separates advertising from the other forms of media writing is the financial aspect. In public relations, practitioners use various tools to influence news publications to promote content that matters to the practitioners and their clients. Despite practitioners' best efforts, these groups can decline to provide coverage on those topics. Even more, the practitioners cannot control how the news organizations cover the issue or what the reporters will publish.

Advertising offers a more direct route for information dissemination, as professionals in this field pay for the right to publish a message within established media outlets. Paid communication is the core of what distinguishes advertising from news and public relations. As noted in the ethics chapter, reporters are forbidden from receiving anything of value from sources or organizations in exchange for coverage or favorable treatment. That chapter also outlines the ethical behavior standards for PR practitioners as they seek to persuade and influence various audiences.

Advertising, however, differentiates itself from these other forms of media in that the payment for space is clear and known. Whether it is a 30-second TV ad during the Super Bowl, a **sponsored link** on a Facebook feed or a billboard on the side of the road, advertising costs money. The actual costs are based on the reach of the medium, the media platform the advertiser uses, the amount of space purchased and the amount of time the advertiser keeps the ad in circulation. Networks, publications and websites often have rules associated with what is and is not acceptable advertising content. The management at these media outlets often reserves the right to reject advertising for specific reasons, including taste, accuracy and fairness. However, advertisements carry with them a general understanding: Advertisers buy a chunk of media space and place a message they deem important into that space.

Known Sponsor

The source of the advertisement is key to understanding how it will attempt to persuade you and the underlying values associated with those attempts. For example, U.S. federal law requires all political committees to include disclaimers on public communication that explicitly states they were "paid for by (the name of the source)." This allows the public to understand who is sending the information and what amount of credence they should lend to that message.[1] If an independent organization criticizes Sen. John Smith for his stance on crime, it is likely to have more weight than if the criticism comes from Smith's opponent, Jane Jones. This is why having a known sponsor is crucial.

The **Federal Trade Commission**, which oversees much of the advertising law in the United States, places a premium on the importance of "prohibiting unfair or deceptive acts or practices." One of the key elements associated with creating fair and honest advertising, according to the law, is making clear who is sending the message.[2]

Information Plus Persuasion

Advertising law also requires that companies back their claims with information as they attempt to persuade people. Most professionals in this field do an inordinate amount of research to determine how best to sell their products in an honest and straightforward manner. Pharmaceutical companies spend millions of dollars on testing to determine if a product can create specific benefits that will not only improve people's lives but also draw consumers. They then couple this information with persuasion techniques to increase sales of this product.

When companies refer to something as "miraculous," "amazing" or "the best ever," this is traditionally known as puffery, which runs counter to what good advertising should do. The FTC defines puffery as exaggerations regarding a product that are subjective and thus "the truth or falsity of which cannot be precisely determined."[3] In 2014, the U.S. Senate questioned TV host Mehmet Oz about his claims of finding "a revolutionary fat buster" called Garcinia cambogia and his statement regarding "magic beans" called green coffee beans that will lead to weight loss. Dr. Oz, as he is known to viewers, said he often used "flowery language" to describe products, but senators noted that scientific studies showed the products failed to work as promised.[4]

Companies can get into trouble when advertisements have too few facts behind their claims. In April 2017, Arla Foods promoted its dairy products as healthy and pure by denouncing the use of rbST, a bovine growth hormone that increases milk production. Eli Lilly, the company that markets rbST, filed suit against the company for its representation of the hormone as unsafe. A 30-second commercial at the center of the suit portrayed rbST as a giant monster with six eyes, razor-sharp horns and electrified fur.[5] A court enjoined the dairy company from using the advertisement, dismissing Arla's claims of puffery and noting that the advertising was likely to mislead viewers as to the hormone's safety.[6]

When it comes to properly structuring your advertising messages, you should rely on facts and reputable sources so you can deliver clear and honest messages. When you couple this core of information with persuasive techniques, you will communicate effectively and reach your audience better.

Delivered to an Audience

The best messages in the world won't have any impact if they don't reach the proper readers and viewers. People within the advertising community often refer to reaching an audience as "buying eyeballs" or "going where the eyeballs are."[7] The underlying notion here is that an ad must be seen for it to be effective.

Newspapers used to run into the hundreds of pages, with sections simply for classified advertising as well as the giant display ads that helped fuel the news industry. However, fewer people read papers these days, and thus not only have the ads disappeared, but the papers themselves have shrunk. Putting ads on television was once the golden ticket to reaching potential consumers; three networks dominated the TV landscape, and everyone who saw a program did so at the exact same time. However, with the explosion of cable television, Internet channels and time-shifting devices such as DVRs, consumers can ignore, miss or speed past your messages without a second thought.

The delivery mechanism you choose should allow you to "find the eyeballs" of people you want to reach, so you need to consider your audience carefully. For example, if you wanted to send a message to senior citizens, you might still advertise in the newspaper. A 2016 Pew study found that 48 percent of people age 65 or older said they often get their news from a newspaper. The same study found that only 5 percent of people 18 to 29 said they often read a newspaper for news, thus making it a fairly weak channel for reaching those consumers.[8]

The better you understand your audience, the better you will be at delivering the message to the people in it.

Promotes Products, Services or Ideas

An advertisement should persuade people to enact a behavior that will benefit both the consumer and the advertiser. This can be anything from purchasing a product to voting for a candidate. Advertising should demonstrate to interested audience members why a product, a service or an idea is worth their time. How best to promote these items and thoughts will be the focus of the rest of this chapter.

PROFESSIONAL THOUGHTS
KATE MORGAN

Kate Morgan has crisscrossed the state of Indiana as she has climbed the communications ladder as an editor, a magazine writer, a public relations staffer, an advertising account manager and more before landing at the University of Notre Dame.

Morgan is the director of communications for the Division of Student Affairs, where she helps develop the division's messaging strategy, streamline its content and rework the informational material the office provides to the public.

At each career stop, she said, writing was a common denominator for her.

"For as long as I can remember, I've told my interns, coordinators, student workers and so on that as long as they can write, they can do just about anything," she said. "I'm a perfect example. I don't have any classical training in public relations or advertising. Everything I know about marketing I've learned on the job. I had never written a press release until I started working in the agency, and I hadn't the faintest idea what b-roll was until I was on my first video shoot. But because I knew how to write, I was able to work my way up."

Morgan said a crucial aspect of writing is understanding who is in your audience and how best to reach those people.

"Grammar and voice and sentence structure are all essential, don't get me wrong, but if you don't know your audience and how to speak to their needs, a 500-word essay on the Immaculate Conception for a blog geared toward undergraduate students won't mean a thing," she said. "So while being a good writer is something anyone working in journalism or advertising or public relations should strive to be, having a handle on

Kate Morgan

your audience is almost just as important. Engagement is the end game in each of these areas, but you're not going to engage anyone if you're writing for the wrong crowd."

During her time as a senior account manager for an Indianapolis-based marketing firm, Morgan said she often had to fine-tune advertising campaign strategies to address the needs of specific niches in her audience.

"One of my biggest clients at the agency was a hospital based in northern Indiana, and given the number of service lines offered by the hospital, including cardiovascular care, maternity services, oncology and emergency medicine, our audiences differed quite a bit," she said. "While we could easily create one campaign for the hospital in general ('come to our hospital for all your medical needs'), we couldn't very well create one message to promote each of these service lines individually. Persuading a middle-aged man to come to our hospital for his cardiac surgery after suffering a heart attack is much different than convincing a woman in her mid-20s to come to us to deliver her first baby. Their priorities are completely different."

Before she crafts a message, Morgan said, she starts with several ideas and fleshes them out. After she is happy with what she wants to say, she then determines how to make her message platform specific.

"I typically start by coming up with at least three messages to communicate with any one audience," she said. "I add a few supporting statements to each message and from there I can go in any number of directions. I can write a news release about any topic using my messages as support. I can condense all three messages into something that allows me to give someone a brief summary of what I'm trying to accomplish. I can write copy for an entire website and then condense it all into 140 characters or less. Knowing your goals and identifying your audience will help you to both adapt to the medium and connect with your reader."

One Last Thing

Q: If you could tell students anything about media writing or anything you have seen in your time in the field, what would it be?

A: There isn't a job I can think of that doesn't involve writing in some capacity. Take emails. If a vendor emails me a quote with spelling and grammatical errors, my level of faith in his ability to adequately meet my needs diminishes significantly. Perhaps this makes me a snob, but that's not my problem. I'm not going to lower my expectations just because someone else is too lazy to write a complete sentence. Given my level of experience in this industry thus far, I'm almost positive I'm not the only one who feels this way.

THE CREATIVE BRIEF

Before you can launch an advertising campaign for the public, you need to pitch it to a number of other people inside and outside of your organization. The **creative brief** is an organized format that allows you to put your ideas before other members of your agency, your boss and eventually your client. It offers a coherent examination of how best to reach the audience with your pitch and why this approach will work.

According to the book "Contemporary Advertising and Integrated Marketing Communications," professional agencies like Leo Burnett and Procter & Gamble use a simple three-part approach to the brief.[9] Below, you can see an explanation of each of those parts as well as a fictional example that illustrates how each step of the process works:

Objective Statement

Here's where you outline what you are trying to accomplish. The **objective statement** is where you can explain simply that X is happening, and we want X to occur more or less. Then you can outline the ways in which the campaign will address this goal:

> EXAMPLE: *As people continue to suffer financial losses as a result of the recent recession, they are looking for ways to stretch their food dollar while still feeling like they are rewarding themselves. This campaign for Pasta Town's "Eat Like a King" promotion will meet that need by providing quality food and a luxurious dining experience while keeping costs low for consumers.*

Support Statement

Here is where you describe the evidence that explains why your approach to this promotion makes sense. The **support statement** can show how others have succeeded at this task or why your research suggests this approach should work.

EXAMPLE: Restaurant promotions that have done well are those that offer unlimited food for little money. Our research suggests that Red Lobster's "Endless Shrimp" promotion more than doubles its standard share of customers each day during the promotion with sharp drop-offs right after the end of the promotion. In addition, Golden Corral saw a recent spike in traffic after it added "All-You-Can-Eat Seafood" to its menu as part of a "surf-and-turf spectacular."

Our approach will offer customers whatever they want on our menu for only $14.99 for singles and $24.99 for couples. The endless-food angle and full access to our entire menu should provide customers with a sense of being able to eat what they want and how much of it they desire. Theoretically, we should not only be able to make up our costs on customer volume but also offer additional beverage service to those who wait in the bar. Increased wine and beer service during dinner should provide supplemental revenue as well.

Tone or Brand

This is the brief statement as to how you plan to do this and how you plan to give people the information in an acceptable fashion.

*EXAMPLE: Because we want to avoid the "you're poor" feel on this, we won't use an overly serious message of gloom and doom. However, humor likely won't work either in this situation. Thus, we are planning a "**benefit deserved**" approach to the topic, in which we highlight how hard the consumers are working and how they really deserve a reward for their efforts. This will be akin to the McDonald's "You deserve a break today" ads of the 1980s but will be more elegant and focus on the unlimited nature of choice and amount.*

ADAPT
A "LEAD" APPROACH TO THE CREATIVE BRIEF

The creative brief has a number of names, including copy platform and creative strategy, but essentially, a creative brief is like a broader version of a news lead. It attempts to answer the 5W's and 1H, even though it does so in a different way than a news lead. When you think about it this way, you can adapt some of the skills discussed in lead writing and information prioritization to pitch your ideas to others in a straightforward and clear fashion.

Let's take a look at the 5W's and 1H as they apply to the creative brief:

Who

Who is the target audience, which is based on the kinds of things we have discussed throughout the book, such as demographics and psychographics. Beyond that, you want to examine preferred message characteristics for certain personality types. Some people like humor, while others like things to be played straight. Some people enjoy a lot of excitement, while others prefer a down-to-earth approach. As you study the "who," personification can help you explain the target audience to others associated with your campaign.

What

This explains some of the features that will get the message across and how to use those features in a creative fashion. For example, if you want to show automobile safety, you could buckle a dozen eggs into the front seat and show how they don't crack when a car gets into a head-on collision. Since each ad has to have a singular, focused topic, you need to clearly explain what you want to showcase in your work.

When

The "when" element can take into account everything from the time of day you will run the ads to the time of year you will run them. Ads for tropical cruises don't draw a lot of attention during the dog days of summer. Ads for local eateries don't do well at 2 a.m., when people might be hungry, but the restaurants are closed. The purpose of the ad, the time of day your target audience will most likely see the ad and the time of year the ad will have the most impact all matter in your brief.

Where

The "where" element encompasses geography and platform concerns. The geography issue will matter when you think of a company that sells lawn mowers and snow blowers. Lawn mowers might do well anywhere within the United States, but the snow blower ads will probably fare poorly in Texas. In terms of platforms, "where" could mean digital or traditional media as well as print or broadcast. The physical placement of an ad on a platform has as much to do with the ad's success or failure as does the geographic placement.

Why

Here you explain to your audience members the value of your product and outline the ways you can do it. Some ads and audiences require a **rational appeal**, which requires you to use logic and reason to sway people. An example of this might be something like the great gas mileage a car gets. You can use an ad that logically explains that gasoline is expensive, this car uses less of it and people like to save money. Other ads rely on **emotional appeals**, which use psychological triggers or socializing elements to draw people toward a product. This can be anything from using sex appeal to sell beer to the use of ego enhancement to sell high-end watches. In either case, the advertisement explains why people should value the product and the benefits it provides.

How

In some cases, you might view the "how" as a platform concern, as in "How will we get the message out to people?" However, since that has been discussed more within the "where" explanation, it is actually better to think about "how" as an issue of tone and approach. Certain products can rely on energy and excitement to sell a product or service. A place that caters children's birthday parties would best be served with a high-energy approach, which talks to kids in an excited and dynamic fashion. However, a funeral home or a life-insurance service would do poorly with a similar approach.

These six elements can help you organize your thinking, clarify your intent and create a strong pitch that will lead to a good advertisement and a quality campaign.

GIVE IT A TRY: Pick a product for which you would like to build a creative brief. Do as much research as you think is necessary to understand the company, the product line and the goals associated with this product. Then, work through the 5W's and 1H as you put together your approach to this brief. Make sure to touch on the various aspects of each W and H outlined above. Then, walk through the three-step formula to create a simple pitch for marketing the product.

MESSAGE FORMATION

After you conceptualize your approach to your message, you need to outline how best to build that message. This is a multistep process that requires you to apply a number of the skills outlined in the first half of the book, including research, planning and audience identification. With those things in mind, here are the key steps you need to take as you start to shape your message:

Plan First, Then Write

Most writers dive right into their work in hopes of finding inspiration among the keystrokes. As we have discussed throughout the book, however, the best way to make media writing valuable and on point is to figure out the purpose of the writing before getting into it. This is particularly important in advertising, where you have to make a single point that

Charlese Watson/SCAN Magazine

matters to your audience in a quick and clear way. In most cases, trying to write before you plan is like trying to shoot before you aim.

Start with the basics outlined in the research chapter so that you can understand what you want to accomplish. Then use some of the inverted-pyramid basics outlined in Chapter 4 to determine what is the most important thing you want to get across to your audience. Use this information to create a plan that will guide you as you write. If you have a plan, it becomes much easier to craft a message.

Determine Your Audience

As noted in Chapter 1, the audience matters most in all forms of media. You can use a lot of that research information you gather to determine the demographic, psychographic and geographic aspects of your audience. Take a look at the Sam Flax advertisement, and you can see how the writer took those issues into account. The copy targets a clear demographic group, namely, students and faculty who attend the Savannah College of Art and Design in Atlanta, Georgia. The store promotes its geographic value when it notes that it is "just two minutes away from SCAD!" In addition, it targets students through financial benefits ("Students receive a 10 percent discount") and the psychographic values associated with potential customers (the importance of creativity, given the school's reputation as "The University for Creative Careers").

In building advertising copy, consider these issues for determining your audience:

Target Audience

The target audience is the group of people you have in mind for an advertisement or an ad campaign. Other people might see the advertisement, but they aren't the intended consumers. For example, if a 12-year-old boy is browsing through a parenting magazine in the dentist's office, he might run across an ad for a baby monitor or some new type of baby formula. He isn't the person intended to receive that message, and it is unlikely that he will act based on seeing it. However, a new parent who sees that same magazine in a pediatrician's office would likely fit into the target audience, as there is a need and possibly an intent to purchase associated with that person.

Experts in the field often differentiate between a **target market** and a **target audience**, each of which is important as you go further into the field of advertising. David Ingram of Demand Media noted that a target market is "a specific well-defined segment of consumers that a company plans to target with its products, services and marketing activities." He distinguishes this from a target audience by noting that the audience is more narrow because it refers to the specific group of consumers that ads will target, thus making it more well defined.[10] For example, a target market might be "girls age 12 to 14 who have an interest in horseback riding," while a target audience might be "girls age 12 to 14 who participate in horseback riding in the state of Kansas."

For the purposes of this book, the underlying principle remains the same: You need to figure out who is likely to be interested in your product, service or idea. This will allow you to shape your message to fit their needs and wants.

Actual Audience

In many cases, ads miss their target audiences because advertisers misinterpret the consumer landscape or the message falls on deaf ears. However, in some cases, advertisers market their products to one group—the target audience—and draw a different group of consumers. This is known as the **actual audience**, or the actual consumers.

One such example is the case of Mitchell and Ness and the company's "throwback" jersey line. According to the company's website, in 1983 a customer entered the store and asked to have two of his old game-worn jerseys repaired. As the employees attempted to do so, they discovered thousands of yards of old fabric in a warehouse, which inspired them to create retro jerseys.[11] The target audience for the jerseys was middle-aged men with disposable income who would want to wear the jerseys of their boyhood heroes. Instead, younger people, especially those in the hip-hop community and urban-based communities, became enamored with the product. Spike Lee wore a Brooklyn Dodgers jersey commemorating Jackie Robinson during his movie "Do the Right Thing." Young entertainers began wearing Willie Mays jerseys in videos as well. Although the jerseys continue to sell well, the target audience and the actual audience weren't one and the same.

One Ad, One Idea

You have many ways to showcase your product, which range from practical benefits to image and status. If you know enough about your product, you probably have 1,001 ways you would like to tell people how great it is. However, the more you try to cram into an ad, the more lost your readers and viewers will be.

When it comes to an ad, you should look for one main thing that you want to promote and focus solely on that. Much like a news story has a lead that keeps the attention on a main idea, an ad should pick a primary idea and drive it home throughout the ad. In most cases, campaigns pick multiple ways of reaching the same goal of promoting a product or idea, but each ad has a simple message.

Consider these two ads that serve as part of an awareness campaign for the Rambler Media Group on the campus of Texas Wesleyan University. Both advertisements promote a single idea ("Engage us" and "Watch Rambler TV") while keeping the focus on why the audience should do so ("for the latest in sports, campus news, arts, entertainment and local news"). However, the second ad clearly places the emphasis on the television station, while the first ad touches on the other media platforms as well. In the TV ad, no other media elements (newspaper or computer) are present, thus honing the focus.

Present an Option for Action

Ads are meant to direct action, whether that action is immediate or delayed. In writing advertising copy, you will always want to convince your readers and viewers that your point is valid. However, you need to take that next step for them and present them with an option for action. In short, if you do your job, your readers will be thinking "Exactly right! What now?" If you don't answer that question, you will leave a lot of people energized with nowhere to go.

In the Hallowfest ad, the option for action is clear: Go to the event. The advertisement lists the time and place for the event and offers compelling reasons to attend (music, food, festivities). The clarity here is solid, and the readers can easily understand what the ad asks of them.

For **immediate-action items**, you want to provide people with basic information about how to buy a product or purchase a service. The local Ford dealership might have a one-day, half-off sale on all year-end models. The advertising copy for this sale should tell people when the sale is and where the car lot is located. For **delayed-action items**, you want to create a broader sense of what to do when the time comes to act. In the case of the Ford Motor Co., advertisements are meant to make people think Fords are the best cars available. Thus, when the time comes for the audience members to buy a car, they will think of the Ford brand and purchase a car from a local Ford dealer.

Focus on Desired Outcome

You need to figure out what you want your writing to do in terms of the advertising message. This is where you must have a discussion with your client to determine what the ad should do. In other words, what will happen if the ad "works"? The client and you need to have a shared understanding of what "working" means in terms of your desired outcomes.

For example, an advertiser who is opening a comic book store wants to alert people to that store's big opening-day event, which will include local artists and special celebrity appearances. Your advertising content might create a huge buzz about the store and its grand opening, thus drawing many people to the store. However, the store might not make a lot of money on that day, as a lot of people will come through for the autographs and to meet the famous people rather than to buy comics.

If the desired outcome was to have people show up at the event, you succeeded. You would then create additional ads to draw on people's positive experiences with that event and get them to come back to the store and purchase items. However, if the goal of your initial advertising campaign was to create a financial windfall for your client, you failed.

You need to lay out your objectives in a clear and concise fashion. This will help you determine if you have succeeded in your campaign. Most campaigns have multiple objectives, such as trying to increase brand awareness as well as improving the audience members' intent to purchase. Whatever your goal is, everyone involved should have a clear understanding of the advertising objectives before, during and after the campaign.

Understand How to Measure the Outcome

This element goes hand in hand with the issue of selecting a desired outcome. Figuring out what you want to do is important, but figuring out how well you did it is even more crucial. Here are some things to keep in mind when looking at your outcomes:

Be idealistic but be practical: A big mistake young advertising writers make is to assume they can solve all the world's problems with their advertising. It's not going to happen, and if you start with this goal, you will never learn to appreciate your true gains.

Set the bar at a challenging and yet reasonable level: Think about what you can actually accomplish. If you aren't sure what is logical in terms of accomplishments, this means you didn't do enough research before you started, and you need to start digging again. If the previous campaign for this client raised sales by X percent, it's reasonable to assume that you can do X plus a couple percentage points if you really put your mind to it. Don't say "We can triple X with no problem!" All that does is set you up to fail.

Establish a concrete benchmark: People in the field don't like to establish a specific benchmark, because it means someone will hold them to a standard they might not meet. Politicians, for example, don't like to say, "I will create 250,000 new jobs in my first term in office," because if those jobs don't materialize, their opponents will beat that issue to death in the next election.

However, you can't let fear of failure prevent you from determining what you will do in this field. If you don't set the goals, you'll never know if you met them. Even more, if you don't set the goals with your clients, you might have a serious disconnect that costs you your job. If you hoped for a 5 percent increase in sales but didn't say anything, your client might be assuming a 20 percent increase is the goal. When you hit 15 percent, you end up feeling over-the-moon happy about this, and your client is really disappointed. A concrete goal that all participants share will keep this from becoming problematic.

Don't confuse measurements: This is crucial when you decide to examine how well you did with your advertising campaign. People often run into trouble when they decide to measure the wrong goal with the wrong tool. The impact of the Ford Motor Co. ads noted earlier in the chapter that seek to create brand awareness shouldn't be analyzed in terms of sales increases. The goal of those ads wasn't to improve sales, so asking if they succeeded based on how many cars dealers sold last week makes no sense. It's like saying you drove your car 500 miles this weekend and you are upset that you didn't lose any weight. The two things are unrelated.

Make sure you understand the goal of your advertising campaign before you attempt to measure it. You should establish your measurement option at the same time you start working with your client on the overall campaign. This will make sure you all are on the same page.

Figure out a time frame: In the world of instant gratification, people expect results immediately, if not sooner. Unfortunately, that's not how advertising works, and campaigns will take time to see results based on what you are trying to sell. An ad that pitches a $1 hamburger at a local restaurant will have a shorter time frame than an ad trying to sell a $1 million home in a posh subdivision. The product type, the audience and the price are just a few of the factors that will inform upon your time frame for success.

This is again where research can be your best friend. If you see that every other campaign like yours has taken a week or a month to really gain traction, you can help your client see this before you launch the campaign. By setting these goals in concrete terms, you can help determine when you can declare something truly a success or a failure.

CONNECT
NATIVE ADVERTISING

One of the best ways to connect with your audience is to tell them stories in a way they enjoy. However, when it comes to advertising, the question becomes a bit more gray in terms of what is and is not acceptable behavior.

In recent years, **native advertising** has become popular, as it appears to take advantage of the story-telling tools and approaches people most like. The idea of creating "sponsored content" is not a new one. The **advertorial**, a term that dates back to the 1940s, is an advertising approach that blends advertising messages with an editorial approach in hopes of drawing readers.

In the 1950s, Camel cigarettes presented "The Camel News Caravan," a 15-minute television program produced and aired by NBC News. In the 1960s, Winston cigarettes served as a sponsor for "The Flintstones" cartoon, a sponsorship made even more clear when Fred and Barney snuck away from yard work to enjoy "the best tasting cigarette" on the market.

As technology continued to evolve, the idea of sponsorships, pay-for-play arrangements and other "native" approaches became more widely applied. The Interactive Advertising Bureau lists a number of key native advertising applications in its "Native Advertising Playbook."[12]

One such application is the in-feed unit, where advertisers post material that mimics the editorial content of a site. For example, on BuzzFeed in July 2017, a post that offered "10 Ways to Upgrade Your Apartment So It Looks Elegant AF" was sandwiched between a quiz that noted "Only a True Cat Lover Will Get 7/10 on This Quiz" and a list of "18 Cringeworthy Times a Parent Wanted to Yell, 'That's Not My Kid!'" The headline, the photo size, and the font choices for all three pieces were identical, but the middle one was actually native advertising. Once you clicked on it, you were taken to a list of ways to improve apartment elegance, complete with links to Parachute Home's website, where you can buy everything the list suggests. The other items on the list were similar to those you would expect to find in nonsponsored content.

Other forms of native advertising include paid search units, "recommended" content widgets and promoted listings. In each case, the advertising is structured to look like editorial content and is

32 Things No British Person Will Ever Be Able To Forget
The Animals of Farthing Wood > Game of Thrones.
Robin Edds   3 hours ago   38 responses

11 Pick-Up Lines Pizza Would Totally Use On You
Let's be real: Pizza has GAME. Check out Newman's Own **delicious** frozen pizzas — it would *definitely* woo you into eating it.
PROMOTED BY
Newman's Own

29 Women Who'd Probably Like To Forget They Covered Maxim
Too bad the internet never forgets.
Dorsey Shaw   22 hours ago   128 responses

www.buzzfeed.com

intertwined with other editorial elements to draw readers who might otherwise skip past a traditional advertising message.

The Federal Trade Commission is grappling with the issue of whether this form of advertising is legal. The FTC defines deceptive advertising as content that will likely mislead reasonable consumers and it is important to the consumer's decision to buy or use the product.[13] Under that definition, these forms of advertising run a risk. It is unlikely that a person would click on a banner advertisement for Parachute Home, but many college students looking at a "demolisticle" might click on it to see what the author had to say.

The goal of native advertising, and every other form of advertising, is to reach readers and viewers. In using this form of content-based connection, you can more easily contact readers and find ways to make them see the value in your products. However, as with every other form of advertising, native advertising runs the risk of alienating audience members who think this approach is too sneaky. As this form of advertising continues to evolve, you will want to stay abreast of the law and the restrictions associated with it.

GIVE IT A TRY: Select a product or company and construct a native advertisement that mirrors the content on a site like BuzzFeed. The goal is to mimic the approach the site takes for its editorial content as to entice readers while still integrating tips and sales opportunities for your organization. This could be a quiz, a demolisticle or any other item that you see as being representative of both the site's content and your product's values.

WRITING IN ADVERTISING

Creativity is to advertising what a catchphrase is to announcing: It's a good thing, but without a strong core of quality material, it doesn't matter. When you write for advertising, in a lot of cases you won't just be writing advertising copy. You will also be expected to pitch clients through a creative brief and write persuasive messages to your superiors. In all of these areas, you can do well if you follow some of the simple hints listed below.

Focus on Benefits and Characteristics

Products often have specific **benefits** and **characteristics** you can highlight to entice readers and viewers who might find a use for your products or services.

A characteristic can be a physical attribute, a societal reputation or a historical attachment that you can use to draw in consumers. A physical characteristic can be something like the size of an engine in a car or the reach of a wireless telephone network. The value placed on these characteristics can change over time. For example, stereo speakers used to operate on a "bigger is better" philosophy, in which giant towers of audio power dominated the industry. However, as technology improved, smaller speakers matched the output of their giant predecessors, thus making older stereos obsolete.

You can promote characteristics such as the longevity of the company, the commitment the company has made to quality or the innovative nature of a company's products. These elements often imply specific benefits that will be passed on to the users.

A benefit is something that will enrich the life of the consumer. It can be as simple as "This is cheaper than the product you are currently buying, therefore allowing you to save money," or it can be as complex as "Using this product will enhance your current social position in a way that will allow you to ascend to higher levels of interpersonal engagement with valued people." Everything advertising does should focus on the benefits the product, service or concept provides.

This is where the idea of audience centricity really matters most. Advertisers often want people to buy their products because this will lead to higher levels of profitability. In the case of advertisements for politicians, charities, organizations and the like, the goals may vary slightly, but the underlying aspect of "this will benefit me as an advertiser" remains rock solid. However, advertisements that pitch this concept will fall on deaf ears because most people want to know "What's in this for me?"

When you look at writing for advertising, you want to focus on the characteristics of the products and the benefits they can provide to the audience members. You need to have a good answer to the "What's in it for me?" question your readers and viewers will likely ask. Highlight the benefits to help your audience members see what you have for them and why it matters.

Show, Don't Tell

As is the case with a lot of the writing forms we have discussed in this book, the more you try to tell people something, the less effective you will be. In news writing, you can get away with a little more "telling" because of the audience's expectation that your writing will be objective. When a reporter writes about how horrible a car accident is or how incredibly fun an amusement park can be, the readers will give that person a little leeway because they know the reporter isn't trying to sell them something.

If you show people how something works and why it matters, you won't come across like a carnival barker.

In the case of advertising, people have come to be suspicious of claims that lack concrete support. If you "show" them how something works, they can see it with their own eyes and they might be more likely to buy into your claims. You will want strong research and clear information to support you as you outline those benefits. Why should consumers believe that your toothpaste will lead to fewer cavities or a whiter smile than the toothpaste they are using now? If you have a set of facts at the ready to back your claim, you will be much more convincing. Writing in a way that shows people how something works or that outlines how you determined the benefits you are espousing has a strong "don't take my word for it" feel. This will allow the readers to come to their own conclusions and thus internalize the messages you deliver.

Avoid Hyperbole

As noted earlier in the chapter, you can get into a lot of trouble if you try to sell products with "miracle" claims or ridiculous statements. However, because many organizations try to sell things as "the biggest" or "the most amazing," the verbal arms race continues to escalate every time advertising professionals try to promote a new product or service. Things have to be even bigger than the product claiming to be "the biggest" or even more amazing than the thing that a previous ad said is "the most amazing."

Unfortunately, the more you act like a carnival barker or an Old West traveling salesman, the more people tend to tune you out. Few people are attracted to hyperbolic claims or overblown statements of fancy. What they tend to want is to see how something works and understand why it will benefit them. If you rely on the two previous points (showcase benefits/characteristics and show, don't tell), you don't have to create a hype machine to sell people on something.

Write Clearly and Plainly

In both a metaphoric and physical sense, people won't buy things they don't understand. If they feel lost or unsure, most people will become cautious and thus back away from a potential purchase. If they don't understand the value of a product, they won't purchase it. If they get lost in the language an ad uses to pitch an idea, they won't buy into it.

This is where language comes into play. Clarity is crucial in helping people see both the tangible benefit of an item as well as the argument you are making in your advertisements. Simplicity tends to lead to clarity, so you are in much better shape if you can find a way to put your pitch into simple, straightforward language.

As mentioned earlier, writers who lack confidence often overwrite, relying on jargon, vague language and a thesaurus to mask their insecurities. However, when you start using $5 words that aren't worth a dime, you can arouse suspicion in your readers. To avoid these problems, do heavy research, have confidence in your ability to make sense and then tell the people what they need to know in plain and clear language. This will lead the readers and viewers to come to their own conclusions regarding your work and lead to heavier buy-in.

Embrace the Platform

The use of digital advertising is something that can help you reach a new audience, but only if you are able to successfully transition your approach to meet the needs of this new platform. What works for a standard print ad or 30-second television spot won't necessarily work for an ad on a website or one sent via social media. Shovelware, the concept of just moving content from traditional media to digital media without altering, isn't only a news journalist's problem. Advertising professionals must adjust their approach to telling stories and reaching audience members as well when working on a digital platform.

Social media like Twitter can be extremely valuable to advertisers attempting to reach potential consumers, as it requires very little production work, is accessible to millions of people and can be shared among peers. Companies seek specific demographic and psychographic profiles and then provide "sponsored tweets" to websites and apps that are placed within users' feeds, much like regular tweets. Advertisers use traditional "banner and block" advertisements on platforms like Facebook, where products are microtargeted to users based on browsing history and individual profiles. In addition, they rely on sponsored posts that appear in users' news feeds based on individuals' interests and computer-based algorithms. YouTube has placed advertisements at the front of popular videos, and some news sites require users to complete short marketing surveys before reading articles. The opportunities to reach audience members goes far beyond a simple "buy this now" ad sent to everyone using a particular medium.

Good advertising professionals will use multiple platforms, such as vehicle wraps, to reach interested audiences.

However, a link to a giant newspaper-style ad or a 30-second ad before a 10-second video will only seek to irritate users and thus diminish the value of the advertiser in their minds. You need to tailor your approach to best meet the platform. Twitter operates in 280 characters, with options available for links and visuals. Users who click those links expect the content to be valuable and interactive, much like anything else on the web. They should feel like they know where they're going and that it's worth going there. Video advertisers have the option of letting viewers skip an ad after 5 seconds, but a better approach is to trim down the content to prevent users from feeling the need to "get past" the commercial.

For example, the insurance giant Geico turned away from its famous "gecko" advertisements that worked well on TV and built a campaign specifically for YouTube ads. The "Unskippable" campaign used 5-second cliché situations like families eating dinner or a backyard barbeque to simply set a scene and say how Geico saved the people money. The narrator then noted, "You can't skip this ad because it's already over" before providing the company's signature claim of how it can save users 15 percent on insurance in 15 minutes. The advertising, created by the Martin Agency, received wide acclaim for this approach and earned Advertising Age's 2016 Campaign of the Year award.[14]

As we discussed throughout the book, understanding the benefits and drawbacks associated with the tools at your disposal can provide you with an edge as you reach out to your audience. However, failing to understand how best to use a tool or which tool is most applicable in a particular situation can lead to serious problems from which you might not recover.

THE BIG THREE

Here are the three key things you should take away from this chapter:

1. **Advertising is about reaching people:** Many advertising professionals have used the term "buying eyeballs" to explain their goal in placing ads. The idea is to find a way to reach consumers and grab their attention. The most creative ads or the most innovative pitches won't matter if you can't figure out how best to reach audience members and grab them by the eyeballs.

2. **Plan first, then write:** The use of research, planning and audience analysis will help you determine how best to put your message out for your consumers. It will also help you to determine

your **tone**, your approach and your preferred platform. Although writing seems like the "fun" part of advertising, a lot of hard work needs to happen before you craft your message. In addition, that planning phase can help you set goals for your advertising campaign and assist you in determining whether you were successful in your efforts.

3. **Focus on benefits, not hyperbole:** Don't give in to the desire to scream the praises of your product

from every mountaintop. Instead, avoid superlatives and inflated claims as you focus on what makes your item valuable to the consumers. You can do this through comparisons with other products, accentuating the product's key characteristics and showing consumers how it will benefit them. The more you try to push your product through superlative language, the more your audience members will resist your efforts.

KEY TERMS

actual audience 231

advertorial 234

benefit deserved 228

benefits 235

characteristics 235

creative brief 227

delayed-action items 232

emotional appeal 229

Federal Trade Commission 225

immediate-action items 232

native advertising 234

objective statement 227

rational appeal 229

sponsored link 224

support statement 227

target audience 230

target market 230

tone 238

DISCUSSION QUESTIONS

1. How does advertising affect your intent to purchase? Do you think the ads that attempt to reach you and others in your "target audience" do a good job of persuading you? Why or why not?

2. Do you think most ads are written well? How did you determine this? What would you do to improve the overall writing in advertising?

3. What do you think about native advertising? Is it effective in reaching you? Is it an acceptable format to reach audience members? Support your thoughts with examples.

WRITE NOW!

1. Find a product line or a company that markets a product that interests you. Research the company and the product, and then briefly describe what audience it serves and its overall approach to reaching that market. Explain your thoughts on its

marketing approach. Then select another audience you think could benefit from this product. Briefly describe this audience and explain how you would alter the company's advertising approach to reach that audience.

2. Select an advertisement for a well-known national or international company. This can be from a magazine, newspaper or website, but it should be a still image. Describe the ad briefly and then identify the target audience or target market for the product. Do you think the ad does a good job of reaching that market? Why or why not?

3. Choose a product that you think would be valuable to someone in your demographic and geographic areas. Use the "lead" approach to outline your approach to writing a creative brief for selling this product. Finally, walk through the three steps of a creative brief as outlined in the chapter and explain how you would market this product. Use examples like those outlined in the chapter.

NOTES

1. A full version of the rules pertaining to political advertisements and solicitations can be found here: http://www.fec.gov/pages/brochures/notices.shtml.

2. Here is a brief review of the FTC's look at advertising and consumer protection: http://www.ftc.gov/about-ftc/what-we-do/enforcement-authority.

3. W. M. Pride and O. C. Ferrell (2010). "Marketing." Mason, OH: Cengage Learning.

4. M. Fox (2014, June 17). "The 'Dr. Oz Effect': Senators Scold Mehmet Oz for Diet Scams." NBC News. Accessed at: http://www.nbcnews.com/health/diet-fitness/dr-oz-effect-senators-scold-mehmet-oz-diet-scams-n133226.

5. R. Barrett (2017, June 6). "Lawsuit Says Dairy Ads Portray Bovine Growth Hormone rbST as a Six-Eyed Monster." Milwaukee Journal-Sentinel. Accessed at: http://www.jsonline.com/story/money/business/2017/06/06/lawsuit-says-dairy-ads-portray-bovine-growth-hormone-rbst-six-eyed-monster/375498001/.

6. Venable, LLP. (2017, July 17). "Arla's Dairy Campaign Goes Sour After Court Enjoins Ad Claims Attacking rbST." Accessed at: http://www.lexology.com/library/detail.aspx?g=6b05d639-a048-4056-aa3d-13b28b6d42d8.

7. B. Sheehan (2017, Jan. 13). "Long Live Reach: Buying Eyeballs Still Works if It's Done Right." Advertising Age. Accessed at: http://adage.com/article/guest-columnists/long-live-reach-buying-eyeballs-works/307490/.

8. A. Mitchell, J. Gottfried, M. Barthel, and E. Shearer. (2016, July 7). "The Modern News Consumer." Accessed at: http://www.journalism.org/2016/07/07/pathways-to-news/.

9. W. F. Arens, M. F. Weigold, and C. Arens (2013). "Contemporary Advertising and Integrated Marketing Communications" (14th ed.). New York: McGraw-Hill.

10. D. Ingram. "Target Market vs. Target Audience." Houston Chronicle. Accessed at: http://smallbusiness.chron.com/target-market-vs-target-audience-10247.html.

11. Mitchell & Ness. "About." Accessed at: https://www.mitchellandness.com/about.

12. Interactive Advertising Bureau. "Native Advertising." Accessed at: http://www.iab.net/nativeadvertising.

13. J. C. Miller (1983). "FTC Policy Statement on Deception." Accessed at: http://www.ftc.gov/public-statements/1983/10/ftc-policy-statement-deception.

14. A. Diaz (2016, Jan. 25). "Geico's 'Unskippable' From the Martin Agency is Ad Age's 2016 Campaign of the Year." Accessed at: http://adage.com/article/special-report-agency-alist-2016/geico-s-unskippable-ad-age-s-2016-campaign-year/302300/.

14

MARKETING

Marketing is the process of using various media platforms to reach audience members in hopes of selling them goods or services. A large part of marketing comes from advertising, which was discussed in the previous chapter, but it also involves other promotional efforts. Marketing establishes and reinforces the overall brand of your group or your client. When it is successful, marketing helps people think in a certain way about individual media campaigns and the overall organization. In many cases, integrated marketing communication blends the skills outlined in the previous two chapters: advertising and public relations.

At the core of marketing **campaigns** and **branding** is quality writing. The ability to accurately and clearly communicate can create a bridge between the readers and the client. Although all of the media specialties we discussed in this book involve audience centricity, writing as part of a marketing strategy requires additional effort in this regard. Copywriters don't really operate as either senders or receivers, but they serve more as translators between clients and readers. In addition, they have to engage their persuasive and creative sides.

This chapter will discuss what branding is and why it matters within a marketing campaign. It will also outline how you can craft a successful marketing message and various ways you can reach your readers effectively. Finally, it will outline the benefits and drawbacks associated with creativity as part of your marketing efforts.

BRANDS AND BRANDING

Within the field of marketing, your job as a media professional is to define and differentiate your company, product and ideology from those of your competitors. You want to situate your organization so that consumers will view you in a specific fashion. In short, your work in this field will establish, reinforce or enhance your organization's brand.

A brand incorporates a variety of elements, including your organization's name, its logos, its activities and its relationships. In his book on copywriting, Mark Shaw refers to brands as being the qualities of your organization plus the essence that ties it to a broader framework of understanding.[1] A well-established brand dominates the thoughts of the consumers, and it can prompt reflexive reactions. This is why people who ask for something to drink at a restaurant ask for a "Coke" or a "Pepsi" instead of "a sweet, cola-flavored carbonated beverage."

CAMPAIGNS VERSUS BRANDS

In most cases, you will not establish a brand but rather work to enhance it through the development of a campaign. Campaigns allow marketing professionals to establish relationships with audiences via various forms of outreach. A campaign can be a series of advertisements, social media connections, public relations efforts or a combination of these approaches. The purpose of a campaign is to feature an aspect of the organization, promote a product or highlight a cause.

The primary difference between brands and campaigns is the longevity and depth associated with each. The brand is a permanent aspect of the organization and is deeply rooted in every aspect of how that group acts. A campaign works in the short term to provide audience members with information about a single element or idea within the brand. Campaigns traditionally work as subsets of the brand, reinforcing the dominant identity of the brand while still emphasizing something new or different that emerges from that brand.

A well-branded organization can operate multiple campaigns simultaneously, each of which can draw readers' attention to specific elements of the brand. For example, a clothing manufacturer might brand itself as producing quality clothing in the United States for an affordable price. Its brand might also present itself as clothing for rugged individualists and blue-collar workers. The essence of the brand is strength, conviction and national pride. This company could create several campaigns that emphasize that brand from a variety of angles. One campaign could be a "buy American" approach that promotes its position as a company that hasn't shipped jobs to other countries. A second campaign could use a "cost-benefit analysis" tone to emphasize the high quality and low prices of the products. A third campaign could be more of an "ego appeal," in which the copy showcases tough, strong people who work in labor-intensive fields.

USEFUL MARKETING PLATFORMS AND TOOLS

In promoting your organization or your client's brand, you have many tools and platforms available to you. Unlike other forms of media, you aren't limited to a single print product, a video channel or a website. You can pick from blogs and websites as well as mailers and posters. Marketing expert Theo Theobald argues that you should have a multichannel strategy from the start and rely on strong cross-promotion efforts to keep people engaged and to improve your message.[2]

The important thing is to have a clear vision for the role of each marketing piece you create. As discussed in Chapter 6, you don't want to engage in shovelware, randomly moving content from platform to platform without a broader sense as to the unique values those platforms provide. You need to know what you are doing and why you are doing it. You also need to have a sense as to how the pieces interlock to create a complete picture for the campaign as well as the overall brand. We discussed blogging, Twitter and other social media options earlier in the book, so these items won't be repeated here. Below are a few additional tools that marketers can use as they craft their campaigns:

Email Blasts

Marketers spend a lot of time and money gathering email addresses of potential customers so they can alert these people when something important comes along. One of the benefits of developing a well-managed **opt-in** email list is that these people are likely to be receptive to your messages. When you buy giant mailing lists or simply sign up anyone who ever clicks on your website, you run the risk of having a lot of your messages fall on deaf ears.

An **email blast** is meant to alert your list of audience members to an opportunity you want them to consider. You should use a strong subject line to alert them to what benefit you are offering them while avoiding vague verbiage. The body of the message should be short, tight and to the point. Some experts note that you should restrict your pitch to one screen of text, as many readers will not scroll unless they are extremely interested. The professionals at MayeCreate have a longer set of "dos" and "don'ts" listed on the organization's website.[3]

One-Sheets

Snail mail has become less prominent, thanks to the explosion of websites, e-commerce and digital bill paying. That said, a stock postcard or simple **one-sheet mailer** can have a powerful impact if done right. These mailers can be anything from a postcard to a small magazine-style piece. In addition, the approaches you take with these can be easily applied to posters, table tents and other materials.

As is the case with the other tools mentioned here, keeping a short, tight writing focus is crucial. In this example, the organization presented a simple message to promote the student newspaper at Northwest Missouri State University. The material relies on the simple ideas outlined elsewhere in the book: a solid main idea, an audience-centric message and a call to action via contact information.

Brochures

Whether you mail them to potential customers, feature them in a rack of information or leave them behind after a sales call, brochures offer you an opportunity to inform and persuade people. Professional copywriter John Kuraoka says the biggest mistake people make in building brochures is that they forget that these are selling tools.[4] Kuraoka argues that the purpose of the brochure is to give people a persuasive message in hopes of inspiring action. To that end, the writing needs to start from a persuasive angle and build in information to support the persuasion. The design and visual elements should work with the text to sell the idea the brochure is promoting.

In many cases, brochures use a **multifold** approach, which allows the designer to treat the front panel as a cover. As you build your piece, you should work from a singular theme, which is evident on that cover. A solid headline will help you explain the theme. The interior panels can each discuss a specific aspect of your main idea, thus allowing you to write the text on each panel as a freestanding chunk of information.

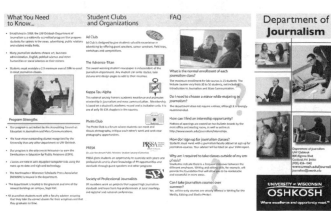

For example, the brochure shown here uses each panel to highlight a different aspect of the overall organization. One panel outlines the history of the department, while a second section discusses the various curricular areas within the discipline. Another panel outlines the frequently asked questions associated with the program, and each major portion of the brochure includes a "call to action" option: the organization's website.

ADAPT
BUILDING COPY

When you write marketing copy, you want to tell your readers a simple story. To help you do this, you can borrow some of the key elements outlined in the previous chapters regarding story structure. Here is a solid example of how to tell a simple story through a marketing piece:

Regardless of your faith background, Campus Ministry is here to assist you as you grow at Notre Dame into the person God created you to be. Through undergraduate, graduate, liturgical and music ministries, Campus Ministry fosters spiritual growth, encourages participation in sacramental and liturgical life, supports worship and personal prayer, provides opportunities for retreats and service, and seeks to enhance and develop lifelong faith formation.

University of Notre Dame Office of Campus Ministry

BE COMPLETE

CAMPUSMINISTRY
mind. heart. zeal. family. hope.

Headline

The headline should serve as a dominant element in your piece. It will not only be a large item from a font-size perspective, but it should provide your readers with a large, mental "poke" to get their attention. Notice the use of size in this headline. It also offers a simple and yet intriguing message: "BE COMPLETE."

Opening Lines

The first sentence or two of your body copy works like a lead in some ways, so use it to present the most important information to your readers right away. You should also use this paragraph to reinforce and explain the headline, because creative headlines often need some clarification. The headline and the opening lines must work together to tell your story.

In this example, the opening sentence reinforces the "BE COMPLETE" message from the headline with the explanation that Campus Ministry is "here to assist you as you grow." The use of growth helps solidify the idea of completion, as noted in the headline. In addition, the opening sentence helps the reader learn who is providing the message (Campus Ministry) and the intent of the sender ("We want to help you grow in spirituality, regardless of your faith background.").

Main Body Copy

The remainder of the body copy should deliver on the promises outlined in the headline and the first paragraph, reinforcing the theme and carrying through the tone of voice. Use those initial elements as a checklist for your remaining paragraphs. At each stage you want to tell the readers something that typifies those initial two points. As you progress, you can also introduce further promises and deliver on them as well, but keep your focus sharp.

The remainder of the body copy in this piece provides the ways in which the ministry program serves students at the University of Notre Dame. The list is expansive and yet specific, as the writer provides a full explanation of the purpose of the program.

Closing Elements

People tend to remember the last thing they see or hear, so it is at this point that you want to remind them of your primary theme and offer them a solid call to action. It is here that you can reflect on the initial promises you made in the headline and the first paragraph. You can also take this opportunity to provide them with opportunities to do something, such as visit a website, make a donation or purchase a product.

In this case, the closing element is the reminder of who sent the message and the core values the organization espouses. This is done neatly at the end with the Campus Ministry logo and the notation of "mind. heart. zeal. family. hope."

GIVE IT A TRY: Sketch out a basic poster for a topic of your choice. This could be a pitch for a local fundraiser, a call to have people join a campus group or an awareness-raising opportunity for a political interest you have. Focus more on the text elements than the dominant visuals you want to use (at least at first). Incorporate the key aspects of marketing copy outlined above (headline, opening lines, body copy, closing elements) as you build your piece. At this point, the goal is to focus most on telling a story via the writing. Once you have text you think does this, you can worry about visuals and structure. (If you have access to design software and an interest in doing so, complete the task with visuals, font choices and design elements.)

COPYWRITING FOR A BRAND

As a copywriter for an organization, your job is to create clear messages that target a defined audience. The message should prompt readers to act in a way that benefits them and your client at the same time. Copywriting is about promotion and selling, thus you have to understand who wants to "buy" what you are trying to "sell." In addition, you have to articulate why you think readers should care and how they can take action.

Shaw notes in his book on marketing that copywriters borrow their storytelling approach from various disciplines in media. He states that news journalists build copy from scratch, using research and facts to build writing that is forced into tightly defined structures. Copywriters also rely on heavy research as they use a simple format to create content. In addition, marketing expert Ardi Kolah notes that copywriters are on a quest for creative expression that will serve the client's interests and connect with readers.[5] Here are some issues you should consider as you craft your copy:

Audience Needs

Copywriters need to understand their audience members just as much as anyone else in the field of media. Beyond being able to operationalize the group from a demographic, psychographic and geographic perspective, these writers must determine the needs of their readers. This broader sense of understanding will allow the writer to pinpoint how best to approach the readers and accentuate the ways in which the client can satisfy those needs.

In some cases, audience members can clearly articulate what they need or want, thus allowing you to easily determine how to present your goods and services. In other situations, you need

LATINO FRESHMAN RETREAT

SOMOS ND SOMOS LATINOS

SEPTEMBER 6–7, 2013

Register online at CampusMinistry.nd.edu or in the Coleman-Morse Center, Room 114

CAMPUSMINISTRY

University of Notre Dame Office of Campus Ministry

to dig deeper to understand what motivates people in the context of what you are pitching to them.

In this example, you can see how this organization is reaching out to the Latino population at the University of Notre Dame. The opening headline promotes the Latino Freshman Retreat, which alerts interested members of that target audience. The main element of the piece is the giant text, written in Spanish, that states, "Somos ND, Somos Latinos," or "We Are Notre Dame, We Are Latinos." The use of Spanish and the use of demographic elements (Latinos, members of the university community) help reach the audience in a direct and meaningful way.

Benefits and Features

Your content must demonstrate value and quality by outlining not just the aspects of what you are promoting but also the benefits of those features. To distinguish between the two elements, you can think of features as the "what" elements of what you are selling and the benefits as the "why" elements associated with those features.

A car you are promoting could have four-wheel drive or a hybrid engine that offers improved fuel economy. These features have benefits, such as the ability to maintain traction in the snow or the ability to save gas. By pairing the benefits and features in your writing, you offer people information on your product or service but also you persuade them to buy it. Each time you write about a feature, ask yourself, "Why does this feature matter?" When you answer it in your own mind, pair that answer with the feature to offer clear benefits to your readers.

Call to Action

As noted in Chapter 13, it isn't enough to convince people something is good. You need to give your readers a call to action. Each piece you write that attempts to market your goods or services should have a final element in it that provides readers with a way to use the information you gave them. The call to action should serve not only the audience members but should reflect what your client wants.

This is why it is crucial for you and your client to be on the same page. If the client is looking to see an increase in sales, your call to action should drive traffic to a point of purchase for the client's organization. If the client wants to gauge the group's public image, the call to action should prompt audience members to explain their feelings regarding that group. When you and your client are on the same page you can determine what kind of tone your call to action should have.

Tone of Voice

Each brand has a particular essence to it, and that essence should be reflected in the way each campaign presents itself. Some clients will try to have a down-to-earth feel to their brand, while others will have an over-the-top approach. Some will promote luxury, while others will promote toughness. Your campaign needs to reflect the voice of the brand, providing readers with a sense of how they should feel upon buying the product or using the service.

PROFESSIONAL THOUGHTS
JONATHAN FOERSTER

When Jonathan Foerster took over as the communication director at Artis–Naples, the leading arts center in southwest Florida, he found that his voice had to change.

"I think the biggest change for me was learning to remove voice from my writing," he said. "No longer was I 'Jonathan Foerster, reporter.' Now I was the voice of an organization and needed to recalibrate my communications to better speak with the authority of that position and with a voice closer to that of the CEO."

Foerster spent much of his early journalism career in newspapers and magazines. He was the executive editor of a city-regional magazine and an entertainment editor at a newspaper. He also covered features, higher education and health care as a reporter. Even with this wide range of experience, he said the change to corporate communication and marketing was a tough adjustment.

"I never really imagined writing in a different voice than my own," he said. "Sure, I would use different language to create different moods in feature stories. But as journalistic writing has become increasingly more personal and less formal, it was challenging at first to separate how I would attack a journalistic piece of writing from formal corporate communications."

Foerster also said good writers must apply their skills in different ways based on the needs of the readers.

"Good writing isn't always effective writing, and that's the biggest thing most media professionals need to learn," he said. "The strategies you use for a 15-inch daily (story) aren't the same as you use for a powerful Facebook brand post nor the same as a potent fundraising mailer."

Even with the changes he worked through, ranging from learning specialized language for public radio to building databases for press releases, he said the underlying aspects of his media-based skills

Jonathan Foerster

helped him make the transition to this position.

"I know from my years of reporting what press releases, news alerts and story pitches I read and what I deleted before they even showed up in my preview pane in Outlook," Foerster said. "Understanding your audiences is the first key to any successful communication. I also think that going beyond the basics of news writing and actually getting some hands-on experience helps your ability as a storyteller. And really in any form of communication, be it journalistic or marketing, your mission is to tell a compelling story."

One Last Thing

Q: If you could tell students anything about media writing or anything you have seen in your time in the field, what would it be?

A: My best advice is to dabble in everything. My first big project at my current job was to produce a two-minute video for our youth education programs. I had no idea what I was doing. My second project was to come up with a social media strategy. Needless to say, I spent a lot of time reading up on both so I could put something good together. Even just some basic training in video production and some cross training in branding and marketing would have saved me a lot of time and headaches going forward. It's not enough to simply study for the job you think you want. Media professionals need to have a bit of MacGyver in them, enough smarts and skills in a variety of disciplines to work your way out of sticky situations until you get on more familiar terrain.

CONNECT
TOOLS AND TRICKS FOR BRIDGING THE GAP

In copywriting, the clients will define how the brand should be presented, and it is your job to build a marketing campaign that meets those needs. In the same vein, you must effectively communicate the essence of the brand to readers in a way that reaches them on their level. To connect these two seemingly incongruent needs, here are some suggestions and tools to help you:

Keep It Simple

People tend to distrust things they don't understand, so the more complex your approach to your copy is, the more likely people will shy away from it. Work on simplifying each aspect of your writing, starting with sentence structure. Build noun-verb and noun-verb-object structures first, and then add descriptors to them. Exchange complex words for common ones. Focus on one key point per sentence and place the most important information highest in your copy.

Use a Word Bank and a Brand Dictionary

These tools are among the most helpful in copywriting because they help you make sense of confusing terms while still keeping the focus on the brand's essence.[6] A **brand dictionary** is a tool that organizations develop over time that defines jargon in user-friendly terms. This helps you effectively translate generic terms used within the field for your readers.

A **word bank** contains a list of terms that should be used within copy to maintain the overall feel of the brand. The use and repetition of these terms will tie your campaign back to the overall brand identity. The terms tend to evoke a feel that the client sees as crucial to the brand's essence.

If your client or your organization doesn't have a word bank or a brand dictionary, work with your colleagues to brainstorm the terms for inclusion in each of these tools. This will save you time later and assure your client that everyone working on the campaign is on the same page.

Write for One Person

As mentioned in Chapter 1, you can personify your audience if you know it well enough. Thinking of that individual person as a representative of the larger whole can make your copywriting much stronger. Only one person reads your copy at a time, making this more of a one-on-one style of writing. Much as broadcast is viewed as an interpersonal medium, copywriting fits the same mold because of how it is consumed and the platforms you use to convey your information. If you engage the reader directly, you will have a greater chance of persuading the individual to take action, especially if you have a firm grasp of who that individual is and what he or she needs.

Edit, Edit and Edit Again

Editing is where you can win the battle for clarity, thus improving the likelihood of effectively reaching your readers. When you edit your work, you want to examine it several times for specific things. The initial edit should help you find big problems, such as factual accuracy or missing information. A second edit can help you assess the overall flow of the piece. You can also look at word usage and branding language at this point. A third edit gives you the chance to pick at spelling, grammar and style issues. Each time you look through your work, you will improve your overall copy.

Ask "Would I Buy This?" Before You Publish

You aren't always a member of the target audience, but you do have the ability to analyze your own content effectively. With that in mind, look back over what you wrote and see if you put your best foot forward in your persuasive efforts. Make sure you are attaching benefits to features. Assess your tone to see if you are too weak or too pushy. Examine the call to action to see if you properly laid the foundation in your copy to inspire people to act. When you are satisfied, release your content to your audience and see what happens.

GIVE IT A TRY: Pick out a marketing piece, such as a one sheet, a poster or a brochure, and analyze it for the elements listed above. Define the audience you suspect is the target for the piece, and explain to what degree you think this piece would work for those readers. Seek keywords that might be part of that organization's word bank or brand dictionary. What thoughts or emotions do they evoke? See if this piece relates to an individual reader (write for one person) or if it doesn't. What makes this work or fail at this level? Examine the piece for any edits that the organization should have made before producing the piece. How does this affect the readability of the piece and the credibility of the organization? Finally, ask if you were a part of the target audience, would you buy what this piece is selling? Why or why not?

WRITING CREATIVELY FOR MARKETING

Creativity is an important component of writing for marketing that is often misunderstood. As Novell Senior Vice President John Dragoon once noted, "Business is not about creative self-actualization for its own sake. And marketing, in particular, is not about fonts and colors." He also noted that CEOs are desperate for more creative people who can communicate effectively.[7]

To properly apply creativity to marketing material, you need to start with the writing and then work your way outward. Although applying fonts, colors and design gimmicks may seem like a better or easier way to apply creativity, the writing is where everything really starts for you.

Several variables will constrain your creative efforts, including your client's wishes, your audience's expectations and your overall ability to execute a creative strategy. In addition, you have to straddle a fine line between practical and creative if you hope to keep everyone happy. If you come across too weak in terms of creativity, the message will lack the value that innovation can provide. If you go overboard, you can offend or lose your readers in the process. Here are a few suggestions to consider when it comes to developing and applying creativity to your marketing work:

Adapt and Innovate

Creative people are said to think "outside of the box," meaning they don't conform to conventional thinking standards. This is only partially true, in that creative people are able to both think about better ways to work in the box and break out of it when necessary.

Adaptors are people who look to "build a better mousetrap," so to speak. They see what others have done and look for better ways to do it. They rework processes to streamline them. They see other ways to use current products in hopes of reaching new markets. **Innovators** are people who break the mold entirely, seeing things that have yet to be done and that others can't see. They don't make evolutionary changes but rather revolutionary ones.

Both of these strategies have merit when it comes to creative efforts. In some cases, rethinking how to reach an audience is a matter of tweaking a standard campaign. For example, in the 1980s, Duracell batteries ran ads in which they had a series of bunny toys beating on tiny drums, each of which eventually stopped working except for the one powered by a Duracell. Marketers at Energizer used an adaptive approach to react to the claim that Duracell outlasted all other batteries. D.D.B. Chicago Advertising put together an ad in which the small Duracell bunny was interrupted by a giant "Energizer Bunny," which wore sunglasses and pounded a bass drum. The campaign not only successfully counteracted the Duracell ads but gave the Energizer battery a long-lasting mascot.

The Energizer Bunny, a longstanding icon of the battery maker's marketing efforts, actually began as a response to a competitor's advertisement.

Innovative efforts require marketers to use an untested formula to engage audience members. HubSpot took a look at seven examples of guerrilla marketing, which was meant to create dissonance among people who encountered creative efforts. For example, Bounty paper towels did a form of installation art in which it placed giant versions of common messes on the city streets, including a knocked-over coffee cup and a melting popsicle. Next to these items was a sign noting that Bounty "makes small work of BIG spills." Other similar marketing efforts included a Burger King campaign using supposed "relationship break-up" exchange on Instagram and GoldToe's placement of underwear on giant statues all throughout New York City.[8]

Apply Strategic Relevance

Creativity for the sake of creativity will always fail. What makes creativity a valuable marketing tool is the concept of **strategic relevance**. This term refers to the idea of making the creative aspects relate to the product itself or to the overall marketing strategy. In the mid-2000s, Nationwide Financial Services built an advertising campaign meant to promote saving for retirement through the purchasing of the company's annuities. The creative angle was to take celebrities who had fallen on hard times and use humor to show how quickly their fortunes could disappear.[9] The tagline on the ads was "Life comes at you fast," after which the announcer noted that a Nationwide annuity could guarantee a person income for life. What made these ads work was the level of strategic relevance because they showed how even wealthy entertainers could use some financial help.

Seek a Tagline

Creativity emerges when you are able to show people how they should remember your product through the use of a **tagline**. Some people in the industry refer to this as a punch line, which makes it sound more like a joke than a creative endeavor, but the underlying value still applies. A memorable line or catchphrase in each campaign will tie your product or organization to the minds of your readers and viewers. This will increase recall among audience members and can help your clients differentiate themselves from other similar products and services.

CREATIVE PYRAMID

FIGURE 14.1 ■

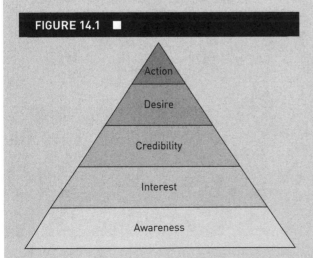

To help reach their creative potential, many experts in the field rely on the creative pyramid to guide them through a marketing process. This tool can aid you in crafting advertisements, but it also works well with other marketing elements, such as mailers and brochures. Here are the basic stages, starting from the bottom and working to the top:

Awareness

The first stage serves to stimulate the readers and get them engaged in what you want to tell them. This stage is akin to a headline in newspapers or a lead in broadcast. If you do this creatively enough, you can have readers asking "What is that all about?" before they read on.

Interest

This gets to the heart of your message and provides your readers with the core information you want to offer them. You can incorporate writing, visuals, audio or a combination of these elements to draw people in. Remember, however, that your writing is what will sell your audience members on what you are trying to get across. Don't assume you can blow off creativity in your writing and let a bunch of video or audio retain your audience.

Credibility

Once people are interested, you need to show them why they should believe you. This stage is one of the least creative in the pyramid, as you have to offer readers a logical and valuable set of information to establish credibility. Still, you can use celebrity endorsements, user testimonials or supporting data in a creative way to make your work more credible.

Desire

Once you establish the overall value of your product or service, you need to entice people in a way that heightens their desire for it. It is at this point that you can fill in the readers as to the overall benefits that they can receive or you can offer them an emotional message that pulls at their heartstrings.

Action

At this point, you want to give them simple ways to enact a behavior. You can show them a website where they can buy a product or give them a telephone number to call so they can get more information on your organization. This is the "Now what?" element of your creative work. Once you draw people in, get them interested and convince them they should do something, you want to funnel them toward a final action that will benefit them and you (or your client).

You will notice that this pyramid mimics a lot of what we discussed earlier in terms of the writing aspects of message creation. The benefit of this is that it offers you a broader understanding of how creativity can develop as you construct a message. Even more, you can overlay this pyramid onto the overall writing structure noted earlier and simultaneously engage in quality writing and creative efforts.

THE BIG THREE

Here are the three key things you should take away from this chapter:

1. **Focus on selling:** Marketing copy should promote the overall value of the goods or services you are selling. Information is crucial to support the persuasive efforts you are making, but you should outline the benefits of your product, not just the features.

2. **Add creativity in a coherent fashion:** Humor, innovation and other creative options can help your promotional effort, but only if they are used in the right way. Adhere to the basic principle of strategic relevance: The creative elements have to make sense and apply clearly to what you are pitching to your audience members. If creativity and persuasion don't work together, your readers will be lost or annoyed.

3. **You are a bridge:** The purpose of the copywriter is to connect the interests of the client with the needs of the audience. Although other forms of media writing also focus on audience centricity, this one requires you to serve more as a direct conduit between the people hiring you and the people who will read your work. The brand will be there long after you and your campaign are gone, so you must focus on conveying the essence of the brand in your work as well as meeting the needs of your audience members.

KEY TERMS

adaptors 249
brand dictionary 248
branding 241
campaign 241
email blast 243

innovators 249
marketing 241
multifold 243
one-sheet mailer 243
opt-in 242

strategic relevance 250
tagline 250
word bank 248

DISCUSSION QUESTIONS

1. Define and differentiate brands and campaigns. How do they work together to get a message out to an audience? What are some of the ways in which brands can help campaigns and what are some of the ways brands can limit campaign efforts?

2. Look at the three types of marketing materials discussed in the chapter (email blasts, mailers and brochures). What are some of the benefits and drawbacks associated with each of these tools?

Give an example of where you think each one would be helpful. Which tool is most appealing to you and why?

3. What is the difference between adapting and innovating? What do you see as some of the benefits associated with each approach to marketing? What do you see as some potentially problematic outcomes associated with each?

WRITE NOW!

1. Collect several pieces of marketing material from an organization. These can be brochures, mailers, press releases or anything else you can find. Then examine them for both campaign and brand characteristics as part of an essay that answers the following questions: What are the specific aspects of the brand that get typified in each piece of material? What are some of the distinct promotional aspects each piece of material provides? Do the themes differ from piece to piece? If so, how? Then summarize your overall feelings regarding how well the organization did in its promotional and branding efforts.

2. Use the creative pyramid to analyze a piece of marketing literature from an organization of your choosing. Define each stage of the pyramid clearly and then discuss how it applies to the literature you selected. Then summarize how well or how poorly you think the copywriter did to apply the stages of the pyramid to his or her writing.

3. Research an organization of your choosing and then write copy for an email blast, a brochure or a mailer. Follow the pattern for copywriting outlined earlier in the book. Then write a short essay that explains the rationale behind your approach to the content and where you think you could have improved.

NOTES

1. M. Shaw (2012). "Copywriting" (2nd ed.). London: Laurence King.

2. T. Theobald (2013). "On Message: Precision Communication for the Digital Age." Philadelphia: Kogan Page.

3. MayeCreate (2013, March). "E-Blast, Don't E-Bomb: The Dos and Don'ts of Email Marketing." Accessed at: http://www.mayecreate.com/2013/03/newsletter-dos-and-donts/.

4. J. Kuraoka. "How to Write a Brochure: Advice From an Advertising Copywriter." Accessed at: http://www.kuraoka.com/how-to-write-a-brochure.html.

5. A. Kolah (2013). "Guru in a Bottle: High Impact Marketing That Gets Results." Philadelphia: Kogan Page.

6. M. Shaw (2012). "Copywriting" (2nd ed.). London: Laurence King.

7. J. Dragoon (2010, Oct. 4). "What Is Creativity's Value—In Marketing, in Business?" Accessed at: http://www.forbes.com/2010/10/04/facebook-zuckerberg-twitter-wendy-kopp-creativity-advertising-cmo-network.html.

8. A. Zantal-Wiener (2017, March 20). "What Is Guerrilla Marketing? 7 Examples to Inspire Your Brand." Accessed at: https://blog.hubspot.com/marketing/guerilla-marketing-examples.

9. P. Thomasch (2007 Jan. 29). "K-Fed Pokes Fun at Himself in Super Bowl Ad." Reuters. Accessed at: http://www.washingtonpost.com/wp-dyn/content/article/2007/01/29/AR2007012901010_pf.html.

GLOSSARY

5W's and 1H: The staple crop of an inverted-pyramid lead: the "who," "what," "when," "why," "where" and "how" of the story a writer wishes to tell.

Absolute privilege: A legal standard that allows officials to make statements in their official roles without fear of libel.

Accuracy: A journalistic standard that requires content to be correct.

Action statement: One of three key needs writers strive to satisfy among readers. It assesses the degree to which the writer can explain what the readers can do with the information the writer just gave them. This is usually done through an action statement.

Active voice: A form of sentence structure that places the subject in a position where it is performing the action in the verb. The noun-verb-object structure denotes active voice: "Bill hit the ball."

Actual audience: The group of consumers who, in spite of an advertiser's intentions, actually attend to the advertising messages. An actual audience can be the exact group of people the advertiser intended or a group of people the advertiser did not initially consider to be potential consumers.

Actual damages: Real losses an individual can demonstrate during a libel case while seeking financial restitution. If a libelous statement led to someone's being fired, that person can show a financial loss of salary and benefits, thus demonstrating actual damages.

Actual malice: A standard of fault in libel cases that requires the plaintiff to show that the publisher of the content acted with a reckless disregard for the truth. This is the standard used for public figures in libel suits, and it is more difficult to prove than negligence.

Actuality: See **soundbite**.

Adaptors: People who see what others have done and look for better ways to do it.

Advertorial: A traditional-media form of selling in which an advertiser formats the content to mimic an editorial piece of copy, thus masking its nature.

Announcement: A form of a press release that allows practitioners to notify the media and the public about things like changes in personnel, product launches, employment opportunities and legal actions.

Antecedent-pronoun agreement: The requirement that nouns and their pronouns be parallel in terms of singularity or plurality.

App: A shortened version of "application" that refers to downloadable programs, traditionally associated with mobile devices, that serve a specific purpose, such as presenting news content, playing a game or capturing photos.

Attribution: Information included with a quote to help readers understand the source of the content.

Audience: The group of people media practitioners hope to reach with their content. The members of this group have characteristics that make them similar in some ways.

Audience segmentation: The ways in which media practitioners divide people into groups based on a series of physical, psychological and geographic characteristics in hopes of better defining the members of the audience and targeting the people in it more effectively.

Beats: Areas of specific news coverage.

Benefit deserved: An advertising approach that seeks to convince audience members that they have earned the reward showcased in the advertisement.

Benefits: Elements of a good or service that will enrich the life of a consumer.

Bill of Rights: The first 10 amendments to the U.S. Constitution.

Blog: A shortened version of "web log." It refers to a storytelling approach that uses short posts and bits of information logged on a website in reverse chronological order.

Brand dictionary: A tool that organizations develop to define jargon in user-friendly terms.

Branding: The process of creating identifying characteristics that come to mind when consumers think of an organization or its goods and services.

Breaking news: An event that takes place without prior notice and requires journalistic coverage. Fires, robberies and shootings fit into this category.

Bridge: The second paragraph of an expanded inverted-pyramid story that helps move readers from the lead into the body of the story.

Byline: A name placed on a piece of copy to identify the author.

Campaign: A series of promotional pieces, including but not limited to advertisements, public relations copy and marketing efforts, that promote a product or service.

Categorical limitations: Restrictions placed on freedom of expression germane to the content people wish to share. Threats, obscenity and false advertising are some categories of expression that courts have refused to protect.

Characteristics: Physical attributes, societal reputations and historical attachments that can be used in advertising to draw in consumers.

Clarity: The essence of being easily understood.

Cliché: An overused statement that lacks imagination.

Clips: A journalistic term for pieces of published copy that hearkens to the days in which newsroom librarians would "clip" stories out of the daily paper and store them based on their topics.

Closed-ended question: An inquiry meant to induce a simple, nonelaborative answer. "Did you win the game?" is an example of a closed-ended question.

Communications Decency Act of 1996: A piece of U.S. legislation passed in 1996 in an initial attempt to regulate pornography online. Section 230 of this act provides the owners of websites with legal protection against libelous comments posted there by people who don't work for the sites, such as commenters.

Conceptual beat: An area of news coverage based on more ethereal concepts, such as multiculturalism or data-driven journalism.

Conflict: One of the five key interest elements. This element emphasizes situations in which two or more people or groups are competing for a mutually exclusive goal.

Contraction: A grammatical construct that uses an apostrophe to combine two words.

Copyright: The exclusive legal right of people who create content to use the content or allow others to use it.

Creative brief: An organized document that pitches a creative marketing strategy to colleagues and/or clients. A simple, traditional brief includes an objective statement, support statements and a discussion of tone.

Creative commons: A licensing option for intellectual property that allows content creators to dictate how others can use that content without forcing the users to obtain express permission from the creators.

Credibility: The degree to which you and your content can be trusted.

Dangling modifier: See **misplaced modifier**.

"Dead-tree" publications- News products published on paper, referring to the tree pulp used to create the medium itself.

Defamation: The act of damaging the reputation of someone.

Delayed-action items: Products and services that advertisers promote in a way that is meant to strengthen brand awareness, thus inspiring people to purchase a product from that company when they decide it is time to buy. A television ad promoting the overall quality of Ford automobiles fits into this definition.

Demographics: Measurable aspects of a group you hope to reach. Demographics commonly include age, gender, race, education and relationship status.

Direct object: The element of the sentence that is acted upon. In the sentence "Bill hit Bob," the direct object is "Bob" because he is receiving the action of the sentence (being hit).

Direct quotes: Information taken from a source in a word-for-word fashion, placed between quotation marks and attributed to that source.

Email blast: A mass digital mailing sent out to a list of potential consumers or interested parties.

Emotional appeal: An advertising technique that uses psychological triggers or socializing elements to persuade people to use a good or a service.

Empty phrase: A cluster of words that fails to add information to a sentence. Example: "Despite the fact that tuition increased 10 percent...." The phrase "the fact that" fails to add value and can be eliminated: "Although tuition increased 10 percent...."

Empty subject: An opening of a sentence that lacks value but takes up space. These traditionally start with "There" or "It." Example: "There is an angry dog in the park." This could be rewritten as "An angry dog is in the park."

Empty word: A vague term that fails to add information to a sentence. "Very" is a descriptor that fits this definition.

Engagement: One of three key needs writers strive to satisfy among readers. It assesses the degree to which the writer can explain the information to the reader in an interesting way.

Event lead: A lead format used to highlight important aspects of a meeting, a speech, a news conference or another gathering. These should highlight the action of an event (the board voted to do X), as opposed to the existence of the event (the board held a meeting).

Fact check: A process writers and editors use to verify information before publication.

Fact sheet: A public relations release that provides media representatives with the basic information about a topic, a company, a group, an event or an idea.

Fair use: The right of media professionals to use copyrighted material without the permission of the copyright holder for educational and information processes.

Fake news: A term that emerged in the mid-2010s to describe content that is purposefully false in hopes of drawing audience members through partisan ideology or shocking headlines. It is also used to describe content that individuals dislike in an attempt to discredit the material.

Fame: One of the five key interest elements. This element emphasizes the overall importance of the individual involved in the content. Subjects who fit into this interest area can be important over an extended period of time or be living out their "15 minutes of fame."

Fault: An element of a libel case that requires a person to show that a publisher did something wrong or failed to act appropriately, thus leading to the publication of the libelous content.

Federal Trade Commission: An independent government agency in the United States that oversees corporate practices to protect consumers from dishonest forms of business, including deceptive advertising and unfair practices.

First Amendment: The first of 10 amendments outlined in the Bill of Rights. It guarantees freedom of speech, freedom of the press, freedom to peaceably assemble, freedom to petition the government for redress of grievances and freedom of religion.

Flow: The smoothness of movement among elements of a story or through questions within an interview.

FOCII: A memory device helpful in remembering the five interest elements: fame, oddity, conflict, immediacy and impact.

Gatekeeping: A process of news filtering that helps determine what information the general public gets to see. David Manning White's study on an editor he dubbed "Mr. Gates" helped popularize the term "content-selection process." Editors are occasionally referred to as "gatekeepers," meaning that they choose what information is published and what information is not.

Gender neutral: A grammatical term indicating that an item is neither male nor female.

Geographic beat: An area of news coverage based on specific regions of a state or city.

Geographic information: An audience characteristic media practitioners rely on to target audience members based on their physical location.

Gotcha journalism: A negative term that describes a method of reporting intended to trap and embarrass sources.

Hashtag: A social media tool that allows users to include a pound sign (#) at the front of a term to identify content on a given topic. Users can then choose to follow the hashtag to remain informed on that issue.

Holes: A writing term that pertains to how complete a piece of copy is. When the writing misses key facts or perspectives, it is said to have holes.

Hyperbole: A statement that is so ridiculously overblown that it could not be reasonably believable.

Hyperlink: A digital tool that allows readers to directly access content elsewhere on a site or on the web.

Identification: An element of a libel claim that requires the person claiming to be libeled to be clearly identifiable in the potentially libelous material.

"Imagine" lead: A lead that offers readers a hypothetical as opposed to a point of fact to begin a piece of copy. These leads often produce clichés and should be avoided.

Immediacy: One of the five key interest elements. This element emphasizes the timely nature of content, with the newest information being seen as the most important.

Immediate-action items: Products and services advertisers promote with the intention for the consumer to purchase the product right away. A television commercial for a sale this weekend at a used-car lot fits into this definition.

Impact: One of the five key interest elements. This element emphasizes the degree to which the information will affect the audience members. It can be measured quantitatively and qualitatively.

Indirect object: The element of the sentence that is indirectly affected by the action of the verb. In the sentence "Jim gave Betty the candy," the indirect object is "Betty," as she is indirectly receiving the action of the sentence in relation to the direct object (getting the candy).

Indirect quotes: Information taken from a source and boiled down into basic information and attributed to that source. This form of quoting is also known as paraphrase.

Innovators: People who break the mold entirely and make revolutionary changes, as opposed to evolutionary ones.

Interest elements: Informational aspects of content that are used to draw audience members to content.

Interesting-action lead: A form of summary lead in which the author relies on the value of the "what" to draw readers into the story. These are used when oddity, conflict or impact is a key interest element in a piece of copy.

Inverted pyramid: A format of journalistic writing in which information is provided in descending order of importance. The higher a fact is in the copy, the more valuable the writer thinks it is.

Jargon: Terminology that is specific to a field that people outside that field have difficulty understanding.

KISS: A broadcast acronym to remind writers to keep their pieces short and simple. It stands for "Keep it short and simple" or "Keep it simple, stupid."

Lead: Occasionally spelled "lede," this is the first sentence in an inverted-pyramid piece of copy. It traditionally outlines the most important facts of the overall piece in 25 to 35 words.

Lead-in: The portion of a script that an anchor or reporter reads to introduce the upcoming story.

Legacy media: Occasionally called "old media" or "traditional media," these outlets operate primarily in the realm of newspapers, television and radio, even if they maintain complementary websites.

Libel: A false published statement that damages a person's reputation.

Limited-purpose public figures: People who aren't as famous as politicians or celebrities but have become known in relation to a specific topic or issue.

Loaded question: An inquiry that includes a faulty presumption or intends to trap a source into answering in an unfair way. "Senator, have you stopped beating your wife yet?" is an example of a loaded question because it doesn't offer the source a chance to proclaim innocence. "Yes" means the senator had beaten his wife but has since stopped. "No" means that the beatings continue at the senator's house.

Localization: A story format in which a reporter covers a broader issue from a local angle. A story that explores how the Affordable Care Act will affect doctors within a newspaper's audience is an example of this form of story.

Logical lapses: A breakdown in assessing the accuracy of a statement brought about by the inclusion of an erroneous statement.

LOS: This stands for live on set or live on the scene and is a more complex version of a package. This form of storytelling includes live interaction between the anchor and the reporter who is either speaking from the TV studio or a remote scene that plays a role in the story. These live elements bookend the traditional broadcast-news package.

Main assertion: The key point of any news story. Completing the sentence "This matters because…" is one way to locate it.

Many-to-many model: The digital media approach in which content is shared socially among many publishers and consumed by many readers. In this approach, people can be both senders and receivers of content.

Marketing: The process of using various media platforms to reach audience members in hopes of selling them goods or services.

Media alert: A form of a public relations release that blends the lead-writing approach associated with the inverted pyramid and the bulleted approach common to fact sheets.

Medium-based limitations: Restrictions placed on freedom of expression germane to the platform used to share information. The First Amendment guarantees freedom of the press, which traditionally translates to printed products. Other platforms, such as broadcast, receive less protection than do newspapers and magazines.

Microtargeting: An approach in which marketers use extremely specific demographic characteristics to target a tiny group of an overall population. An example of this would be targeting people who graduated from St. Louis Park High School in Minnesota from 1988 to 1992.

Misplaced modifier: A structural deficiency in a sentence that results in a word or phrase that can be misapplied to the description of another word or phrase. A classic example is "While typing, the dog bit me," as the ambiguity of the structure makes it seem as if the dog was typing. This is also known as a dangling modifier.

Morgue: An older newsroom term used to describe a newsroom's library and archives.

Multifold: A form of a brochure that uses a single piece of paper folded into multiple panels. Each panel is demarcated by the folds and usually contains a single idea that reinforces the overall intent of the brochure.

Name-recognition lead: A form of summary lead in which the author relies on the importance of the "who" to draw readers into the content. These are used when fame is a key interest element in a piece of copy.

Native advertising: A form of online selling in which the promotional content is formatted to mirror the other content on the site, thus masking its nature.

News peg: The aspect of a story that justifies why a reporter is covering the topic now and for this audience.

News release: See **press release**.

Niche: A small, specialized area of information on which a media outlet might provide coverage.

Notebook emptying: A poor journalistic practice in which every piece of information a writer gathered is wedged into a piece of copy.

Noun: The simple subject of a sentence that explains who or what the sentence is about.

Obituary: A profile story written about a person who has died.

Objective statement: An element of a creative brief that outlines what an advertising campaign is attempting to accomplish.

Objectivity: A journalistic standard that requires news writers to avoid taking sides or infusing their opinions into stories.

Oddity: One of the five key interest elements. This element emphasizes rare feats, strange occurrences and "news of the weird."

One-party consent: A standard for recording conversations that requires only one of the people involved in the conversation to be aware of the recording in order for it to be legal.

One-sheet mailer: A promotional tool sent through the mail or distributed in person that contains a list of important information about goods or services on a single page of paper.

One-to-many model: The traditional mass media approach in which one source provided content to a large audience in a one-way conduit of information. Newspapers and broadcast-news reports are examples of this model.

Open-ended question: An inquiry meant to induce an elaborative answer. Interviewers often use "how" or "why" as part of the question to draw more information from a source. "How did you get the bill passed?" is an example of an open-ended question.

Opt-in: A marketing technique that allows interested consumers to notify an organization that they wish to receive additional information from that group via email or social media.

Outlet: The source of information disseminated to an audience. It differs from a platform, in that an outlet can use more than one platform. For example, ESPN uses print, broadcast and online platforms to disseminate content, but the content all comes from the ESPN organization.

Pace: The speed at which the reader can move through a story based on how it is structured. This speed is also influenced by the use of punctuation and the length of sentences in the piece.

Package: A traditional news-story format in broadcast television. Reporters create these stories in advance of the newscast, and they include the voice track of the reporter, video that matches the script, two or more soundbites and a sign-off. These last between 1:30 and 2 minutes.

Paraphrase: See **indirect quotes**.

Parrot: A negative term that describes how a writer takes incoherent content from a source and passes it along to the audience in a verbatim format.

Partial quotes: A mix of direct and indirect quoting in which a fragment of information is taken directly from a source and placed between quotation marks, with the rest of the information surrounding it written in paraphrase. This form of quoting is used to place emphasis on a key element of a statement a source made.

Passive voice: A form of sentence structure that places the subject of the sentence in a position in which it is receiving the action of the verb: "The ball was hit by Bill."

Payola: A term made popular in the 1950s, when on-air personalities took money to play certain songs. It now more generally refers to freebies and enticements people offer to media professionals in hope of gaining favorable coverage.

Personality profile: A feature story that explores the life of an individual through in-depth reporting and observation.

Personification: A way to view an audience by creating a prototypical audience member who is infused with most prevalent demographic, psychographic and geographic elements of the entire group. This approach to understanding an audience can help a media professional better reflect on what the audience wants and needs from that person's writing.

Pitch: A suggestion of ideas for stories proposed to an outlet.

Plagiarism: Taking content someone else created and claiming it to be your own.

Platforms: The media methods used to deliver content, including but not limited to print, broadcast and online dissemination.

Podcast: A downloadable audio file that is the digital equivalent of a talk-radio broadcast.

Possessive: A grammatical construct that indicates ownership: "Bill's toys." "The three brothers' bedroom."

Post: A bit of information placed on a blog or social networking site.

Preposition: A word that indicates geographic or temporal placement.

Prepositional phrase: A series of words that begins with a preposition and concludes with an object of a preposition. Examples of prepositional phrases include "to the store," "around 9 p.m." and "under the tarp."

Press release: A form of public relations material that is issued to the media to give them information on a specific topic.

Primary source: Documents, people and objects that can provide a firsthand account of an event, activity or outcome. A diary written during the Civil War and a person who witnessed a fire are examples of primary sources.

Pronouncer: A phonetic explanation included in a broadcast script to help reporters and anchors say a word properly.

Psychographics: A set of characteristics audience members hold, including but not limited to personality traits, values, interests and attitudes.

Public figures: People frequently in the public eye, such as politicians and celebrities. People included in this category must demonstrate actual malice in order to win a libel suit.

Publication: An element of a libel claim that requires the potentially libelous content to be sent to someone other than the person claiming to be libeled.

Puffery: A term often associated with advertising in which media professionals can "puff up" the value of a product without relying on facts or in a way that cannot be objectively disproved. This is akin to hyperbole and is often viewed as legally protected speech.

Punitive damages: Financial penalties a court assesses to a libel defendant to punish the person or organization for acting irresponsibly.

Qualified privilege: A legal standard that allows journalists to quote officials acting in their official capacity without fear of libel.

Qualitative: A measurement that assesses the severity of an impact.

Quantitative: A measurement that assesses the numerical reach of an impact.

Question leads: A lead that asks the readers something instead of making a declarative statement. These leads are risky because they presuppose that the reader and the writer view the topic in a similar fashion.

Quote lead: A lead that uses a famous quotation or a bit of text taken directly from a story source to begin a piece of copy. These leads are often confusing or rely on cliché.

Rational appeal: An advertising technique that uses logic and reason to persuade people to purchase a good or service.

Reaction release: A form of a press release that allows public-relations practitioners to respond to newsworthy events and statements that affect your audience.

Reader: The simplest type of broadcast story. It has an anchor or reporter reading a script while on air. These last 10 to 20 seconds each.

Robert's Rules of Order: A set of guidelines used to conduct many meetings. The rules are based on parliamentary procedure and meant to keep order.

Said: The preferred verb of attribution, as it is nonjudgmental.

Script: The text of a broadcast story used to help reporters narrate a story. It will also include references to the use of video when applicable.

Secondary source: Documents, people and objects that provide a secondhand account of an event, activity or outcome. A recently written textbook on the Civil War and a person recalling a parent's stories about serving in World War II are examples of secondary sources.

Second-day lead: A lead format used to update readers about an ongoing event or process. This format promotes the immediacy interest element, as it focuses on the newest developments on the topic.

Sentence diagramming: A process in which a writer physically dissects a sentence to assess its grammatical structure.

Shell: A basic set of information elements associated with a story that can be typed up in advance of an event.

Shiny-object syndrome: A term that describes how new, shiny or fancy items easily distract people from what they are doing, regardless of the value of those new items. Think of a bird chasing a foil gum wrapper across a lawn for no good reason, and you get the idea.

Short Message Service (SMS): Also known as simple messaging service, this is another term for text messaging, referring to the way in which users can send short digital messages to one another via mobile devices.

Shovelware: The process of treating a website like a storage bin for content that has been "shoveled" from traditional platforms onto the web. This approach to web use fails to take into account the ways in which web readers and traditional-media users consume content or the differences between how the platforms can present content.

Sign-off: A portion of a broadcast story in which a reporter signals the end of a piece by noting his or her name and the station's call sign ("For W-X-Y-Z, I'm Bill Smith.")

Social media: Digital information-sharing tools and approaches that allow people to gain information based on their interests from a variety of sources in a many-to-many media model.

Soundbite: Also known as a bite or actuality, this element of a broadcast story allows the source to speak to the audience in his or her own words on camera. This is the audio and video version of a direct quote in a text story.

Sources: People or documents from which media professionals can garner information on a given topic.

Spin: A negative term associated with public relations that refers to the way in which practitioners interpret an event in a way that benefits their client, in spite of the reality of the situation.

Split infinitive: A grammatical construct in which the writer places words between "to" and the verb within an infinitive verb form: "She seemed to really hate John."

Sponsored link: A form of digital advertising that shows up on search result pages or in advertising spaces on websites that contract with third-party advertising organizations.

Spot announcement: A form of a press release that alerts the media to breaking news items that affect the company or organization, such as a fire at a job site or a power outage at a stadium.

Storify: A social media tool that allows the user to create stories or timelines by selecting posts from Twitter, Instagram and Facebook.

Strategic relevance: The requirement in advertising that the creative aspects of an advertisement relate to the product itself or to the overall marketing strategy.

Summary lead: An inverted-pyramid-style lead that seeks to sum up the important elements of a piece of copy. It relies heavily on the 5W's and 1H to determine which aspects of the piece are highlighted.

Support statement: An element of a creative brief that provides evidence that the objective statement within the brief will work.

Tagline: A memorable line or catchphrase in a campaign that ties your product or organization to the minds of your readers and viewers.

Target audience: A more concrete version of a target market, denoted by its more narrow focus and higher level of definitional specificity.

Target market: The group of people an advertiser has in mind as potential consumers of a specific good or service promoted by a marketing campaign.

Thematic beat: An area of news coverage based on specific topics, such as education, courts and religion.

Time-place-manner limitations: Restrictions placed on freedom of expression germane to when, where and how people wish to express themselves.

Tone: An element of a creative brief that explains how the objective statement will be presented so it is acceptable to the audience members.

Trade press: Newspapers, magazines and websites that focus on specific industries or "trades."

Transparency: A public-relations approach that allows everyone within your audience to see what happened in a situation and why it happened.

True threat: A legally unprotected form of communication where an individual announces a violent or dangerous action that is likely to occur. This is distinct from a threat made as a joke, such telling a friend, "I'll travel back in time and kill you as a newborn if you burn my hamburger."

Twibel: A merging of the terms "Twitter" and "libel" to describe libelous acts perpetuated on social media platforms.

Twitter: A social media tool that allows users to tell stories to followers, primarily in short bursts of texts.

Two-party consent: A standard for recording conversations that requires both of the people involved in the conversation to be aware of the recording in order for it to be legal.

Value-: One of three key needs writers strive to satisfy among readers. It assesses the degree to which something matters to a reader by outlining a clear personal impact for the readers.

Verb: The simple predicate of a sentence that provides the action for the sentence.

Vlog: A video blog (see also **blog**).

Voice-over: Also known as a VO. This form of broadcast story has a reporter or anchor reading a script on air while video on the topic is rolling for the audience members to see.

VO/SOT: Stands for voice-over/sound on tape and is a more complex version of a VO. This form of broadcast story operates like a VO, but includes one or more soundbites. VO/SOTs last about 35 to 40 seconds each.

Wallpaper: A derogatory term for video that doesn't enhance the storytelling of a story. This video that only provides visual elements for the sake of having video. For example, a story on a city budget might include images of buildings or signs that feature the city's name.

Word bank: A list of terms that should be used within copy to maintain the overall feel of the brand.

Writing to video: When a journalist produces script text that matches video. An example would be when a script says "The fair featured hot-air balloon races and a rodeo," and visuals of the balloon race and the rodeo appear on the screen.

"You" lead: A lead format that uses second-person point of view to address the audience directly. Although second-person writing is more accepted in broadcast format, text-based platforms often avoid this form of lead, as it often comes across as presumptive.

INDEX